STUDIES IN ISLAM

STUDIES IN ISLAM

Amir Ansari

CYBER TECH PUBLICATIONS
4264/3, Ansari Road, Daryaganj, New Delhi-110002 (India)
Ph.: 011-23244078, 011-43559448 Fax: 011-23280028
E-Mail: cyberpublicationsdelhi@yahoo.com
Website: www.cybertechpublications.com

STUDIES IN ISLAM

Amir Ansari

First Edition 2011

Published by :

G.S. Rawat for **Cyber Tech Publications**
4264/3, Ansari Road, Daryaganj, New Delhi-110002 (India)
Ph.: 011-23244078, 011-43559448 Fax: 011-23280028
E-Mail: cyberpublicationsdelhi@yahoo.com
Website: www.cybertechpublications.com

CONTENTS

Preface

In this book, you will learn why Arabia was such fertile ground for the emergence of a new faith. In its prehistorical period (3000 BCE–500 CE), the dry Arabian Peninsula, most of which was unfavourable for settled agriculture, derived great wealth from its prime location at an important trade crossroads: caravans crisscrossed the desert bringing goods from China, India, and Africa in the East to trade as far as Spain in the West. For hundreds of years, Arabia's residents served as middlemen in this trade; thus, although agricultural opportunity may have been limited, commercial opportunity was almost limitless.

In 570, Muhammad was born in Mecca, already an important Arabian trading and religious centre, in what is known as Islam's formation and orientation period (500-634 CE). Muhammad was a serious young man whose parents had died when he was young; he was raised for a short time by his grandfather, and then by his uncle, Abu Talib.

He later worked for a wealthy businesswoman named Khadijah, whom he married at age 25. Full of spiritual questions, Muhammad often sought the solitude of the desert to think and pray. It was on one such trip that the 40-year-old Muhammad had a revelation. The angel Gabriel came to him, saying three times "Recite!" and told Muhammad that he was the messenger of God. Muhammad went home, relating to Khadijah what had happened. Soon she became Islam's first convert.

— *Author*

1 Introduction

Around 610 CE, a merchant meditating in a cave outside Mecca began to receive a series of revelations. From that vision grew Islam, one of the world's great religions. What Islam's prophet, Muhammad, began gave rise to a number of mighty empires. Islam proved to be such a powerful force that today, 1,400 years after a vision appeared to the Prophet, it is the world's second largest religion. With more than one billion adherents, Islam has deep roots in the Asia, Africa, and Europe. More than half of today's Muslims live in Asia alone, from Turkey to Indonesia. Worldwide, a tremendous variety of people follow Islam—from blue-eyed Bosnians to African Americans to the Uighurs of western China. After fourteen centuries, Islam remains one of the world's fastest-growing faiths.

But Islam, by virtue of extremist acts that pressed its name into the consciousness of many as the 21st century was just beginning, faces a new hurdle. With the terrorist attacks of September 11, 2001 in the United States—and subsequent attacks in Bali, London, Madrid, and elsewhere—radical Islam seized global attention. The images, headlines, and aftermath of each attack indelibly linked those events with the name of Islam. In spite of the attention seized by Muslim extremists in recent history, however, the broader history of Islam is one of astonishing growth and great achievement. Islam itself is complex and multifaceted, and its faithful have, over centuries, been massively prolific in works of science, philosophy, theology, and the arts. From the luminous symmetry of the Taj Mahal to algebraic equations, from the tales of *The Thousand and One Nights* to the collected works of poets such as Rumi or Hafiz, Islam has provided a rich tapestry of contributions to world culture. What binds Muslims? Muslims believe in one God and affirm Muhammad as His prophet. They hold Islam to be the third revelation of monotheism—after Judaism and Christianity—and as such revere many of the prophets honoured in Jewish and Christian tradition, including Abraham, Noah, Moses, and Jesus. Muslims also share several spiritual guides. One is the Qur'an, the sacred scripture of Islam revealed by God to Muhammad and, for all Muslims, the very word of God. Another is the Hadith, the record of the traditions or sayings of the Prophet, revered by Muslims as a major source of religious law and moral guidance and second only to the authority of the Qur'an. Incumbent upon every Muslim are five duties known collectively as the Five Pillars of Islam. First among these is the recitation of a profession of faith called the *shahadah* ("There is no god but God and Muhammad is His prophet"), which must be recited by a Muslim at least once in his or her lifetime. In addition, observant Muslims say prayers fve times a day, give to charity, fast during the holy month of Ramadan, and, if they are able, make a pilgrimage to Mecca, Muhammad's birthplace. In addition to the Five Pillars, many Muslims around the world also study the Qur'an.

In this book, you will learn why Arabia was such fertile ground for the emergence of a new faith. In its prehistorical period (3000 BCE–500 CE), the dry Arabian Peninsula, most of which was unfavourable for settled agriculture, derived great wealth from its prime location at an important trade crossroads: caravans crisscrossed the desert bringing goods from China, India, and Africa in the East to trade as far as Spain in the West. For hundreds of years, Arabia's residents served as middlemen in this trade; thus, although agricultural opportunity may have been limited, commercial opportunity was almost limitless.

In 570, Muhammad was born in Mecca, already an important Arabian trading and religious centre, in what is known as Islam's formation and orientation period (500-634 CE). Muhammad was a serious young man whose parents had died when he was young; he was raised for a short time by his grandfather, and then by his uncle, Abu Talib. He later worked for a wealthy businesswoman named Khadijah, whom he married at age 25. Full of spiritual questions, Muhammad often sought the solitude of the desert to think and pray. It was on one such trip that the 40-year-old Muhammad had a revelation. The angel Gabriel came to him, saying three times "Recite!" and told Muhammad that he was the messenger of God. Muhammad went home, relating to Khadijah what had happened. Soon she became Islam's first convert.

The revelations persisted, and after several years of preaching to his family and friends, Muhammad started delivering his revelations to others in the form of public recitations. Although a number of prominent Meccans became believers, many others harassed his supporters, forcing some of them into a period of exile. During this diffcult time, Muhammad faced the deaths of two of his dearest companions: Khadijah, his wife and confdant, as well as his beloved uncle and protector, Abu Talib. And yet, in spite of the challenges, Muhammad's fock continued to grow. In 622 he moved his followers in small, inconspicuous groups to the city of Yathrib (Medina) in an emigration known as the Hijrah. In Medina Muhammad established Islam as a religious and social order. From there, Muhammad later led campaigns against his opponents, including Mecca; by 629 he was able to lead his followers on the first peaceful pilgrimage to that city. He continued to receive revelations until his death in 632.

After the Prophet Muhammad's passing, the Muslim faithful learned to survive as a community in the period of conversion and crystallization (634–870 CE). First, four "rightly guided" caliphs, all friends or relatives of Muhammad, ruled from 632 to 661. These leaders stretched Islam's borders by taking over Palestine, Egypt, Syria, and parts of Iraq. They also organized the government.

One important event was a controversy over 'Ali, the pious cousin and son-in-law of Muhammad, who was the last of these caliphs. 'Ali faced many diffculties, including the opposition of Mu'awiyah, the governor of Syria. But 'Ali had supporters, too, called the Shi'at 'Ali, or Partisans of 'Ali. In 661, 'Ali was murdered. After 'Ali's assassination, Mu'awiyah assumed the caliphate, founding the Umayyad dynasty. That injustice—and later the murder of 'Ali's son al-Husayn by Umayyad troops—angered the Shi'ites. They opposed the Umayyads' more secular rule and decided to follow spiritual leaders called imams. Thus began a separation between two branches of Islam: the Sunni, who make up 85 percent of Muslims today, and the Shi'ah, who constitute the remainder.

Meanwhile, the Umayyad empire fourished. The Umayyads, who ruled from Damascus, Syria, expanded their empire all the way from the western Mediterranean into Central Asia. They also made use of the *dhimmi* system in managing their heterogenous empire. Under this arrangement, Jews and Christians were not forced to convert to Islam, but they did have to pay a special tax for living in the empire. This way, the empire encouraged but did not force religious conversion. In fact, most of the future Islamic empires had systems in place that made room for religious minorities in their midst. In many of these empires, Christians and Jews would even have privileged places in the government and the military. In 750 a new dynasty, the 'Abbasids, overthrew the Umayyads and began to rule from a new capital city, Baghdad.

During the period of fragmentation and forescence (fowering) that took place between 870 and 1041, the 'Abbasid empire became a centre for art and science. After Chinese papermakers were captured in battle in 751, Muslim artisans learned how to make paper for books. Literature spread quickly. Great works were translated from ancient Greek, Sanskrit, Syriac, and other languages into Arabic. These new ideas encouraged the development of schools of philosophy (*falsafah*, adapting the word from Greek). Muslim scholars made contributions to the sciences in felds such as algebra, astronomy, botany, chemistry, and medicine. They became experts at map-making and navigation. Over time, regional dynasties began to develop, too, such as the Fatimids, who captured Egypt and created a new capital, Cairo.

Although Islam was blooming, it faced obstacles and hostilities that ultimately caused it to redirect and thrive in new ways. During the period of migration and renewal, from 1041 to 1405, broad in-migration and assimilation played an especially crucial role. As part of this trend, a number of Muslim cities were attacked by outsiders. Christian Crusaders captured Jerusalem, a city holy to Christians, Muslims, and Jews, in 1099. The Crusaders were fnally forced from Jerusalem by Saladin, a powerful Muslim leader, in 1187. In 1258, the Mongols—pagan, horse-riding tribes of the Central Asian steppe—invaded Baghdad, where they slaughtered hundreds of thousands of residents and terminated the caliphate. Ironically, after several generations, the Mongols themselves converted to Islam, spreading the faith across their vast empire.

Three powerful empires rose during the period of consolidation and expansion (1405–1683). Babur, a descendent of Mongol leader Genghis Khan, started taking over India in 1519, founding the Mughal dynasty. At its greatest extent, the Mughal empire covered most of the Indian subcontinent. Mughal ruler Shah Jahan had the Ta j Mahal, one of the architectural wonders of the world, built in memory of the favourite of his three wives. By contrast, the Shi'ite Safavid dynasty had its origins in a Suf brotherhood in northwestern Iran. After winning the support of local Turkish tribesmen and other disaffected groups, the Safavids were able to expand throughout Iran and into parts of Iraq.

Meanwhile, in what is now Turkey, the Ottoman Empire was on the march. The Ottoman dynasty, which had started at the turn of the 14th century, conquered lands in the Middle East and in Europe, including Hungary, Serbia, Romania, and Bosnia. In 1453 the Ottomans captured Constantinople from the Byzantine Empire and turned it into the new capital, Istanbul. The Ottoman Empire's trade ships controlled much of the Mediterranean Sea. The Ottomans had a sophisticated culture and made alliances with European powers such as France and Great Britain. Then, in 1683, the Ottomans reached a limit. In that year, they invaded Austria, penetrating all the way to Vienna, where their ambitious campaign failed. It was a turning point, and a telling marker for the future.

As the Islamic world entered its next phase, reform, dependency, and recovery (1683 to the present), it faced a new challenge—the rising power of Europe.

In the 1800s the British took over India as a colony, fnally snuffng out the crumbling Mughal empire. The Ottoman Empire survived longer, but over time it weakened as well. As it did, colonial powers such as France and Britain took control, both directly and indirectly, of more and more territory in Africa, Asia, and the Middle East.

Western powers grew increasingly interested in infuenc-ing the Middle East when they learned of the vast stores of oil that lay underneath such countries as Iran, Iraq, and Saudi Arabia. Eventually, colonized lands became new countries, in some cases more constructs than organic nations, with arbitrary boundaries and markedly different groups of people suddenly designated as countrymen. Such acts led to many questions about what kind of identity should matter most—national or religious.

As you read this book you will learn much more about the Islamic world. Yo u will have the opportunity to explore the perils and promise of great empires, to discover a profound and diverse cultural heritage, and to learn what unites and separates different branches of the Islamic faith. And you will gain a new perspective on one of the world's greatest and most enduring religions.

2

The Precursors of Islam

Adherence to Islam is a global phenomenon: Muslims predominate in some 30 to 40 countries, from the Atlantic eastward to the Pacific and along a belt that stretches across northern Africa into Central Asia and south to the northern regions of the Indian subcontinent. Although many in the West consider Arabs and Muslims synonymous, Arabs account for fewer than one-fifth of all Muslims, more than half of whom live east of Karachi, Pakistan. Despite the absence of large-scale Islamic political entities, the Islamic faith continues to expand, by some estimates faster than any other major religion.

A very broad perspective is required to explain the history of today's Islamic world. This approach must enlarge upon conventional political or dynastic divisions to draw a comprehensive picture of the stages by which successive Muslim communities, throughout Islam's 14 centuries, encountered and incorporated new peoples so as to produce an international religion and civilization.

In general, events referred to here are dated according to the Gregorian calendar, and eras are designated BCE (before the Common Era or Christian Era) and CE (Common Era or Christian Era), terms which are equivalent to BC (before Christ) and AD (Latin: *anno Domini*). In some cases the Muslim reckoning of the Islamic era is used, indicated by AH (Latin: *anno Hegirae*). The Islamic era begins with the date of Muhammad's emigration (Hijrah) to Medina, which corresponds to July 16, 622 CE, in the Gregorian calendar.

The term *Islamic* refers to Islam as a religion. The term *Islamicate* refers to the social and cultural complex that is historically associated with Islam and the Muslims, even when found among non-Muslims. *Islamdom* refers to that complex of societies in which the Muslims and their faith have been prevalent and socially dominant.

The prehistory of Islamdom is the history of central Afro-Eurasia from Hammurabi of Babylon to the Achaemenid Cyrus II in Persia to Alexander the Great to the Sasanian emperor Nushirvan to Muhammad in Arabia; or, in a Muslim view, from Adam to Noah to Abraham to Moses to Jesus to Muhammad. The potential for Muslim empire building was established with the rise of the earliest civilizations in western Asia. It was refned with the emergence and spread of what have been called the region's Axial Age religions – Abrahamic, centred on the Hebrew patriarch Abraham, and Mazdean, focused on the Iranian deity Ahura Mazda – and their later relative, Christianity. It was facilitated by the expansion of trade from eastern Asia to the Mediterranean and by the political changes thus effected. The Muslims were heirs to the ancient Egyptians, Babylonians, Persians, Hebrews, even the Greeks and Indians; the societies they created bridged time and space, from ancient to modern and from east to west.

THE RISE OF AGRARIAN-BASED CITIED SOCIETIES

In the 7th century CE a coalition of Arab groups, some sedentary and some migratory, inside and outside the Arabian Peninsula, seized political and fiscal control in western Asia, specifically of the lands between the Nile and Oxus (Amu Darya) rivers – territory formerly controlled by the Byzantines in the west and the Sasanians in the east. The factors that surrounded and directed their accomplishment had begun to coalesce long before, with the emergence of agrarian-based citied societies in western Asia in the 4th millennium BCE. The rise of complex agrarian-based societies, such as Sumer, out of a subsistence agricultural and pastoralist environment, involved the founding of cities, the extension of citied power over surrounding villages, and the interaction of both with pastoralists.

This type of social organization offered new possibilities. Agricultural production and intercity trading, particularly in luxury goods, increased. Some individuals were able to take advantage of the manual labour of others to amass enough wealth to patronize a wide range of arts and crafts. Of these, a few were able to establish territorial monarchies and foster religious institutions with wider appeal. Gradually the familiar troika of court, temple, and market emerged. The new ruling groups cultivated skills for administering and integrating non-kin-related groups. They benefted from the increased use of writing and, in many cases, from the adoption of a single writing system, such as the cuneiform, for administrative use. New institutions, such as coinage, territorial deities, royal priesthoods, and standing armies, further enhanced their power.

In such town-and-country complexes the pace of change quickened enough so that a well-placed individual might see the effects of his actions in his own lifetime and be stimulated to self-criticism and moral reflection of an unprecedented sort. The religion of these new social entities reflected and supported the new social environments. Unlike the religions of small groups, the religions of complex societies focused on deities, such as Marduk, Isis, or Mithra, whose appeal was not limited to one small area or group and whose powers were much less fragmented. The relationship of earthly existence to the afterlife became more problematic, as evidenced by the elaborate death rites of pharaonic Egypt. Individual religious action began to compete with communal worship and ritual; sometimes it promised spiritual transformation and transcendence of a new sort, as illustrated in the pan-Mediterranean mystery religions. Ye t large-scale organization had introduced social and economic injustices that rulers and religions could address but not resolve. To many, an absolute ruler uniting a plurality of ethnic, religious, and interest groups offered the best hope of justice.

Cultural Core Areas of the Settled World

By the middle of the 1st millennium BCE the settled world had crystallized into four cultural core areas: Mediterranean, Nile-to-Oxus, Indic, and East Asian. The Nile-to-Oxus, the future core of Islamdom, was the least cohesive and the most complicated. Whereas each of the other regions developed a single language of high culture—Greek, Sanskrit, and Chinese, respectively— the Nile-to-Oxus region was a linguistic palimpsest of Irano-Semitic languages of several sorts: Aramaic, Syriac (eastern or Iranian Aramaic), and Middle Persian (the language of eastern Iran).

The Nile-to-Oxus Region

In addition to its various linguistic groups, the Nile-to-Oxus region also differed in climate and ecology. It lay at the centre of a vast arid zone stretching across Afro-Eurasia from the Sahara to the Gobi. It favoured those who could deal with aridity – not only states that could control fooding (as in Egypt) or maintain irrigation (as in Mesopotamia) but also pastoralists and oasis dwellers. Although its agricultural potential was severely limited, its commercial possibilities were virtually unlimited. Located at the crossroads of the trans-Asian trade and blessed with numerous natural transit points, the region offered special social and economic prominence to its merchants.

The period from 800 to 200 BCE has been called the Axial Age because of its pivotal importance for the history of religion and culture. The world's first religions of salvation developed in the four core areas. From these traditions – for example, Judaism, Mazdeism, Buddhism, and Confucianism – derived all later forms of high religion, including Christianity and Islam. Unlike the religions that surrounded their formation, the Axial Age religions concentrated transcendent power into one locus, be it symbolized theistically or nontheistically. Their radically dualistic cosmology posited another realm, totally unlike the earthly realm and capable of challenging and replacing ordinary earthly values. The individual was challenged to adopt the right relationship with that "other" realm, so as to transcend mortality by earning a final resting place, or to escape the immortality guaranteed by rebirth by achieving annihilation of earthly attachment.

In the Nile-to-Oxus region two major traditions arose during the Axial Age: the Abrahamic in the west and the Mazdean in the east. Because they required exclusive allegiance through an individual confession of faith in a just and judging deity, they are called confessional religions. This deity was a unique all-powerful creator who remained active in history, and each event in the life of every individual was meaningful in terms of the judgment of God at the end of time. The universally applicable truth of these new religions was expressed in sacred writings. The traditions reflected the mercantile environment in which they were formed in their special concern for fairness, honesty, covenant keeping, moderation, law and order, accountability, and the rights of ordinary human beings. These values were always potentially incompatible with the elitism and absolutism of courtly circles. Most often, as in the example of the Achaemenian Empire, the conflict was expressed in rebellion against the crown or was adjudicated by viewing kingship as the guarantor of divine justice.

Although modern Western historiography has projected an East-West dichotomy onto ancient times, Afro-Eurasian continuities and interactions were well established by the Axial Age and persisted throughout premodern times. The history of Islamdom cannot be understood without reference to them. Through Alexander's conquests in the 4th century BCE in three of the four core areas, the Irano-Semitic cultures of the Nile-to-Oxus region were permanently overlaid with Hellenistic elements, and a link was forged between the Indian subcontinent and Iran. By the 3rd century CE, crosscutting movements like Gnosticism and Manichaeism integrated individuals from disparate cultures. Similarly organized large, land-based empires with official religions existed in all parts of the settled world. The Christian Roman Empire was locked in conflict with its counterpart to the east, the Zoroastrian-Mazdean Sasanian empire. Another Christian empire in East Africa, the Abyssinian, was involved alternately with each of the others. In the context of these regional interrelationships, inhabitants of Arabia made their fateful entrance into international political, religious, and economic life.

The Arabian Peninsula

The Arabian Peninsula consists of a large central arid zone punctuated by oases, wells, and small seasonal streams and bounded in the south by well-watered lands that are generally thin, sometimes mountainous coastal strips. To the north of the peninsula are the irrigated agricultural areas of Syria and Iraq, the site of large-scale states from the 4th millennium BCE. As early as the beginning of the 1st millennium BCE the southwest corner of Arabia, the Yemen, was also divided into settled kingdoms. Their language was a South Arabian Semitic dialect, and their culture bore some affinity to Semitic societies in the Fertile Crescent. By the beginning of the Common Era (the 1st century AD in the Christian calendar), the major occupants of the habitable parts of the arid centre were known as Arabs. They were Semitic-speaking tribes of settled, semi-settled, and fully migratory peoples who drew their name and apparently their identity from what the camel-herding Bedouin pastoralists among them called themselves: *'arab*.

Until the beginning of the 3rd century CE the greatest economic and political power in the peninsula rested in the relatively independent kingdoms of the Yemen. The Yemenis, with a knowledge of the monsoon winds, had evolved an exceptionally long and profitable trade route from East Africa across the Red Sea and from India across the Indian Ocean up through the peninsula into Iraq and Syria, where it joined older Phoenician routes across the Mediterranean and into the Iberian Peninsula. Their power depended on their ability to protect islands discovered in the Indian Ocean and to control the straits of Hormuz and Aden. It also depended on the Bedouin caravanners who guided and protected the caravans that carried the trade northward to Arab entrepôts like Petra and Palmyra. Participation in this trade was in turn an important source of power for tribal Arabs, whose livelihood otherwise depended on a combination of intergroup raiding, agriculture, and animal husbandry.

By the 3rd century, however, external developments began to impinge. In the early 3rd century, Ardashir I founded the Sasanian empire in Fars. Within 70 years the Sasanian state was at war with Rome, a conflict that was to last up to Islamic times. The Roman Empire was reorganized under Constantine the Great, with the adoption of a new faith, Christianity, and a new capital, Constantinople. These changes exacerbated the competition with the Sasanian empire and resulted in the spreading of Christianity into Egypt and Abyssinia and the encouraging of missionizing in Arabia itself. In Arabia Christians encountered Jews who had been settling there since the 1st century, as well as Arabs who had converted to Judaism. By the beginning of the 4th century the rulers of Abyssinia and Ptolemaic Egypt were interfering in the Red Sea area and carrying their aggression into the Yemen proper. In the first quarter of the 6th century the proselytizing efforts of a Jewish Yemeni ruler resulted in a massacre of Christians in the major Christian centre of Najran. This event invited Abyssinian Christian reprisal and occupation, which put a virtual end to indigenous control of the Yemen. In conflict with the Byzantines, the Zoroastrian-Mazdean Sasanians invaded Yemen toward the end of the 6th century, further expanding the religious and cultural horizons of Arabia, where membership in a religious community could not be apolitical and could even have international ramifcations. The connection between communal affliation and political orientations would be expressed in the early Muslim community and in fact has continued to function to the present day. The long-term result of Arabia's entry into international politics was paradoxical: it enhanced the power of the tribal Arabs at the expense of the "superpowers." Living in an ecological environment that favoured tribal independence and small-group loyalties, the Arabs had never established lasting large-scale states, only transient tribal confederations. By the 5th century, however, the settled powers needed their hinterlands enough to foster client states: the Byzantines oversaw the Ghassanid kingdom; the Persians oversaw the Lakhmid; and the Yemenis (prior to the Abyssinian invasion) had Kindah. These relationships increased Arab awareness of other cultures and religions, and the awareness seems to have stimulated internal Arab cultural activity, especially the classical Arabic, or *mudari,* poetry, for which the pre-Islamic Arabs are so famous. In the north, Arabic speakers were drawn into the imperial administrations of the Romans and Sasanians. Soon certain settled and semi-settled Arabs spoke and wrote Aramaic or Persian as well as Arabic, and some Persian or Aramaic speakers could speak and write Arabic. The prosperity of the 5th and 6th centuries, as well as the intensif cation of imperial rivalries in the late 6th century, seems to have brought the Arabs of the interior permanently into the wider network of communication that fostered the rise of the Muslim community at Mecca and Medina.

FORMATION AND ORIENTATION

A critical period of formation and orientation between the emergence of the Islamic faith and the death of Abu Bakr (reigned 632-634), the first of the Rashidun (Arabic: "Rightly Guided") caliphs, centred first on the city of Mecca (Makkah) and swiftly unfolded toward Yathrib (later known as Medina) and beyond. Although strong bonds of faith within the nascent community of believers were accentuated by the experience of persecution in Mecca, it was only after the emigration of the community in 622 to Yathrib, that the Islamic community-state began to emerge in earnest.

THE CITY OF MECCA: CENTRE OF TRADE AND RELIGION

Although the 6th-century client states were the largest Arab polities of their day, it was not from them that a permanently significant Arab state arose. Rather, it emerged among independent

Arabs living in Mecca at the junction of major north-south and west-east routes, in one of the less naturally favoured Arab settlements of the Hejaz (al-Hijaz). The development of a trading town into a city-state was not unusual, but, unlike many other western Arabian settlements, Mecca was not centred on an oasis or located in the hinterland of any non-Arab power. Although it had enough well water and springwater to provide for large numbers of camels, it did not have enough for agriculture; its economy depended on long-distance as well as short-distance trade.

Mecca Under the Quraysh Clans

Sometime after the year 400 CE Mecca had come under the control of a group of Arabs who were in the process of becoming sedentary; they were known as Quraysh and were led by a man remembered as Qusayy ibn Kilab (called al-Mujammi', "the Unifier"). During the generations before Muhammad's birth in about 570, the several clans of the Quraysh fostered a development in Mecca that seems to have been occurring in a few other Arab towns as well. They used their trading connections and their relationships with their Bedouin cousins to make their town a regional centre whose influence radiated in many directions. They designated Mecca as a quarterly *haram,* a safe haven from the intertribal warfare and raiding that was endemic among the Bedouin. Thus, Mecca became an attractive site for large trade fairs that coincided with pilgrimage (Arabic: *hajj*) to a local shrine, the Ka'bah. The Ka'bah housed the deities of visitors as well as the Meccans' supra-tribal creator and covenant-guaranteeing deity, called Allah. Most Arabs probably viewed this deity as one among many, possessing powers not specific to a particular tribe; others may have identified this figure with the God of the Jews and Christians.

The building activities of the Quraysh threatened one non-Arab power enough to invite direct interference: the Abyssinians are said to have invaded Mecca in the year of Muhammad's birth. But the Byzantines and Sasanians were distracted by internal reorganization and renewed conflict; simultaneously the Yemeni kingdoms were declining. Furthermore, these shifts in the international balance of power may have dislocated existing tribal connections enough to make Mecca an attractive new focus for supra-tribal organization, just as Mecca's equidistance from the major powers protected its independence and neutrality.

The Meccan link between shrine and market has a broader signifcance in the history of religion. It is reminiscent of changes that had taken place with the emergence of complex societies across the settled world several millennia earlier. Much of the religious life of the tribal Arabs had the characteristics of small-group, or "primitive," religion, including the sacralization of group-specific natural objects and phenomena and the multifarious presence of spirit beings, known among the Arabs as *jinn*. Where more-complex settlement patterns had developed, however, widely shared deities had already emerged, such as the "trinity" of Allah's "daughters" known as al-Lat, Manat, and al-'Uzza. Such qualified simplification and inclusivity, wherever they have occurred in human history, seem to have been associated with other fundamental changes— increased settlement, extension and intensification of trade, and the emergence of lingua francas and other cultural commonalties, all of which had been occurring in central Arabia for several centuries.

NEW SOCIAL PATTERNS AMONG THE MECCANS AND THEIR NEIGHBOURS

The sedentarization of the Quraysh and their efforts to create an expanding network of cooperative Arabs generated social stresses that demanded new patterns of behaviour. The ability of the Quraysh to solve their problems was affected by an ambiguous relationship between sedentary and migratory Arabs. Tribal Arabs could go in and out of sedentarization easily, and kinship ties often transcended lifestyles. The sedentarization of the Quraysh did not involve the destruction of their ties with the Bedouin or their idealization of Bedouin life. Thus, for example, did wealthy Meccans, thinking Mecca unhealthy, often send their infants to Bedouin foster mothers. Yet the settling of the Quraysh at Mecca was no ordinary instance of sedentarization. Their commercial success produced a society unlike that of the Bedouin and unlike that of many other sedentary Arabs. Whereas stratifca-tion was minimal among the Bedouin, a hierarchy based on wealth appeared among the Quraysh. Although a Bedouin group might include a small number of outsiders, such as prisoners of war, Meccan society was markedly diverse, including non-Arabs as well as Arabs, slave as well as free. Among the Bedouin, lines of protection for in-group members were clearly drawn; in Mecca, sedentarization and socioeconomic stratification had begun to blur family responsibilities and foster the growth of an oligarchy whose economic objectives could easily supersede other motivations and values. Whereas the Bedouin acted in and through groups and even regularized intergroup raiding and warfare as a way of life, Meccans needed to act in their own interest and to minimize conflict by institutionalizing new, broader social alliances and interrelationships.

The market-shrine complex encouraged surrounding tribes to put aside their conflicts periodically and to visit and worship the deities of the Ka'bah; but such worship, as in most complex societies, could not replace either the particularistic worship of small groups or the competing religious practices of other regional centres, such as al-Ta'if.

Very little in the Arabian environment favoured the formation of stable large-scale states. Therefore, Meccan efforts at centralization and unification might well have been transient, especially because they were not reinforced by any stronger power and because they depended almost entirely on the prosperity of a trade route that had been formerly controlled at its southern terminus and could be controlled elsewhere in the future, or exclude Mecca entirely. The rise of the Meccan system also coincided with the spread of the confessional religions, through immigration, missionization, conversion, and foreign interference. Alongside members of the confessional religions were unaffliated monotheists, known as *hanifs*, who distanced themselves from the Meccan religious system by repudiating the old gods but embracing neither Judaism nor Christianity. Eventually in Mecca and elsewhere a few individuals came to envision the possibility of effecting supra-tribal association through a leadership role common to the confessional religions, that is, prophethood or messengership. The only such individual who succeeded in effecting broad social changes was a member of the Hashim (Hashem) clan of Quraysh named Muhammad ibn 'Abd Allah ibn 'Abd al-Muttalib. One of their own, he accomplished what the Quraysh had started, first by working against them, later by working with them. When he was born, around 570, the potential for pan-Arab unification seemed nil, but after he died, in 632, the first generation of his followers were able not only to maintain pan-Arab unification but also to expand far beyond the peninsula.

3

The Prophet Muhammad

MUHAMMAD'S YEARS IN MECCA

Spiritual Awakening

Any explanation of such an unprecedented development must include an analysis not only of Muhammad's individual genius but also of his ability to articulate an ideology capable of appealing to multiple constituencies. His approach to the role of prophet allowed a variety of groups to conceptualize and form a single community. Muhammad was, according to many students of social behaviour, particularly well placed to lead such a social movement; in both ascribed and acquired characteristics he was unusual. Although he was a member of a high-status tribe, he belonged to one of its less well-placed clans.

He was fatherless at birth; his mother and grandfather died when he was young, leaving him under the protection of an uncle. Although he possessed certain admirable personality traits to an unusual degree, his commercial success derived not from his own status but from his marriage to a much older woman, a wealthy widow named Khadijah. During the years of his marriage, his personal habits grew increasingly atypical. He began to absent himself in the hills outside Mecca to engage in the solitary spiritual activity of the *hanifs*. At age 40, while on retreat, he saw a figure, whom he later identified as the angel Gabriel, who asked him to "recite" (*iqra'*), then overwhelmed him with a very strong embrace. Muhammad told the stranger that he was not a reciter. But the angel repeated his demand and embrace three times before the verses of the Qur'an, beginning with "Recite in the Name of thy Lord, who created," were revealed. Although a few individuals, including his wife Khadijah, recognized his experience as that of a messenger of God, the contemporary religious life of most of the Meccans and the surrounding Arabs did not prepare them to share in this recognition easily.

Arabs did recognize several other types of intermediaries with the sacred. Some of the kings of the Yemen are said to have had priestly functions. Tribal leaders, sheikhs, in protecting their tribes' hallowed custom (Sunnah), had a spiritual dimension. Tribal Arabs also had their *kahins*, religious specialists who delivered oracles in ecstatic rhymed prose (*saj'*) and read omens. And they also had their *sha'irs*, professionally trained oral poets who defended the group's honour, expressed its identity, and engaged in verbal duels with the poets of other groups. The power of the recited word was well established; the poets' words were even likened to arrows that could wound the unprotected enemy. Because Muhammad's utterances seemed similar, at least in form, to those of the *kahins*, many of his hearers naturally assumed that he was one of the fgures with whom they were more familiar. Indeed, Muhammad might not even have attracted attention had he not sounded like other holy men. But, by eschewing any source other than the one supreme being, whom he identifed as Allah ("God") and whose message he regarded as cosmi-cally significant and binding, he was gradually able to distinguish himself from all other intermediaries. Like many successful leaders, Muhammad broke through existing restraints by what might be called transformative conservatism. By combining familiar leadership roles with a less familiar one, he expanded his authority; by giving existing practices a new history, he reoriented them; by assigning a new cause to existing problems, he resolved them. His personal characteristics ft his historical circumstances perfectly.

Public Recitations

Muhammad's first vision was followed by a brief lull, after which he began to hear messages frequently, entering a special physical state to receive them and returning to normalcy to deliver them orally. Soon he began publicly to recite warnings of an imminent reckoning by Allah that disturbed the Meccan leaders. Muhammad was one of their own, a man respected for his personal qualities. Yet weakening kinship ties and increasing social diversity were helping him attract followers from many different clans and also from among tribeless persons, giving all of them a new and potentially disruptive affiliation. The fundamentals of his message, delivered often in the vicinity of the Ka'bah itself, questioned the very reasons for which so many people gathered there. If visitors to the Ka'bah assumed, as so many Arabs did, that the deities represented by its idols were all useful and accessible in that place, Muhammad spoke, as had Axial Age figures before, of a placeless and timeless deity that not only had created human beings, making them dependent on him, but would also bring them to account at an apocalypse of his own making. In place of time or chance, which the Arabs assumed to govern their destiny, Muhammad installed a final reward or punishment based on individual actions. Such individual accountability to an unseen power that took no account whatsoever of kin relationships and operated beyond the Meccan system could, if taken seriously, undermine any authority the Quraysh had acquired. Muhammad's insistence on the protection of the weak, which echoed Bedouin values, threatened the unbridled amassing of wealth so important to the Meccan oligarchy.

Efforts to Reform Meccan Society

Yet Muhammad also appealed to the town dweller by describing the human being as a member of a polis (city-state) and by suggesting ways to overcome the inequities that such an environment breeds. By insisting that an event of cosmic significance was occurring in Mecca, he made the town the rival of all the greater cities with which the Meccans traded. To Meccans who believed that what went on in their town and at their shrine was hallowed by tribal custom, Sunnah, Muhammad replied that their activities in fact were a corrupt form of a practice that had a very long history with the God of whom he spoke. In Muhammad's view, the Ka'bah had been dedicated to the aniconic worship of the one God (Allah) by Abraham, who fathered the ancestor of the Israelites, Ishaq (Isaac), as well as the ancestor of the Arabs, Isma'il (Ishmael). Muhammad asked his hearers not to embrace something new but to abandon the traditional in favour of the original. He appealed to his fellow Quraysh not to reject the Sunnah of their ancestors but rather to appreciate and fulfill its true nature. God should be worshipped not through offerings but through prayer and recitation of his messages, and his house should be emptied of its useless idols.

In their initial rejection of his appeal, Muhammad's Meccan opponents took the first step toward accepting the new idea: they attacked it. For it was their rejection of him, as well as his subsequent rejection by many Jews and Christians, that helped to forge Muhammad's followers into a community with an identity of its own and capable of ultimately incorporating its opponents. Muhammad's disparate following was exceptionally vulnerable, bound together not by kinship ties but by a "generic" monotheism that involved being faithful (*mu'min*) to the message God was sending through their leader. Their vulnerability was mitigated by the absence of formal municipal discipline, but their opponents within the Quraysh could apply informal pressures ranging from harassment and violence against the weakest to a boycott against Muhammad's clan, members of which were persuaded by his uncle Abu Talib to remain loyal even though most of them were not his followers. Meanwhile, Muhammad and his closest associates were thinking about reconstituting themselves as a separate community in a less hostile environment. In about 615, some 80 of his followers made an emigration (Hijrah) to Abyssinia, perhaps assuming that they would be welcome in a place that had a history of hostility to the Meccan oligarchy and that worshipped the same God who had sent Muhammad to them, but they eventually returned without establishing a permanent community. During the next decade, continued rejection intensified the group's identity and its search for another home. Although the boycott against Muhammad's clan began to disintegrate, the deaths of his wife and his uncle, about 619, removed an important source of psychological and social support. Muhammad had already begun to preach and attract followers at market gatherings outside Mecca; now he intensified his search for a more hospitable environment. In 620, he met with a delegation of followers from Yathrib, an oasis about 200 miles (320 km) to the northeast. In the next two years their support grew into an offer of protection.

Muhammad's Emigration to Yathrib (Medina)

Like Mecca, Yathrib was experiencing demographic problems: several tribal groups coexisted, descendants of its Arab Jewish founders as well as a number of pagan Arab immigrants divided into two tribes, the Aws and the Khazraj. Unable to resolve their conflicts, the Yathribis invited Muhammad to perform the well-established role of neutral outside arbiter (*hakam*). In September

622, having discreetly sent his followers ahead, he and one companion, Abu Bakr, completed the community's second and final emigration, barely avoiding Quraysh attempts to prevent his departure by force. By the time of the emigration, a new label had begun to appear in Muhammad's recitations to describe his followers: in addition to being described in terms of their faithfulness (*iman*) to God and his messenger, they were also described in terms of their undivided attention—that is, as *muslims*, individuals who assumed the right relationship to God by surrendering (*islam*) to his will. Although the designation *muslim*, derived from *islam*, eventually became a proper name for a specifc historical community, at this point it appears to have expressed commonality with other monotheists. Like the others, *muslims* faced Jerusalem to pray; Muhammad was believed to have been transported from Jerusalem to the heavens to talk with God; and Abraham, Noah, Moses, David, and Jesus, as well as Muhammad, all were considered to be prophets (*nabis*) and messengers of the same God. In Yathrib, however, conflicts between other monotheists and the *muslims* sharpened their distinctiveness.

The Forging of Muhammad's Community

As an autonomous community, *muslims* might have become a tribal unit like those with whom they had affliated, especially because the terms of their immigration gave them no special status. Ye t under Muhammad's leadership they developed a social organization that could absorb or challenge everyone around them. They became Muhammad's *ummah* ("community") because they had recognized and supported God's emissary (*rasul Allah*). The *ummah*'s members differed from one another not by wealth or genealogical superiority but by the degree of their faith and piety, and membership in the community was itself an expression of faith. Anyone could join, regardless of origin, by following Muhammad's lead, and the nature of members' support could vary. In the concept of *ummah*, Muhammad supplied the missing ingredient in the Meccan system: a powerful abstract principle for def ning, justifying, and stimulating membership in a single community.

Muhammad made the concept of *ummah* work by expanding his role as arbiter so as to become the sole spokesman for all residents of Yathrib, hereafter called Medina. Even though the agreement under which Muhammad had emigrated did not obligate non-Muslims to follow him except in his arbitration, they necessarily became involved in the fortunes of his community. By protecting him from his Meccan enemies, the residents of Medina identifed with his fate. Those who supported him as Muslims received special designations: the Medinans were called *ansar* ("helpers"), and his fellow emigrants were distinguished as *muhajirun* ("emigrants"). He was often able to use revelation to arbitrate.

Because the terms of his emigration did not provide adequate fnancial support, he began to provide for his community through caravan raiding, a tactic familiar to tribal Arabs. By thus inviting hostility, he required all the Medinans to take sides. Initial failure was followed by success, first at Nakhlah, where the Muslims defed Meccan custom by violating one of the truce months so essential to Meccan prosperity and prestige. Their most memorable victory occurred in 624 at Badr, against a large Meccan force; they continued to succeed, with only one serious setback, at Uhud in 625. From that time on, "conversion" to Islam involved joining an established polity, the successes of which were tied to its proper spiritual orientation, regardless of whether the convert shared that orientation completely. During the early years in Medina a major motif of Islamic history emerged: the connection between material success and divine favour, which had also been prominent in the history of the Israelites.

The *Ummah*'s Allies and Enemies

During these years, Muhammad used his outstanding knowledge of tribal relations to act as a great tribal leader, or sheikh, further expanding his authority beyond the role that the Medinans had given him. He developed a network

Battle of Badr

The early military victory of the Prophet Muhammad at the Battle of Badr (624 CE) seriously damaged Meccan prestige while strengthening the political position of Muslims in Medina and establishing Islam as a viable force in the Arabian Peninsula.

Since their emigration from Mecca (622), the Muslims in Medina had depended for economic survival on constant raids on Meccan caravans. When word of a particularly wealthy caravan escorted by Abu Sufyan, head of the Umayyad clan, reached Muhammad, a raiding party of about 300 Muslims, to be led by Muhammad himself, was organized. By filling the wells on the caravan route near Medina with sand, the Muslims lured Abu Sufyan's army to battle at Badr, near Medina, in March 624. Despite the superior numbers of the Meccan forces (about 1,000 men), the Muslims scored a complete victory, and many prominent Meccans were killed. The success at Badr was recorded in the Qur'an as a divine sanction of the new religion: "It was not you who slew them, it was God... in order that He might test the Believers by a gracious trial from Himself" (8:17). Those Muslims who fought at Badr became known as the *badriyun* and make up one group of the Companions of the Prophet. of alliances between his *ummah* and neighbouring tribes, and so competed with the Meccans at their own game. He managed and distributed the booty from raiding, keeping one-ffth for the *ummah*'s overall needs and distributing the rest among its members. In return, members gave a portion of their wealth as *zakat*, a tax paid to help the needy and to demonstrate their awareness of their dependence on God for all of their material benefts. Like other sheikhs, Muhammad contracted numerous, often strategically motivated, marriage alliances. He was also more able to harass and discipline Medinans, Muslim and non-Muslim alike, who did not support his activities fully. He agitated in particular against the Jews, one of whose clans, the Banu Qaynuqa', he expelled.

Increasingly estranged from nonresponsive Jews and Christians, he reoriented his followers' direction of prayer from Jerusalem to Mecca. He formally instituted the *hajj* to Mecca and fasting during the month of Ramadan as distinctive cultic acts, in recognition of the fact that *islam*, a generic act of surrender to God, had become Islam, a proper-name identity distinguished not only from paganism but from other forms of monotheism as well. As more and more of Medina was absorbed into the Muslim community and as the Meccans weakened, Muhammad's authority expanded. He continued to lead a three-pronged campaign—against nonsupporters in Medina, against the Quraysh in Mecca, and against surrounding tribes—and he even ordered raids into southern Syria. Eventually Muhammad became powerful enough to punish non-supporters severely, especially those who leaned toward Mecca. For example, he had the men of the Qurayzah clan of Jews in Medina executed after they failed to help him against the Meccan forces at the Battle of the Ditch in 627. But he also used force and diplomacy to bring in other Jewish and Christian groups. Because they were seen, unlike pagans, to have formed *ummahs* of their own around a revelation from God, Jews and Christians were entitled to pay for protection (*dhimmah*). Muhammad thus set a precedent for another major characteristic of Islamicate civilization, that of qualifed religious pluralism under Muslim authority.

Muhammad's Later Recitations

During these years of warfare and consolidation, Muhammad continued to transmit revealed recitations, though their nature began to change. Some commented

Battle of the Ditch

Victory at the Battle of the Ditch (Arabic: *Al-Khandaq* ["The Ditch"]) in 627 CE ultimately forced the Meccans to recognize the political and religious strength of the Muslim community in Medina.

A Meccan army of 3,000 men had defeated the undisciplined Muslim forces at Uhud near Medina in 625, wounding Muhammad himself. In March 627, when they had persuaded a number of Bedouin tribes to join their cause, the Meccans brought a force of 10,000 men against Medina again. Muhammad then resorted to tactics unfamiliar to the Arabs, who were accustomed to brief, isolated raids. Rather than sally out to meet the enemy in the usual way—the mistake made at Uhud—he had a ditch dug around Medina, according to tradition, at the suggestion of a Persian convert, Salman. The Meccan horsemen were disconcerted and soon grew bored of the siege, and the coalition of Bedouin tribes started breaking up. After an unsuccessful siege, the Meccans dispersed. With the Muslim and Meccan forces now more evenly matched and the Meccans tiring of a war that was damaging their trade, Muhammad used his victory to negotiate greater concessions for the Muslims in a treaty at al-Hudaybiyah (628).

on Muhammad's situation, consoled and encouraged his community, explained the continuing resistance of the Meccans, and urged appropriate responses. Some told stories about fgures familiar to Jews and Christians but cast in an Islamic framework.

Though still delivered in the form of God's direct speech, the messages became longer and less ecstatic, less urgent in their warnings if more earnest in their guidance. Eventually they focused on interpersonal regulations in areas of particular importance for a new community, such as sexuality, marriage, divorce, and inheritance. By this time certain Muslims had begun to write down what Muhammad uttered or to recite passages for worship (*salat*) and private devotion. The recited word, so important among the Arab tribes, had found a greatly enlarged signifcance. A competitor for Muhammad's status as God's messenger even declared himself among a nonmember tribe; he was Musaylimah of Yamamah, who claimed to convey revelations from God. He managed to attract numerous Bedouin Arabs but failed to speak as successfully as Muhammad to the various available constituencies.

Activism in the name of God, both nonmilitary as well as military, would become a permanent strand in Muslim piety. Given the environment in which Muhammad operated, his *ummah* was unlikely to survive without it; to compete as leader of a community, he needed to exhibit military prowess. (Like most successful leaders, however, Muhammad was a moderate and a compromiser; some of his followers were more militant and aggressive than he, and some were less so.) In addition, circumstantial necessity had ideological ramifcations. Because Muhammad as messenger was also, by divine providence, leader of an established community, he could easily defne the whole realm of social action as an expression of faith. Thus, Muslims were able to identify messengership with worldly leadership to an extent almost unparalleled in the history of religion. There had been activist prophets before Muhammad and there were activist prophets after him, but in no other religious tradition does the image of the activist prophet, and by extension the activist follower, have such a comprehensive and coherent justification in the formative period.

ISLAM AT MUHAMMAD'S DEATH

Muhammad's continuing success gradually impinged on the Quraysh in Mecca. Some defected and joined his community. His marriage to a Quraysh woman provided him with a useful go-between. In 628 he and his followers tried to make an Islamized *hajj* but were forestalled by the Meccans. At Al-Hudaybiyah, outside Mecca, Muhammad granted a 10-year truce on the condition that the Meccans would allow a Muslim pilgrimage the next year. Even at this point, however, Muhammad's control over his followers had its limits; his more zealous followers agreed to the pact only after much persuasion. As in all instances of charismatic leadership, persisting loyalty was correlated with continuing success. In the next year the Meccans allowed a Muslim *hajj;* and in the next year, 630, the Muslims occupied Mecca without a struggle. Muhammad began to receive deputations from many parts of Arabia. By his death in 632 he was ruler of virtually all of it.

The Meccan Quraysh were allowed to become Muslims without shame. In fact, they quickly became assimilated to the actual *muhajirun,* even though they had not emigrated to Medina themselves. Ironically, in defeat they had accomplished much more than they would have had they achieved victory: the centralization of all of Arabia around their polity and their shrine, the Ka'bah, which had been emptied of its idols to be flled with an infnitely greater invisible power.

Because intergroup conflict was banned to all members of the *ummah* on the basis of their shared loyalty to the emissary of a single higher authority, the limitations of the Meccan concept of *haram,* according to which the city quarterly became a safe haven, could be overcome. The broader solidarity that Muhammad had begun to build was stabilized only after his death, and this was achieved, paradoxically, by some of the same people who had initially opposed him. In the next two years one of his most significant legacies became apparent: the willingness and ability of his closest supporters to sustain the ideal and the reality of one Muslim community under one leader, even in the face of signifcant opposition. When Muhammad died, two vital sources of his authority ended—ongoing revelation and his unique ability to exemplify his messages on a daily basis. A leader capable of keeping revelation alive might have had the best chance of inheriting his movement, but no Muslim claimed messengership, nor had Muhammad unequivocally designated any other type of successor. The *ansar,* his early supporters in Medina, moved to elect their own leader, leaving the *muhajirun* to choose theirs, but a small number of *muhajirun* managed to impose one of their own over the whole. That man was Abu Bakr, one of Muhammad's earliest followers and the father of his favourite wife, 'A'ishah. The title Abu Bakr took, *khalifah* (caliph), meaning deputy or successor, echoed revealed references to those who assist major leaders and even God himself. To *khalifah* he appended *rasul Allah,* so that his authority was based on his assistance to Muhammad as messenger of God.

ABU BAKR'S SUCCESSION

Abu Bakr soon confronted two new threats: the secession of many of the tribes that had joined the *ummah* after 630 and the appearance among them of other prophet figures who claimed continuing guidance from God. In withdrawing, the tribes appear to have been able to distinguish loyalty to Muhammad from full acceptance of the uniqueness and permanence of his message. The appearance of other prophets illustrates a general phenomenon in the history of religion: the volatility of revelation as a source of authority. When successfully claimed, it has almost no competitor; once opened, it is difficult to close; and, if it cannot be contained and focused at the appropriate moment, its power disperses. Jews and Christians had

The *riddah* wars, or wars of apostasy, were a series of politico-religious uprisings in various parts of Arabia in about 632 CE during the caliphate of Abu Bakr.

In spite of the traditional resistance of the Bedouins to any restraining central authority, by 631 Muhammad was able to exact from the majority of their tribes at least nominal adherence to Islam, payment of the *zakat,* a tax levied on Muslims to support the poor, and acceptance of Medinan envoys. In March 632, in what Muslim historians later called the first apostasy, or *riddah,* a Yemeni tribe expelled two of Muhammad's agents and secured control of Yemen. Muhammad died three months later, and dissident tribes, eager to reassert their independence and stop payment of the *zakat,* rose in revolt. They refused to recognize the authority of Abu Bakr, interpreting Muhammad's death as a termination of their contract, and rallied instead around at least four rival prophets.

Most of Abu Bakr's reign was consequently occupied with *riddah* wars, which under the generalship of Khalid ibn al-Walid not only brought the secessionists back to Islam but also won over many who had not yet been converted. The major campaign was directed against Abu Bakr's strongest opponent, the prophet Musaylimah and his followers in Al-Yamamah. It culminated in a notoriously bloody battle at 'Aqraba' in eastern Najd (May 633), afterward known as the Garden of Death. The encounter cost the Muslims the lives of many *ansar* ("helpers"; Medinan Companions of the Prophet) who were invaluable for their knowledge of the Qur'an, which had been revealed to the Prophet, recited to his disciples, and memorized by them but not yet written down. Musaylimah was killed, the heart of the *riddah* opposition was destroyed, and the strength of the Medinan government was established. Sometime between 633 and 634 Arabia was fnally reunited under the caliph, and the energy of its tribes was diverted to the conquest of Iraq, Syria, and Egypt.

responded to this dilemma in their own ways; now it was the turn of the Muslims, whose future was dramatically affected by Abu Bakr's response. He put an end to revelation with a combination of military force and coherent rhetoric. He defined withdrawal from Muhammad's coalition as ingratitude to or denial of God (the concept of *kufr*. Thus he gave secession (*riddah*) cosmic signifcance as an act of apostasy punishable, according to God's revealed messages to Muhammad, by death. He declared that the secessionists had become Muslims, and thus servants of God, by joining Muhammad. They were not free not to be Muslims, nor could they be Muslims, and thus loyal to God, under any leader whose legitimacy did not derive from Muhammad. Finally, he declared Muhammad to be the last prophet God would send, relying on a reference to Muhammad in one of the revealed messages as *khatm al-anbiya'* ("seal of the prophets"). In his ability to interpret the events of his reign from the perspective of Islam, Abu Bakr demonstrated the power of the new conceptual vocabulary Muhammad had introduced.

Had Abu Bakr not asserted the independence and uniqueness of Islam, the movement he had inherited could have been splintered or absorbed by other monotheistic communities or by new Islam-like movements led by other tribal figures. Moreover, had he not quickly made the ban on secession and intergroup conflict yield material success, his chances for survival would have been very slim, because Arabia's resources could not support his state. To provide an adequate fiscal base, Abu Bakr enlarged impulses present in pre-Islamic Mecca and in the *ummah.* At his death he was beginning to turn his followers to raiding non-Muslims in the only direction where that was possible, the north. Migration into Syria and Iraq already had a long history; Arabs, both migratory and settled, were already present there. Indeed, some of them were already launching raids when 'Umar I, Abu Bakr's acknowledged successor, assumed the caliphate in 634. The ability of the Medinan state to absorb random action into a relatively centralized movement of expansion testifes to the strength of the new ideological and administrative patterns inherent in the concept of *ummah.*

The fusion of two once separable phenomena, membership in Muhammad's community and faith in Islam—the mundane and the spiritual—would become one of Islam's most distinctive features. Becoming and being Muslim always involved doing more than it involved believing.

On balance, Muslims have always favoured orthopraxy (correctness of practice) over orthodoxy (correctness of doctrine). Being Muslim has always meant making a commitment to a set of behavioral patterns because they reflect the right orientation to God. Where choices were later posed, they were posed not in terms of religion and politics, or church and state, but between living in the world the right way or the wrong way. Just as classical Islamicate languages developed no equivalents for the words *religion* and *politics,* modern European languages have developed no adequate terms to capture the choices as Muslims have posed them.

CONVERSION AND CRYSTALLIZATION

The Arab conquests are often viewed as a discrete period. The end of the conquests appears to be a convenient dividing line because it coincides with a conventional watershed, the overthrow of the Umayyad caliphs by the 'Abbasids. To illustrate their role in broader social and cultural change, however, the military conquests should be included in a period more than twice as long, during which the conquest of the hearts and minds of the majority of the subject population also occurred. Between 634 and 870 Islam was transformed from the badge of a small Arab ruling class to the dominant faith of a vast empire that stretched from the western Mediterranean into Central Asia.

SOCIAL AND CULTURAL TRANSFOTRMATIONS

As a result of so long and gradual a period of conversion, Arab cultures intermingled with the indigenous cultures of the conquered peoples to produce Islam's fundamental orientations and identities. The Arabic language became a vehicle for the transmission of high culture, even though the Arabs remained a minority. For the first time in the history of the Nile-to-Oxus region, a new language of high culture, carrying a great cultural florescence, replaced all previous languages of high culture. Trade and taxation replaced booty as the fiscal basis of the Muslim state; a nontribal army replaced a tribal one; and a centralized empire became a nominal confederation, with all of the social dislocation and rivalries those changes imply.

Yet despite continuous internal dissension, virtually no Muslim raised the possibility of there being more than one legitimate leader. Furthermore, the impulse toward solidarity, inherited from Muhammad and Abu Bakr, may have actually been encouraged by persisting minority status. While Muslims were a minority, they naturally formed a conception of Islamic dominance as territorial rather than religious, and of unconverted non-Muslim communities as secondary members. In one important respect the Islamic faith differed from all other major religious traditions: the formative period of the faith coincided with its political domination of a rich complex of old cultures. As a result, during the formative period of their civilization, the Muslims could both introduce new elements and reorient old ones in creative ways.

Just as Muhammad fulfilled and redirected ongoing tendencies in Arabia, the builders of early Islamicate civilization carried forth and transformed developments in the Roman and Sasanian territories in which they first dominated. While Muhammad was emerging as a leader in the Hejaz, the Byzantine and Sasanian emperors were ruling states that resembled what the Islamicate empire was to become. Byzantine rule stretched from North Africa into Syria and sometimes Iraq; the Sasanians competed with the Byzantines in Syria and Iraq and extended their sway, at its furthest, across the Oxus River. Among their subjects were speakers and writers of several major languages—various forms of Aramaic, such as Mandaean and Syriac; Greek; Arabic; and Middle Persian. In fact, a signifcant number of persons were probably bilingual or trilingual. Both the Byzantine and the Sasanian empire declared an offcial religion, Christianity and Zoroastrian-Mazdeism, respectively. The Sasanian empire in the early 7th century was ruled by a religion-backed centralized monarchy with an elaborate bureaucratic structure that was reproduced on a smaller scale at the provincial courts of its appointed governors. Its religious démography was complex, encompassing Christians of many persuasions, including monophysites, Nestorians, Orthodox, and others; pagans; gnostics; Jews; and Mazdeans. Minority religious communities were becoming more clearly organized and isolated. The population included priests; traders and merchants; landlords (*dihqans*), sometimes living not on the land but as absentees in the cities; pastoralists; and large numbers of peasant agriculturalists. In southern Iraq, especially in and around towns like Al-Hirah, it included migratory and settled Arabs as well. Both empires relied on standing armies for their defense and on agriculture, taxation, conquest, and trade for their resources. When the Muslim conquests began, the Byzantines and Sasanians had been in conflict for a century; in the most recent exchanges, the Sasanians had established direct rule in al-Hirah, further exposing its many Arabs to their administration. When the Arab conquests began, representatives of Byzantine and Sasanian rule on Arabia's northern borders were not strong enough to resist.

'UMAR I'S SUCCESSION

The Spirit of Conquest Under 'Umar I

Abu Bakr's successor in Medina, 'Umar I (ruled 634–644), had not so much to stimulate conquest as he had to organize and channel it. He chose as leaders skillful managers experienced in trade and commerce as well as warfare and imbued with an ideology that provided their activities with a cosmic significance. The total numbers involved in the initial conquests may have been relatively small, perhaps less than 50,000, divided into numerous shifting groups. Yet few actions took place without any sanction from the Medinan government or one of its appointed commanders. The fighters, or *muqatilah,* could generally accomplish much more with Medina's support than without. 'Umar, one of Muhammad's earliest and staunchest supporters, had quickly developed an administrative system of manifestly superior effectiveness. He defined the *ummah* as a continually expansive polity managed by a new ruling elite, which included successful military commanders like Khalid ibn al-Walid. Even after the conquests ended, this sense of expansiveness continued to be expressed in the way Muslims divided the world into their own zone, the Dar al-Islam, and the zone into which they could and should expand, the Dar al-Harb, the abode of war. The norms of 'Umar's new elite were supplied by Islam as it was then understood. Taken together, Muhammad's revelations from God and his Sunnah (precedent-setting example) defined the cultic and personal practices that distinguished Muslims from others: prayer, fasting, pilgrimage, charity, avoidance of pork and intoxicants, membership in one community centred at Mecca, and activism (jihad) on the community's behalf.

Forging the Link of Activism with Faithfulness

'Umar symbolized this conception of the *ummah* in two ways. He assumed an additional title, *amir al-mu'minin* ("commander of the faithful"), which linked organized activism with faithfulness (*iman*), the earliest defining feature of the Muslim. He also adopted a lunar calendar that began with the emigration (Hijrah), the moment at which a group of individual followers of Muhammad had become an active social presence. Because booty was the *ummah*'s major resource, 'Umar concentrated on ways to distribute and sustain it. He established a *diwan*, or register, to pay all members of the ruling elite and the conquering forces, from Muhammad's family on down, in order of entry into the *ummah*. The immovable booty was kept for the state. After the government's fifth-share of the movable booty was reserved, the rest was distributed according to the *diwan*. The *muqatilah* he stationed as an occupying army in garrisons (*amsar*) constructed in locations strategic to further conquest: al-Fustat in Egypt, Damascus in Syria, Kufah and Basra in Iraq. The garrisons attracted indigenous population and initiated signifcant demographic changes, such as a population shift from northern to southern Iraq. They also inaugurated the rudiments of an "Islamic" daily life; each garrison was commanded by a caliphal appointee, responsible for setting aside an area for prayer, a mosque (*masjid*), named for the prostrations (*sujud*) that had become a characteristic element in the five daily worship sessions (*salat*s). There the fghters could hear God's revelations to Muhammad recited by men trained in that emerging art. The most pious might commit the whole work to memory. There too, the Friday midday *salat* could be performed communally, accompanied by an important educational device, the sermon (*khutbah*), through which the fighters could be instructed in the principles of the faith. The mosque fused the practical and the spiritual in a special way: because the Friday prayer included an expression of loyalty to the ruler, it could also provide an opportunity to declare rebellion.

The series of ongoing conquests that fueled this system had their most extensive phase under 'Umar and his successor 'Uthman ibn 'Affan (ruled 644–656). Within 25 years Muslim Arab forces created the first empire to permanently link western Asia with the Mediterranean. Within another century Muslim conquerors surpassed the achievement of Alexander the Great, not only in the durability of their accomplishment but in its scope as well, reaching from the Iberian Peninsula to Central Asia. Resistance was generally slight and nondestructive, and conquest through capitulation was preferred to conquest by force. After the Sasanian city of Al-Hirah fell in 633, a large Byzantine force was defeated in Syria, opening the way to the final conquest of Damascus in 636. The next year further gains were made in Sasanian territory, especially at the Battle of al-Qadisiyyah, and in the next the focus returned to Syria and the taking of Jerusalem. By 640 Roman control in Syria was over, and by 641 the Sasanians had lost all their territory west of the Zagros. During the years 642 to 646 Egypt was taken under the leadership of 'Amr ibn al-'As, who soon began raids into what the Muslims called the Maghrib, the lands west of Egypt. Shortly thereafter, in the east, Persepolis fell; in 651 the defeat and assassination of the last Sasanian emperor, Yazdegerd III, marked the end of the 400-year-old Sasanian empire.

'UTHMAN'S SUCCESSION AND POLICIES

Discontent in 'Uthman's Reign

This phase of conquest ended under 'Uthman and ramifed widely. 'Uthman may even have sent an emissary to China in 651; by the end of the 7th century Arab Muslims were trading there. The fscal strain of such expansion and the growing independence of local Arabs outside the peninsula underlay the persisting discontents that surfaced toward the end of 'Uthman's reign. The very way in which he was made caliph had already signaled the potential for competition over leadership and resources. Perceived as pliable and docile, he was the choice of the small committee charged by the dying 'Umar with selecting one of their own number. Once in offce, however, 'Uthman acted to establish the power of Medina over and against some of the powerful Quraysh families at Mecca and local notables outside Arabia. He was accused of nepotism for relying on his own family, the Banu Umayyah, whose talents 'Umar had already recognized. Among his many other "objectionable" acts was his call for the production of a single standard collection of Muhammad's messages from God, which was known simply as the Qur'an ("Recitation" or "Recitations"). Simultaneously he ordered the destruction of any other collections. Although they might have differed only in minor respects, they represented the independence of local communities. Above all, 'Uthman was the natural target of anyone dissatisfed with the distribution of the conquest's wealth, since he represented and defended a system that defned all income as Medina's to distribute.

The diffculties of 'Uthman's reign took more than a century to resolve. They were the inevitable result not just of the actions of individuals but of the whole process initiated by Muhammad's achievements. His coalition had been fragile. He had disturbed existing social arrangements without being able to reconstruct and stabilize new ones quickly. Into a society organized along family lines, he had introduced the supremacy of trans-kinship ties. Ye t he had been forced to make use of kinship ties himself; and, despite his egalitarian message, he had introduced new inequities by granting privileges to the earliest and most intensely devoted followers of his cause. Furthermore, personal rivalries were stimulated by his charisma; individuals like his wife 'A'ishah, his daughter Fatimah, and her husband 'Ali frequently vied for his affection. 'Umar's *diwan* had, then, reinforced old inequities by extending privileges to wealthy high-placed Meccans, and it had introduced new tensions by assigning a lower status to those, indigenous or immigrant to the provinces, who joined the cause later (but who felt themselves to be making an equivalent or greater contribution). Other tensions resulted from conditions in the conquered lands: the initial isolation of Arab Muslims, and even Arab Christians who fought with them, from the indigenous non-Arab population; the discouragement of non-Arab converts, except as clients (*mawali*) of Arab tribes; the administrative dependence of peninsular Arabs on local Arabs and non-Arabs;

and the development of a tax system that discriminated against non-Muslims.

Intra-Muslim Conflicts

The ensuing conflicts were played out in a series of intra-Muslim disputes that began with 'Uthman's assassination in 656 and continued to the end of the period under discussion. The importance of kinship ties persisted, but they were gradually replaced by the identities of a new social order. These new identities resulted from Muslim responses to anti-Muslim activity as well as from Muslim participation in a series of controversies focused on the issue of leadership. Because the *ummah,* unified under one leader, was seen as an earthly expression of God's favour, and because God was seen as the controller of all aspects of human existence, the identities formed in the course of the *ummah*'s early history could fuse dimensions that secular modern observers are able to distinguish—religious, social, political, and economic. Furthermore, intra-Muslim rivalries changed during the conversion period; the meaningfulness of the new identities expanded as non-Muslims contributed to Islam's formation, through opposition or through conversion, and the key issues broadened as the participating constituencies enlarged. At first the disputes were coterminous with intra-Arab, indeed even intra-Quraysh, rivalries; only later did they involve persons of other backgrounds. Thus the faith of Islam was formed in conjunction with the crises that attended the establishment of rule by Muslims. Muslims might have produced an extremely localized and exclusivistic religion; but in spite of, and perhaps because of, their willingness to engage in continuing internal conflicts, they produced one of the most unified religious traditions in human history. THE FOUR *FITNAHS*

By the end of the period of conversion and crystallization, Muslim historians would retrospectively identify four discrete periods of conflict and label them *fitnahs*, trials or temptations to test the unity of the *ummah*. Many historians also came to view some identities formed during the *fitnahs* as authentic and others as deviant. This retrospective interpretation may be anachronistic and misleading. The entire period between 656 and the last quarter of the 9th century was conflict-ridden, and the *fitnahs* merely mark periods of intensifcation; yet the most striking characteristic of the period was the pursuit of unity.

The First *Fitnah*

In the first two *fitnahs* the claimants to the caliphate relied on their high standing among the Quraysh and their local support in either Arabia, Iraq, or Syria. Competition for the caliphate thus reflected rivalries among the leading Arab families as well as regional interests. The first *fitnah* occurred between 'Uthman's assassination in 656 and the accession of his kinsman Mu'awiyah I in 661 and included the caliphate of 'Ali, the cousin and son-in-law of Muhammad. It involved a three-way contest between 'party in Iraq; a coalition of important Quraysh families in Mecca, including Muhammad's wife 'A'ishah and Talhah and Zubayr; and the party of Mu'awiyah, the governor of Syria and a member of 'Uthman's clan, the Banu Umayyah. Ostensibly the conflict focused on whether 'Uthman had been assassinated justly, whether 'Ali had been involved, and whether 'Uthman's death should be avenged by Mu'awiyah or by the leading Meccans. 'Ali and his party (*shi'ah*) at first gained power over the representatives of the other leading Meccan families, then lost it permanently to Mu'awiyah, who elevated Damascus, which had been his provincial capital, to the status of imperial capital. Disappointed at the Battle of Siffn (657) with 'Ali's failure to insist on his right to rule, a segment of his partisans withdrew; another segment of 'Ali's party intensifed their loyalty to him as a just and heroic leader who was one of Muhammad's dearest intimates and the father of his only male descendants.

The Second *Fitnah*

The second *fitnah* followed Mu'awiyah's caliphate (661– 680), which itself was not free from strife, and coincided with the caliphates of Mu'awiyah's son Yazid I (ruled 680– 683), whom he designated as successor, and Yazid's three successors. This *fitnah* was a second-generation reprise of the first; some of the personnel of the former were descendants or relatives of the leaders of the latter. Once again, different regions supported different claimants, as new tribal divisions emerged in the garrison towns; and once again, representatives of the Syrian Umayyads prevailed. In 680, at Karbala' in Iraq, Yazid's army murdered al-Husayn, a son of 'Ali and grandson of Muhammad, along with a small group of supporters, accusing them of rebellion. And even though the Umayyads subdued Iraq,

Battle of Siffn

The series of negotiations and skirmishes during the first *fitnah* is known as the Battle of Siffn (May–July 657 CE). The battle and the arbitration that followed it undermined the authority of 'Ali as fourth caliph and prepared for the establishment of the Umayyad dynasty.

Mu'awiyah, governor of Syria, refused to recognize 'Ali as the new caliph before justice for the murder of his kinsman, the third caliph, 'Uthman, was done. For his part, 'Ali relied on the support of individuals who had been implicated in 'Uthman's murder and was therefore reluctant to prosecute them. 'Ali gathered support in Kufah, where he had established his centre, and invaded Syria. The two armies met along the Euphrates River at Siffn (near the Syrian-Iraqi border), where they engaged in an indecisive succession of skirmishes, truces, and battles, culminating in the legendary appearance of Mu'awiyah's troops with copies of the Qur'an impaled on their lances—supposedly a sign to let God's word decide the conflict. 'Ali agreed to bring the matter to arbitration on the basis of the Qur'an and delegated Abu Musa al-Ash'ari as his representative, while Mu'awiyah sent 'Amr ibn al-'As. By agreeing to arbitration, 'Ali conceded to deal with Mu'awiyah on equal terms, thus permitting him to challenge 'Ali's claim as leader of the Muslim community. This concession aroused the anger of a large group of 'Ali's followers, who protested that "judgment belongs to God alone" (Qur'an 6:57) and believed that arbitration would be a repudiation of the Qur'anic dictum "If one party rebels against the other, fght against that which rebels" (49:9). A small number of these pietists withdrew (*kharaju*) to the village of Harura' and so became known as Kharijites (Arabic: Khawarij).

Accounts of what precisely transpired at the arbitration vary; what is clear, however, is that 'Ali's position was critically weakened as a result. In May 658 Mu'awiyah was proclaimed caliph by some of his Syrian supporters. 'Ali and Mu'awiyah rebellions in the name of this or that relative of 'Ali continued, attracting more and more non-Arab support and introducing new dimensions to his cause. In the Hejaz the Marwanid branch of the Umayyads, descendants of Marwan I who claimed the caliphate in 684, fought against 'Abd Allah ibn al-Zubayr for years; by the time they defeated him, they had lost most of Arabia to Kharijite rebels.During the period of the first two *fitnahs,* resistance to Muslim rule was an added source of conflict. Some of this resistance took the form of syncretic or anti-Islamic religious movements. For example, during the second *fitnah,* in Iraq a Jew named Abu 'Isa al-'Isfahani led a syncretic movement (that is, a movement combining different forms of belief or practice) on the basis of his claim to be a prophet (an option not generally open to Muslim rebels) and forerunner of the messiah. He viewed Muhammad and Jesus as messengers sent not to all humanity but only to their own communities, so he urged each community to continue in its own tradition as he helped prepare for the coming of the messiah. In other areas, such as the newly conquered Maghrib, resistance took the form of large-scale military hostility. In the 660s the Umayyads had expanded their conflict with the Byzantine Empire by competing for bases in coastal North Africa; it soon became clear, however, that only a full-fledged occupation would serve their purposes. That occupation was begun by 'Uqbah ibn Naf ', the founder of al-Qayrawan (Kairouan, in modern Tunisia) and, as Sidi (Saint) 'Uqbah, the f rst of many Maghribi Muslim saints. It eventually resulted in the incorporation of large numbers of pagan or Christianized Amazigh (plural: Imazighen; Berber) tribes, the f rst large-scale forcible incorporation of tribal peoples since the secession of tribes under Abu Bakr. But f rst the Arab armies met f erce resistance from two individuals – one a man, Kusaylah, and one a woman, al-Kahinah – who became Amazigh heroes. Amazigh resistance was not controlled until the end of the 7th century, after which the Imazighen participated in the further conquest of the Maghrib and the Iberian Peninsula.

The Emergent Islamic Civilization

During the caliphate of 'Abd al-Malik ibn Marwan (ruled 685–705), which followed the end of the second *fitnah,* and under his successors during the next four decades, the problematic consequences of the conquests became much more visible. Like their Byzantine and late Sasanian predecessors, the Marwanid caliphs nominally ruled the various religious communities but allowed the communities' own appointed or elected officials to administer most internal affairs. Ye t now the right of religious communities to live in this fashion was justifed by the Qur'an and Sunnah; as peoples with revealed books (*ahl al-kitab*), they deserved protection (*dhimmah*) in return for a payment. The Arabs also formed a single religious community whose right to rule over the non-Arab protected communities the Marwanids sought to maintain.

To signify this supremacy, as well as his co-optation of previous legitimacy, 'Abd al-Malik ordered the construction of the monumental Dome of the Rock in Jerusalem, a major centre of non-Muslim population. The site chosen was sacred to Jews and Christians because of its associations with biblical history; it later gained added meaning for Muslims, who believed it to be the starting point for Muhammad's *mi'raj* (midnight journey to heaven). Although the Dome of the Rock (whose original function remains unclear) and many early mosques resembled contemporary Christian churches, gradually an Islamic aesthetic emerged: a dome on a geometrical base, accompanied by a minaret from which to deliver the call to prayer; and an emphasis on surface decoration that combined arabesque and geometrical design with calligraphic representations of God's Word.

Dome of the Rock

The Dome of the Rock (Arabic: Qubbat al-Sakhrah) is the oldest extant Islamic monument. The rock over which the shrine was built is sacred to both Muslims and Jews: the Prophet Muhammad is traditionally believed to have ascended into heaven from the site; and in Jewish tradition, it is here that Abraham, the progenitor and first patriarch of the Hebrew people, is said to have prepared to sacrifce his son Isaac. The Dome and Al-Aqsa Mosque are both located on the Temple Mount, the site of Solomon's Temple and its successors.

The original purpose of the Dome of the Rock, which was built between 685 and 691 CE by the caliph 'Abd al-Malik ibn Marwan, remains a source of debate. An unprecedented structure, it is virtually the first monumental building in Islamic history and is of considerable aesthetic and architectural importance; it is rich with mosaic, faience, and marble, much of which was added several centuries after its completion. Basically octagonal, the Dome of the Rock makes use of Byzantine techniques but is already distinctly Islamic. A wooden dome— approximately 60 feet (18 metres) in diameter and mounted on an elevated drum—rises above a circle of 16 piers and columns. Surrounding this circle is an octagonal arcade of 24 piers and columns. The outer walls repeat this octagon, each of the eight sides being approximately 60 feet (18 metres) wide and 36 feet (11 metres) high. Both the dome and the exterior walls contain many windows.

Christians and Muslims in the Middle Ages believed the Dome itself to be the Temple of Solomon (Templum Domini). The Knights Templar were quartered there in the Crusades, and Templar churches in Europe imitated its plan.

The Marwanids also depended heavily on the help of non-Arab administrative personnel (*kuttab*, singular *katib*) and on administrative practices (e.g., a set of government bureaus) inherited from Byzantine and, in particular, late Sasanian practice. Pre-Islamic writings on governance translated into Arabic, especially from Middle Persian, infuenced caliphal style. The governing structure at Damascus and in the provinces began to resemble pre-Islamic monarchy, and thus appealed to a majority of subjects, whose heritage extolled the absolute authority of a divinely sanctioned ruler. Much of the inspiration for this development came from 'Abd al-Malik's administrator in the eastern territories, al-Hajjaj ibn Yusuf al-Thaqaf, who was himself an admirer of Sasanian practice.

The Marwanid caliphs, as rulers of Muslims and non-Muslims alike, had thus been forced to respond to a variety of expectations. Ironically, it was their defense of the importance and distinctiveness of the Arabic language and the Islamic community, not their responsiveness to non-Muslim preferences, that prepared the way for the gradual incorporation of most of the subject population into the *ummah*. As the conquests slowed and the isolation of the fighters (*muqatilah*) became less necessary, it became more and more diffcult to keep Arabs garrisoned. The sedentarization of Arabs that had begun in the Hejaz was being repeated and extended outside the peninsula. As the tribal links that had so dominated Umayyad politics began to break down, the meaningfulness of tying non-Arab converts to Arab tribes as clients was diluted; moreover, the number of non-Muslims who wished to join the *ummah* was already becoming too large for this process to work effectively.

Simultaneously, the growing prestige and elaboration of things Arabic and Islamic made them more attractive to non-Arab Muslims and to non-Muslims alike. The more the Muslim rulers succeeded, the more prestige their customs, norms, and habits acquired. Heirs to the considerable agricultural and commercial resources of the Nile-to-Oxus region, they increased its prosperity and widened its horizons by extending its control far to the east and west. Arabic, which occasionally had been used for administrative purposes in earlier empires, now became a valuable lingua franca. As Muslims continued to adapt to rapidly changing circumstances, they needed Arabic to reflect upon and elaborate what they had inherited from the Hejaz. Because the Qur'an, translation of which was prohibited, was written in a form of Arabic that quickly became archaic to Muslims living in the garrisons and because it contained references to life in Arabia before and during Muhammad's time, full understanding of the text required special effort. Scholars began to study the religion and poetry of the *jahiliyyah,* the times of ignorance before God's revelation to Muhammad. Philologians soon emerged, in the Hejaz as well as in the garrisons. Many Muslims cultivated reports, which came to be known as Hadith, of what Muhammad had said and done, in order to develop a clearer and fuller picture of his Sunnah. These materials were sometimes gathered into accounts of his campaigns, called *maghazi.* The emulation of Muhammad's Sunnah was a major factor in the development of recognizably "Muslim" styles of personal piety and public decision making. As differences in the garrisons needed to be settled according to "Islamic" principles, the caliphs appointed arbitrating judges, *qadis,* who were knowledgeable in Qur'an and Sunnah. The pursuit of legal knowledge, *fiqh,* was taken up in many locales and informed by local pre-Islamic custom and Islamic resources. These special forms of knowledge began to be known as *'ulum* (singular *'ilm*) and the persons who pursued them as *ulama* (*'ulama',* singular *'alim*), a role that provided new sources of prestige and infuence, especially for recent converts or sons of converts.

Muslims outside Arabia were also affected by interacting with members of the religious communities over which they ruled. When protected non-Muslims converted, they brought new expectations and habits with them; Islamic eschatology is one area that reflects such enrichment. Unconverted protected groups (*dhimmis*) were equally influential. Expressions of Islamic identity often had to take into account the critique of non-Muslims, just as the various non-Muslim traditions were affected by contact with Muslims. This interaction had special consequences in the areas of prophethood and revelation, where major shifts and accommodations occurred among Jews, Christians, Mazdeans, and Muslims during the first two centuries of their coexistence. Muslims attempted to establish Muhammad's legitimacy as an heir to Jewish and Christian prophethood, while non-Muslims tried to distinguish their prophets and scriptures from Muhammad and the Qur'an. Within the emergent Islamicate civilization, the separate religious communities continued to go their own way, but the influence of Muslim rule and the intervention of the caliphs in their internal affairs could not help but affect them. The Babylonian Talmud, completed during these years, bears traces of early interaction among communities. In Iraq caliphal policy helped promote the Jewish gaons (local rabbinic authorities) over the exilarch (a central secular leader). Mazdeans turned to the Nestorian Church to avoid Islam, or reconceptualized Zoroaster as a prophet sent to a community with a Book. With the *dhimmi* system (the system of protecting non-Muslims for payment), Muslim rulers formalized and probably intensified pre-Islamic tendencies toward religious communalization. Furthermore, the greater formality of the new system could protect the subject communities from each other as well as from the dominant minority. So "converting" to Islam, at least in the Nile-to-Oxus region, meant joining one recognizably distinct social entity and leaving another. One of the most significant aspects of many Muslim societies was the inseparability of "religious" affiliation and group membership, a phenomenon that has translated poorly into the social structures of modern Muslim nations. In the central caliphal lands of the early 8th century, membership in the Muslim community offered the best chance for social and physical mobility, regardless of a certain degree of discrimination against non-Arabs. Among many astounding examples of this mobility is the fact that several of the early governors and independent dynasts of Egypt and the Maghrib were grandsons of men born in Central Asia. The Marwanid Maghrib illustrates a kind of conversion more like that of the peninsular Arabs.

After the defeat of initial Amazigh resistance movements, the Arab conquerors of the Maghrib quickly incorporated the Amazigh tribes en masse into the Muslim community, turning them immediately to further conquests. In 710 an Arab-Amazigh army set out for the Iberian Peninsula under the leadership of Tariq ibn Ziyad (the name Gibraltar is derived from Jabal Tariq, or "Mountain of Tariq"). They defeated King Roderick in 711; raided into and through the Iberian Peninsula, which they called al-Andalus; and ruled in the name of the Umayyad caliph. The Andalusian Muslims never had serious goals across the Pyrenees. In 732 Charles Martel encountered not a Muslim army but a summer raiding party; despite his "victory" over that party, Muslims continued their seasonal raiding along the southern French coast for many years. Muslim Andalusia is particularly interesting because there the pressure for large-scale conversion that was coming to plague the Umayyads in Syria, Iraq, and Iran never developed. Muslims may never have become a majority throughout their 700-year Andalusian presence.

Non-Muslims entered into the Muslim realm as Mozarabs, Christians who had adopted the language and manners, rather than the faith, of the Arabs. Given essentially the same administrative arrangements, the Iberian Christian population was later restored to dominance while the Syrian Christian population was drastically reduced, but the Iberian Jewish population all but disappeared while the Nile-to-Oxus Jewish population survived.

The Imazighen who remained in the Maghrib illustrate the mobility of ideologies and institutions from the central lands to more recently conquered territories. No sooner had they given up anti-Muslim resistance and joined the Muslim community than they rebelled again, but this time an Islamic identity, Kharijism, provided the justifcation. Kharijite ideas had been carried to the Maghrib by refugees from the numerous revolts against the Marwanids. Kharijite egalitarianism suited the economic and social grievances of the Imazighen as non-Arab Muslims under Arab rule. The revolts outlasted the Marwanids; they resulted in the first independent Maghribi dynasty, the Rustamid, founded by Muslims of Persian descent. The direct infuence of the revolts was felt as late as the 10th century and survives among small communities in Tunisia and Algeria.

The Third *Fitnah*

Meanwhile, in the central caliphal lands, growing discontent with the emerging order crystallized in a multifaceted movement of opposition to the Marwanids. It culminated in the third *fitnah*

(744–750), which resulted in the establishment of a new and final dynasty of caliphs, the 'Abbasids. Ever since the second *fitnah,* a number of concerned and self-conscious Muslims had begun to raise serious questions about the proper Muslim life and the Marwanids' ability to exemplify it, and to answer them by reference to key events in the *ummah*'s history. Pious Muslims tried to define a good Muslim and to decide whether a bad Muslim should be excluded from the community, or a bad caliph from office. They also considered God's role in determining a person's sinfulness and final dispensation. The proper relationship between Arab and non-Arab Muslims, and between Muslims and *dhimmis,* was another important and predictable focus of reflection.

The willingness of non-Arabs to join the *ummah* was growing, but the Marwanids had not found a solution that was either ideologically acceptable or fiscally sound. Because protected non-Muslim groups paid special taxes, fiscal stability seemed to depend on continuing to discourage conversion. One Marwanid, 'Umar II (ruled 717–720), experimented unsuccessfully with a just solution. In these very practical and often pressing debates lay the germs of Muslim theology, as various overlapping positions, not always coterminous with political groupings, were taken: rejecting the history of the community by demanding rule by Muhammad's family; rejecting the history of the community by following any pious Muslim and excluding any sinner; or accepting the history of the community, its leaders, and most of its members.

In the course of these debates the Marwanid caliphs began to seem severely deficient to a significant number of Muslims of differing persuasions and aspirations. Direct and implied criticism began to surface. Al-Hasan al-Basri, a pious ascetic and a model for the early Sufs, called on the Marwanids to rule as good Muslims and called on good Muslims to be suspicious of worldly power. Ibn Ishaq composed an account of Muhammad's messengership that emphasized the importance of the *ansar,* the Yathribi tribes that accepted Muhammad, and by implication the non-Arab converts (from whom Ibn Ishaq himself was descended). The Marwanids were accused of *bid'ah,* new actions for which there were no legitimate Islamic precedents. Their continuation of pre-Islamic institutions—the spy system, extortion of deposed officials by torture, and summary execution—were some of their most visible "offenses." To the pious, the ideal ruler, or imam (the word also for a Muslim who led the *salat*), should, like Muhammad, possess special learning and knowledge. The first four caliphs, they argued, had been imams in this sense, but under the Umayyads the caliphate had been reduced to a military and administrative office devoid of *imamah*, of true legitimacy.

This piety-minded opposition to the Umayyads, as it has been aptly dubbed, now began to talk about a new dispensation. Some of the most vocal members found special learning and knowledge only in Muhammad's family. Some defined Muhammad's family broadly to include any Hashimite; others, more narrowly, to include only descendants of 'Ali. As the number of Muhammad's descendants through 'Ali had grown, numerous rebellions had broken out in the name of one or the other, drawing on various combinations of constituencies and reflecting a wide spectrum of Islamic and pre-Islamic aspirations.

In the late Marwanid period, the piety-minded opposition found expression in a movement organized in Khorasan (Khurasan) by Abu Muslim, a semisecret operative of one particularly ambitious Hashimite family, the 'Abbasids. The 'Abbasids, who were kin but not descendants of Muhammad, claimed also to have inherited, a generation earlier, the authority of one of 'Ali's actual descendants, Abu Hashim. Publicly Abu Muslim called for any qualified member of Muhammad's family to become caliph, but privately he allowed the partisans (*shi'ah*) of 'Ali to assume that he meant them. Abu Muslim ultimately succeeded because he managed to link the concerns of the piety-minded in Syria and Iraq with Khorasanian discontent. He played upon the grievances of its Arab tribes against the tribes of Syria and their representatives in the Khorasanian provincial government, and on the millennial expectations of non-Arab converts and non-Muslims disenchanted with the injustices of Marwanid rule.

When in 750 the army organized and led by Abu Muslim succeeded in defeating the last Marwanid ruler, his caliph-designate represented only one segment of this broad coalition. He was the head of the 'Abbasid family, Abu al-'Abbas al-Saffah, who now subordinated the claims of the party of 'Ali to those of his own family and who promised to restore the unity of the *ummah*, or *jama'ah*. The circumstances of his accession reconfgured the piety-minded opposition that had helped bring him to power. The party of 'Ali refused to accept the compromise the 'Abbasids offered.

Their former fellow opponents did accept membership in the reunifed *jama'ah,* isolating the People of the Shi'ah and causing them to defne themselves in terms of more radical points of view. Those who accepted the early 'Abbasids came to be known as the People of the Sunnah and Jama'ah. They accepted the cumulative historical reality of the *ummah*'s first century: all the decisions of the community and all the caliphs it had accepted had been legitimate, as would be any subsequent caliph who could unite the community. The concept of *fitnah* acquired a fully historicist meaning: if internal discord were a trial sent by God, then any unifying victor must be God's choice.

Sunnis and Shi'ites

The historicists came to be known as Sunnis and their main opponents as Shi'ites. These labels are somewhat misleading because they imply that only the Sunnis tried to follow the Sunnah of Muhammad. In fact, each group relied on the Sunnah, but emphasized different elements. For the Sunnis, who should more properly be called the Jama'i-Sunnis, the principle of solidarity was essential to the Sunnah. The Shi'ites argued that the fundamental element of the Sunnah, and one willfully overlooked by the Jama'i-Sunnis, was Muhammad's devotion to his family and his wish that they succeed him through 'Ali. These new labels expressed and consolidated the social reorganization that had been under way since the beginning of the conquests. The vast majority of Muslims now became consensus-oriented, while a small minority became oppositional. The inherent inimitability of Muhammad's role had made it impossible for any form of successorship to capture universal approval.

When the 'Abbasids denied the special claims of the family of 'Ali, they prompted the Shi'ites to define themselves as a permanent opposition to the status quo. The crystallization of Shi'ism into a movement of protest received its greatest impetus during and just after the lifetime of one of the most infuential Shi'ite leaders of the early 'Abbasid period, Ja'far al-Sadiq (died 765). Ja'far's vision and leadership allowed the Shi'ites to understand their chaotic history as a meaningful series of efforts by truly pious and suffering Muslims to right the wrongs of the majority. The leaders of the minority had occupied the office of imam, the central Shi'ite institution, which had been passed on from the first imam, 'Ali, by designation down to Ja'far, the sixth. To protect his followers from increasing Sunni hostility to the views of radical Shi'ites, known as the *ghulat* ("extremists"), who claimed prophet-hood for 'Ali, Ja'far made a distinction that both protected the uniqueness of prophethood and established the superiority of the role of imam. Since prophethood had ended, its true intent would die without the imams, whose protection from error allowed them to carry out their indispensable task.

Although Ja'far did develop an ideology that invited Sunni toleration, he did not unify all Shi'ites. Differences continued to be expressed through loyalty to various of his relatives. During Ja'far's lifetime, his uncle Zayd revolted in Kufah (740), founding the branch of Shi'ism known as the Zaydiyyah (Zaydis), or Fivers (for their allegiance to the fifth imam), who became particularly important in southern Arabia. Any pious follower of 'Ali could become their imam, and any imam could be deposed if he behaved unacceptably. The Shi'ite majority followed Ja'far's son Musa al-Kazim and imams in his line through the 12th, who disappeared in 873. Those loyal to the 12 imams became known as the Imamis or Ithna 'Ashariyyah (Twelvers). They adopted a quietistic stance toward the status quo government of the 'Abbasids and prepared to wait until the 12th imam should return as the messiah to avenge injustices against Shi'ites and to restore justice before the Last Judgment. Some of Ja'far's followers, however, remained loyal to Isma'il, Ja'far's eldest son who predeceased his father after being designated. These became the Isma'iliyyah (Isma'ilis) or Sab'iyyah (Seveners), and they soon became a source of continuing revolution in the name of Isma'il's son Muhammad al-Tamm, who was believed to have disappeared. Challenges to the 'Abbasids were not long in coming. Of particular significance was the establishment in 789 of the first independent Shi'ite dynasty, in present-day Morocco, by Idris ibn 'Abd Allah ibn Hasan II, who had fled after participating in an unsuccessful uprising near Mecca. Furthermore, Kharijite rebellions continued to occur regularly.

The 'Abbasids

Legitimacy was a scarce and fragile resource in all pre-modern societies; in the early 'Abbasid environment, competition to define and secure legitimacy was especially intense. The 'Abbasids came to power vulnerable; their early actions undermined the unitive potential of their office. Having alienated the Shi'ites, they liquidated the Umayyad family, one of whom, 'Abd al-Rahman I, escaped and founded his own state in Andalusia. Although the 'Abbasids were able to buttress their legitimacy by employing the force of their Khorasanian army, by appealing to their piety-minded support, and by emphasizing their position as heirs to the pre-Islamic traditions of rulership, their own circumstances and policies militated against them. Despite their continuing preference for Khorasanian troops, the 'Abbasids' move to Iraq and their execution of Abu Muslim disappointed the Khorasanian chauvinists who had helped them. The non-Muslim majority often rebelled too. Bih'afrid ibn Farwardin claimed to be a prophet capable of incorporating both Mazdeism and Islam into a new faith. Hashim ibn Hakim, called al-Muqanna' ("the Veiled One"), around 759 declared himself a prophet and then a god, heir to all previous prophets, to numerous followers of 'Ali, and to Abu Muslim himself.

The 'Abbasids symbolized their connection with their pre-Islamic predecessors by founding a new capital, Baghdad, near the old Sasanian capital. They also continued to elaborate the Sasanian-like structure begun by the Marwanid governors in Iraq. Their court life became more and more elaborate, the bureaucracy fuller, the inner sanctum of the palace fuller than ever with slaves and concubines as well as the retinues of the caliph's four legal wives. By the time of Harun al-Rashid (ruled 786–809), Europe had nothing to compare with Baghdad, not even the court of his contemporary Charlemagne (ruled 768–814). But problems surfaced too. Slaves' sons fathered by Muslims were not slaves and so could compete for the succession. Despite the 'Abbasids' defense of Islam, unconverted Jews and Christians could be infuential at court. The head (vizier, or *wazir*) of the fnancial bureaucracy sometimes became the effective head of government by taking over the chancery as well. Like all absolute rulers, the 'Abbasid caliphs soon confronted the insoluble dilemma of absolutism: the monarch cannot be absolute unless he depends on helpers, but his dependence on helpers undermines his absolutism. Harun al-Rashid experienced this paradox in a particularly painful way: having drawn into his service prominent members of a family of Buddhist converts, the Barmakids, he found them such rivals that he liquidated them within a matter of years. It was also during Harun's reign that Ibrahim ibn al-Aghlab, a trusted governor in

Tunis, founded a dynasty that gradually became independent, as did the Tahirids, the 'Abbasid governors in Khorasan, two decades later.

The 'Abbasids' ability to rival their pre-Islamic predecessors was enhanced by their generous patronage of artists and artisans of all kinds. The great 7,000-mile (11,265-km) Silk Road from Ch'ang-an (now Xi'an [Sian], China) to Baghdad—then the two largest cities in the world—helped provide the wealth. The ensuing literary forescence was promoted by the capture of a group of Chinese papermakers at the Battle of Talas in 751. The 'Abbasids encouraged translation from pre-Islamic languages, particularly Middle Persian, Greek, and Syriac. This activity provided a channel through which older thought could enter and be reoriented by Islamicate societies. In the field of mathematics, al-Khwarizmi, from whose name the word *algorithm* is derived, creatively combined Hellenistic and Sanskritic concepts. The word

Harun al-Rashid

Harun al-Rashid (ruled 786–809; in full, Harun al-Rashid ibn Muhammad al-Mahdi ibn al-Mansur al-'Abbasi) was the son of al-Mahdi, the third 'Abbasid caliph (ruled 775–785). His mother, al-Khayzuran, was a former slave girl from Yemen and a woman of strong personality who greatly infuenced affairs of state in the reigns of her husband and sons. In 780 and 782 Harun was nominal leader of expeditions against the Byzantine Empire, though the military decisions were doubtless made by the experienced generals accompanying him. The expedition of 782 reached the Bosporus, opposite Constantinople, and peace was concluded on favourable terms. For this success Harun received the honorifc title of al-Rashid, "the one following the right path," and was named second in succession to the throne and appointed governor of Tunisia, Egypt, Syria, Armenia, and Azerbaijan, with his tutor, Yahya the Barmakid, acting as actual administrator. After a brief period of rule by his elder brother al-Hadi, Harun al-Rashid became caliph in September 786, with Yahya as his vizier.

The fabulous descriptions of Harun and his court in *The Thousand and One Nights* are idealized and romanticized, yet they had a considerable basis in fact. Untold wealth had fowed into the new capital of Baghdad since its foundation in 762. The leading men, and still more their wives, vied in conspicuous consumption, and in Harun's reign this reached levels unknown before. Harun's palace was an enormous institution, with numerous eunuchs, concubines, singing girls, and male and female servants. He himself was a connoisseur of music and poetry and gave lavish gifts to outstanding musicians and poets. In the stories of his nocturnal wanderings through Baghdad in disguise, he is usually accompanied by Masrur the executioner as well as friends like Ja'far the Barmakid (Yahya's son) and Abu Nuwas, the brilliant poet.

The less pleasant aspects of Harun's character are highlighted by the fall of the Barmakids, who for more than 16 years had been mainly responsible for the administration of the empire and who had provided the money for the luxury and extravagance of the court. Moreover, Ja'far the Barmakid had become Harun's special friend, so that gossip spoke of a homosexual relationship. Gossip also alleged that Harun had arranged that Ja'far should secretly marry his sister 'Abbasah, on condition that he did not consummate the marriage, but Ja'far fell in love with her, and she had a child. Whether in anger at this or not, Harun had Ja'far executed on Jan. 29, 803. The other members of the family were imprisoned and their goods confscated. Modern historians reject this gossip and instead suggest that Harun felt dominated by the Barmakids and may even have coveted their wealth. Moreover, diverse interests within the empire were being attracted to two opposing poles. On the one side were the "secretaries," or civil servants, many Persians, and many men from the eastern provinces; on the other side were the religious scholars (*ulama*), many Arabs, and many from the western provinces. Since the Barmakids favoured the first group of interests and the new vizier, al-Fadl ibn al-Rabi', favoured the second, it is likely that this political cleavage was involved in the change of ministry.

The struggle between the two groups of interests continued for at least half a century. Harun recognized its existence by assigning Iraq and the western provinces to his son al-Amin, the heir apparent, and the eastern provinces to the second in succession, his son al-Ma'mun. The former was son of the Arab princess Zubaydah and after 803 had al-Fadl ibn al-Rabi' as tutor. Al-Ma'mun was son of a Persian slave girl and after 803 had as tutor a Barmakid protégé, al-Fadl ibn Sahl. Harun has been criticized for so dividing the empire and contributing to its disintegration, for there was war between his two sons after his death; but it may well be that by making the cleavage manifest, he contributed to its eventual resolution after 850.

algebra derives from the title of his major work, *Kitab al-jabr wa al-muqabalah* ("The Book of Integration and Equation"). Movements such as *falsafah* (a combination of the positive sciences with logic and metaphysics) and *kalam* (systematic theological discourse) applied Hellenistic

thought to new questions. The translation of Indo-Persian lore promoted the development of *adab,* a name for a sophisticated prose literature as well as the set of refned urbane manners that characterized its clientele. Soon a movement called *shu'ubiyyah* arose to champion the superiority of non-Arabic tastes over the alleged crudeness of the poetry so dear to Arabic litterateurs. However, the great writer of early 'Abbasid times, al-Jahiz, produced a type of *adab* that fused pre-Islamic and Islamic concerns in excellent Arabic style. Many of these extra-Islamic resources conflicted with Islamic expectations. Ibn al-Muqaffa', an administrator under al-Mansur (ruled 754–775), urged his master to emulate pre-Islamic models, lest the law that the religious specialists (the *ulama*) were developing undermine caliphal authority irrevocably.

The 'Abbasids never acted on such advice completely; they even contravened it by appealing for piety-minded support. Having encouraged conversion, they tried to "purify" the Muslim community of what they perceived to be socially dangerous and alien ideas. Al-Mahdi (ruled 775–785) actively persecuted the Manichaeans, whom he defned as heretics so as to deny them status as a protected community. He also tried to identify Manichaeans who had joined the Muslim community without abandoning their previous ideas and practices. 'Abbasid "purifcation of Islam" ironically coincided with some of the most sig-nifcant absorption of pre-Islamic monotheistic lore to date, as illustrated by the stories of the prophets written by Al-Kisa'i, grammarian and tutor to a royal prince. Even though, like the Marwanids, the 'Abbasids continued to maintain administrative courts, not accessible to the *qadis,* they also promoted the study of *'ilm* and the status of those who pursued it. In so doing they fostered what Ibn al-Muqaffa' had feared—the emergence of an independent body of law, Shari'ah, which Muslims could use to evaluate and circumvent caliphal rule itself.

Shari'ah

A key figure in the development of Shari'ah was Abu 'Abd Allah al-Shaf'i, who died in 820. By his time Islamic law was extensive but uncoordinated, reflecting differing local needs and tastes. Schools had begun to form around various recognized masters, such as al-Awza'i in Syria, Abu Hanifah in Iraq, and Malik ibn Anas, all of whom used some combination of local custom, personal reasoning, Qur'an, and Hadith. Al-Shaf'i was raised in Mecca, studied with Malik, participated in a Shi'ite revolt in the Yemen, and was sent to Baghdad as a prisoner of the caliph. After his release he emigrated to Egypt, where he produced his most famous work. Like most other *faqihs* (students of jurisprudence, or *fqh*), al-Shaf'i viewed Muhammad's community as a social ideal and his first four successors as rightly guided. So that this exemplary time could provide the basis for Islamic law, he constructed a hierarchy of legal sources: Qur'an; Hadith, clearly traceable to Muhammad and in some cases to his companions; *ijma'* (consensus); and *qiyas* (analogy to one of the first three).

The way in which Islamic law had developed had allowed many pre-Islamic customs, such as the veiling and seclusion of women, to receive a sanction not given to them in the Qur'an or Hadith. Al-Shaf'i did not change that entirely. Law continued to be pursued in different centres, and several major "ways" (*madhhabs*) began to coalesce among Sunnis and Shi'ites alike. Among Sunnis, four schools came to be preeminent—Shaf'iyyah (Shafites), Malikiyyah (Malikites), Hanafyyah (Hanaftes), and Hanabilah (Hanbalites)—and each individual Muslim was expected to restrict himself to only one. Furthermore, the notion that the gate of *ijtihad* (personal effort at reasoning) closed in the 9th century was not firmly established until the 12th century. However, al-Shaf'i's system was widely influential in controlling divergence and in limiting undisciplined forms of personal reasoning. It also stimulated the collecting and testing of hadiths for their unbroken traceability to Muhammad or a companion. The need to verify Hadith stimulated a characteristic form of pre-modern Muslim intellectual and literary activity, the collecting of biographical materials into compendiums (*tabaqat*). By viewing the Qur'an and documentable Sunnah as preeminent, al-Shaf'i also undermined those in 'Abbasid court circles who wanted a more fexible base from which the caliph could operate. The Shari'ah came to be a supremely authoritative, comprehensive set of norms and rules covering every aspect of life, from worship to personal hygiene. It applied equally to all Muslims, including the ruler, whom Shari'ah-minded Muslims came to view as its protector, not its administrator or developer. While the caliphs were toying with theocratic notions of themselves as the shadow of God on Earth, the students of legal knowledge were defning their rule as "nomocratic," based only on the law they protected and enforced.

According to the Shari'ah, a Muslim order was one in which the ruler was Muslim and the Shari'ah was enshrined as a potential guide to all; Muslims were one confessional community among many, each of which would have its own laws that would apply except in disputes between members of different communities. The Shari'ah regulated relations and inequities among different segments of society—freeborn Muslim, slave, and protected non-Muslim. The process that produced Shari'ah resembled the evolution of oral Torah and rabbinic law, which the Shari'ah resembled in its comprehensiveness, egalitarianism, and consensualism, in its absorption of local custom, in its resistance to distinguishing the sublime from the mundane, and in its independence from government. Like many Jews, many ultra-pious Muslims came to view the law as a divine rather than human creation.

The Fourth *Fitnah*

During the reign of al-Ma'mun (813–833) the implications of all this *'ilm*-based activity for caliphal authority began to become clear. Al-Ma'mun came to the caliphate as the result of the fourth *fitnah,* which reflected the persisting alienation of Khorasan. Al-Ma'mun's father, Harun al-Rashid, provided for the empire to be divided at his death between two sons. Al-Amin would rule in the capital and all the western domains, and al-Ma'mun, from his provincial seat at Merv in Khorasan, would rule the less signifcant east. When Harun died, his sons struggled to expand their control. Al-Ma'mun won. During his reign, which probably represents the high point of caliphal absolutism, the court intervened in an unprecedented manner in the intellectual life of its Muslim subjects, who for the next generation engaged in the first major intra-Muslim conflict that focused on belief as well as practice. The Muslims, who now constituted a much more sizable proportion of the population but whose faith lacked doctrinal clarity, began to engage in an argument reminiscent of 2nd-century Christian discussions of the Logos. Among Christians, for whom the Word was Jesus, the argument had taken a Christological form. But for Muslims the argument had to centre on the Qur'an and its created or uncreated nature. Al-Ma'mun, as well as his brother and successor al-Mu'tasim (833–842), was attracted to the Mu'tazilah (Mutazilites), whose school had been infuenced by Hellenistic ideas as well as by contact with non-Muslim theologians. If the Qur'an were eternal along with God, his unity would, for the Mu'tazilah, be violated. They especially sought to avoid literal exegesis of the Qur'an, which in their view discouraged free will and produced embarrassing inconsistencies and anthropomorphisms. By arguing that the Qur'an was created in time, they could justify metaphorical and changing interpretation. By implication, Muhammad's position as deliverer of revelation was undermined because Hadith was made less authoritative.

The opponents of the Mu'tazilah, and therefore of the official position, coalesced around the figure of Ahmad ibn Hanbal. A leading master of Hadith, he had many followers, some of them recent converts, whom he was able to mobilize in large public demonstrations against the doctrine of the created Qur'an. Because viewing the Qur'an as created would invalidate its absolute authority, Ibn Hanbal argued for an eternal Qur'an and emphasized the importance of Muhammad's Sunnah to the understanding of it. By his time, major literary works had established a coherent image of the indispensability of Muhammad's prophet-hood. In fact, just before the Mu'tazilite controversy began, Ibn Hisham had produced his classic recension of the *sirah*, or life, of Muhammad, composed half a century earlier by Ibn Ishaq. As in the early Christian church, these were not merely dogmatic issues. They were rooted in the way ordinary Muslims lived, just as affection for a divine Christ had become popular sentiment by the time Arius and Athanasius debated. Although Muslims lacked an equivalent of the Christian church, they resolved these issues similarly; like Jesus for the Christians, the Qur'an for the Muslims was somehow part of God. Hadith-mindedness and emulation of

Muhammad's Sunnah had become such an essential part of the daily life of ordinary people that the Mu'tazilite position, as intellectually consistent and attractive as it was, was unmarketable. In a series of forcible inquiries called *mihnah,* al-Ma'mun and al-Mu'tasim actively persecuted those who, like Ibn Hanbal, would not conform, but popular sentiment triumphed, and after al-Mu'tasim's death the caliph al-Mutawakkil was forced to reverse the stand of his predecessors.

This caliphal failure to achieve doctrinal unity coincided with other crises. By al-Mu'tasim's reign the tribal troops were becoming unreliable and the Tahirid governors of Khorasan more independent. Al-Mu'tasim expanded his use of military slaves, fnding them more loyal but more unruly too. Soon he had to house them at Samarra', a new capital north of Baghdad, where the caliphate remained until 892. For most of this period, the caliphs were actually under the control of their slave soldiery, and, even though they periodically reasserted their authority, rebellions continued. Many were anti-Muslim, like that of the Iranian Babak (whose 20-year-long revolt was crushed in 837), but increasingly they were intra-Muslim, like the Kharijite-led revolt of black agricultural slaves (Zanj) in southern Iraq (869–883). By 870 then, the Baghdad-Samarra' caliphate had become one polity among many; its real rulers had no ideological legitimacy. At Córdoba the Umayyads had declared their independence, and the Maghrib was divided among several dynasties of differing persuasions—the Shi'ite Idrisids, the Kharijite Rustamids, and the Jama'i-Sunni Aghlabids. The former governors of the 'Abbasids, the Tulunids, ruled Egypt and parts of Arabia. Iran was divided between the Saffarids, governors of the 'Abbasids in the south, and the Persian Samanids in the north.

The centrifugal forces represented by these administrative divisions should not obscure, however, the existence of numerous centripetal forces that continued to give Islamdom, from Andalusia to Central Asia, other types of unity. The ideal of the caliphate continued to be a source of unity after the reality waned; among all the new states, no alternative to the caliphate could replace it. Furthermore, now that Muslims constituted a majority almost everywhere in Islamdom, conflict began to be expressed almost exclusively in Islamic rather than anti-Islamic forms. In spite of continuing intra-Muslim conflict, Muslim worship and belief remained remarkably uniform. The annual pilgrimage to Mecca helped reinforce this underlying unity by bringing disparate Muslims together in a common rite. The pilgrimage, as well as the rise of prosperous regional urban centres, enhanced the trade that traversed Islamdom regardless of political conflicts. Along the trade routes that crisscrossed Eurasia, Islamdom at its centre, moved not only techniques and goods but ideas as well. A network of credit and banking, caravansaries, and intercity mercantile alliances tied far-fung regions together. Central was the caravan, then the world's most effective form of transport. The peripatetic nature of education promoted cross-fertilization. Already the *faqir* (fakir), a wandering mendicant Sufi dervish, was a familiar traveler. Across Islamdom, similar mosque-market complexes sprang up in most towns; because municipal institutions were rare, political stability so unpredictable, and government intervention kept to a minimum (sometimes by design, more often by necessity), the Shari'ah and the learned men who carried it became a mainstay of everyday life and social intercourse.

Al-Bukhari

One of the greatest Muslim compilers and scholars of Hadith (the recorded corpus of the sayings and acts of the Prophet Muhammad), al-Bukhari (810–870) began learning the utterances and actions of the Prophet by heart while still a child. His travels in search of more information about them began with a pilgrimage to Mecca when he was 16. He then went to Egypt, and for 16 years he sought out informants from Cairo to Merv in Central Asia. Al-Bukhari was an extremely scrupulous compiler, showing great critical discrimination and editorial skill in his selection of traditions as authentic ones. From the approximately 600,000 traditions he gathered, he selected only about 7,275 that he deemed completely reliable and thus meriting inclusion in his *Al-Jami' al-Sahih* ("The Authentic Collection"). He arranged his collection in sections according to subject so that the reader can compare the soundest accounts of the Prophet's example, in word or deed, on points of law and religious doctrine as diverse as the validity of good deeds performed before conversion to Islam and marriage law.

As a preliminary to his *Sahih*, al-Bukhari wrote *Al-Ta'rikh al-kabir* ("The Large History"), which contains biographies of the persons forming the living chain of oral transmission and recollection of traditions back to the Prophet. Toward the end of his life, he was involved in a theological dispute in Nishapur and left that city for Bukhara, but, following his refusal to give special classes for Bukhara's governor and his children, he was forced into exile in Khartank, a village near Samarkand.

scent to the cut of a beard. Comprehensive and practical, the Sunnah could amuse as well. When asked whether to trust in God or tie one's camel, so a popular hadith goes, the Prophet replied, "Trust in God, then tie your camel." The signifcance of Hadith and Sunnah is represented by the ending date of the period of conversion and crystallization. No one can say exactly when the majority of Islamdom's population became Muslim. Older scholarship looks to the end of the f rst quarter of the 9th century, newer scholarship to the beginning of the third quarter. In 870 a man died whose life's work symbolized the consolidation of Islam in everyday life: al-Bukhari, who produced one of the six collections of Hadith recognized as authoritative by Jama'i-Sunni Muslims. His fellow collector of Hadith, Muslim ibn al-Hajjaj, died about four years later. About the same time, classical thinkers in other areas of Islamicate civilization died, among them the great author of *adab*, al-Jahiz (died 868/869), the great early ecstatic Suf s Abu al-Fayd Dhu al-Nun al-Misri (died 861) and Abu Yazid Bistami (died 874), the philosopher Ya'qub ibn Ishaq al-Sabah al-Kindi (died *c.* 870), and the historian of the conquests al-Baladhuri (died *c.* 892). Men of different religious and ethnic heritages, they signif ed by the last quarter of the 9th century the full and varied range of intellectual activities of a civilization that had come of age.

4

Fragmentation and Florescence

The unifying forces operative at the end of the period of conversion and crystallization persisted during the period of fragmentation and florescence, but the caliphal lands in Iraq became less central. Even though Baghdad remained preeminent in cultural prestige, important initiatives were being taken from surrounding "regions": Andalusia; the Maghrib and sub-Saharan Africa; Egypt, Syria, and the holy cities (Mecca and Medina); Iraq; and Iran, Afghanistan, Transoxania, and, toward the end of the period, northern India.

THE RISE OF COMPETITIVE REGIONS

The rise of competitive regions signified a number of important realities. Increasingly, regional courts could compete with the Abbasids and with each other as patrons of culture. Interregional and intraregional conflicts were often couched in terms of loyalties formed in the period of conversion and crystallization, but local history provided supplemental identities. Although the Abbasid caliphate was still a focus of concern and debate, other forms of leadership became important. Just as being Muslim no longer meant being Arab, being cultured no longer meant speaking and writing exclusively in Arabic. Certain Muslims began to cultivate a second language of high culture, New Persian. As in pre-Islamic times, written as well as spoken bilingualism became important. Ethnic differences were blurred by the effects of peripatetic education and shared languages. Physical mobility was so common that many individuals lived and died far from their places of birth. Cultural creativity was so noticeable that this period is often called the Renaissance of Islam.

Economic changes also promoted regional strengths. Although

Baghdad continued to proft from its central location, caliphal neglect of Iraq's irrigation system and southerly shifts in the trans-Asian trade promoted the fortunes of Egypt. The opening of the Sahara to Maghribi Muslims provided a new source of slaves, salt, and minerals; and Egyptian expansion into the Mediterranean opened a major channel for Islamicate infuence on medieval Europe. Islamdom continued to expand, sometimes as the result of aggression on the part of frontier warriors (*ghazis*) but more often as the result of trade. The best symbol of this expansiveness is Ibn Fadlan, who left a provocative account of his mission in 921, on behalf of the Baghdad caliph, to the Volga Bulgars, among whom he met Swedes coming down the river to trade.

By the beginning of the period of fragmentation and forescence, the subject populations of most Muslim rulers were predominantly Muslim, and nonsedentary peoples had ceased to play a major role. The period gave way to a much longer period (dated 1041-1405) in which migratory tribal peoples were once again critically important. In 1041 the reign of the Ghaznavid sultan Mas'ud I ended. By then the Ghaznavid state had lost control over the Seljuq Turks in their eastern Iranian domains and thus inaugurated Islamdom's second era of tribal expansion. Because localism and cosmopolitanism coexisted in the period of fragmentation and florescence, the period is best approached through a region-by-region survey that underscores phenomena of interregional significance.

ANDALUSIA, THE MAGHRIB, AND SUB-SAHARAN AFRICA

Andalusia, far from the centre of Islamdom, illustrated the extent of 'Abbasid prestige and the assertion of local creativity. In the beginning of the period, Islamicate rule was represented by the Umayyads at Córdoba. Established in 756 by 'Abd al-Rahman I (known as al-Dakhil, "the Immigrant"), a refugee from the 'Abbasid victory over the Syrian Umayyads, the Umayyad dynasty in Córdoba replaced a string of virtually independent deputies of the Umayyad governors in the Maghrib. At first the Cordoban Umayyads had styled themselves emirs, the title also used by caliphal governors and other local rulers. Though refugees from 'Abbasid hostility, they continued to mention the 'Abbasids in the salat al-jum'ah (Friday prayer) until 773. Their independence was not made off-cial, however, until their best-known member, 'Abd al-Rahman III (ruled 912–961), adopted the title of caliph in 929 and began having the Friday prayer recited in the name of his own house.

The fact that 'Abd al-Rahman declared his independence from the 'Abbasids while he modeled his court after theirs illustrates the period's cultural complexities. Like that of the 'Abbasids and the Marwanids, 'Abd al-Rahman's absolute authority was limited by the nature of his army

'Abd al-Rahman I

'Abd al-Rahman I (fourished 750–788) was a member of the Umayyad ruling family of Syria who founded an Umayyad dynasty in Spain. When the 'Abbasids overthrew the Umayyad caliphate in 750 CE and sought to kill as many members of the Umayyad family as possible, 'Abd al-Rahman fed, eventually reaching Spain. The Iberian Peninsula had for some time been occupied by Muslim Arab forces, and he recognized political opportunity for himself in the rivalries of the Qays and Yaman, the dominant Arab factions there. By shifting alliances and using mercenary support, he placed himself in a position of power, attacking and defeating the governor of Al-Andalus in 756 and making Córdoba his capital. As news of his success spread eastward, men who had previously worked in the Umayyad administrative system came to Spain to work with 'Abd al-Rahman, and his administrative system came to resemble that formerly operative in Damascus. 'Abd al-Rahman secured his realm against external attack by defeating armies sent by Charlemagne and the 'Abbasid caliph. Although he faced a series of rebellions by Muslim Spaniards, Imazighen (Berbers) from the mountainous areas, and various Arab clans, his authority and dynasty remained frmly in power.

(Amazigh tribesmen and Slav slaves) and by his dependence on numerous assistants. His internal problems were compounded by external threats, from the Christian kingdoms in the north and the Fatimids in the Maghrib. The Umayyad state continued to be the major Muslim presence in the peninsula until 1010, after which time it became, until 1031, but one of many independent city-states. Nowhere is the connection between fragmentation and forescence more evident than in the courts of these *muluk al-tawa'if*, or "party kings"; it was they who patronized some of

Andalusia's most brilliant Islamicate culture. This florescence also demonstrated the permeability of the Muslim-Christian frontier. For example, the poet and theologian Ibn Hazm (994–1064) composed love poetry, such as *Tawq al-hamamah* (*The Ring of the Dove)*, which may have contributed to ideas of chivalric love among the Provençal troubadours.

In 870 the Maghrib was divided among several dynasties, all but one of foreign origin and only one of which, the Aghlabids, nominally represented the 'Abbasids. The Muslim Arabs had been very different rulers than any of their predecessors—Phoenicians, Romans, Vandals, or Byzantines—who had occupied but not settled. Their interests in North Africa had been secondary to their objectives in the Mediterranean, so they had restricted themselves to coastal settlements, which they used as staging points for trade with the western Mediterranean or as sources of food for their "metropolitan" population.

They had separated themselves from the Imazighen with a fortifed frontier. The Arabs, however, forced away from the coast in order to compete more effectively with the Byzantines, had quickly tried to incorporate the Imazighen, who were also pastoralists. One branch of the Imazighen, the Sanhajah, extended far into the Sahara, across which they had established a caravan trade with blacks in the Sudanic belt. At some time in the 10th century the Sanhajah nominally converted to Islam, and their towns in the Sahara began to assume Muslim characteristics. Around 990 a black kingdom in the Sudan, Ghana, extended itself as far as Audaghost, the Sanhajah centre in the Sahara. Thus was black Africa first brought into contact with the Muslim Mediterranean, and thus were the conditions set for dramatic developments in the Maghrib during the 12th and 13th centuries.

In the late 9th century the Maghrib was unifed and freed from outside control for the first time. Paradoxically, this independence was achieved by outsiders associated with an international movement of political activism and subversion. Driven underground by 'Abbasid intolerance and a maturing ideology of covert revolutionism, the Isma'ili Shi'ites had developed mechanisms to maintain solidarity and undertake political action. These mechanisms can be subsumed under the term *da'wah,* the same word that had been used for the movement that brought the 'Abbasids to power. The *da'wah*'s ability to communicate rapidly over a large area rested on its traveling operatives as well as on a network of local cells. In the late 9th century an Isma'ili movement, nicknamed the Qaramitah (Qarmatians), had seriously but unsuccessfully threatened the 'Abbasids in Syria, Iraq, and Bahrain. Seeking other outlets, a Yemeni operative known as Abu 'Abd Allah al-Shi'i made contact, on the occasion of the *hajj*, with representatives of an Amazigh tribe that had a history of Kharijite hostility to caliphal control. The *hajj* had already become a major vehicle for tying Islamdom's regions together, and Abu 'Abd Allah's movement was only one of many in the Maghrib that would be inaugurated thereby.

In 901 Abu 'Abd Allah arrived in Little Kabylia (in present-day Algeria). For eight years he prepared for an imam, preaching of a millennial restoration of justice after an era of foreign oppression. After conquering the Aghlabid capital al-Qayrawan (in present-day Tunisia), he helped free from a Sijilmassa prison his imam, 'Ubayd Allah, who declared himself the *mahdi*, using a multivalent word that could have quite different meanings for different constituencies. Some Muslims applied *mahdi* to any justice-restoring divinely guided fgure; others, including many Jama'i-Sunnis, to the apocalyptic fgure expected to usher in the millennium before the Last Judgment; and still others, including most Shi'ites, to a returned or restored imam. Abu 'Abd Allah's followers may have differed in their expectations, but the *mahdi* himself was unequivocal: he was a descendant of 'Ali and Fatimah through Isma'il's disappeared son and therefore was a continuation of the line of the true imam. He symbolized his victory by founding a new capital named, after himself, al-Mahdiyyah (in present-day Tunisia). During the next half century the "Fatimids" tried with limited success to expand westward into the Maghrib and north into the Mediter ranean, where they made Sicily a naval base (912–913); but their major goal was Egypt, nominally under 'Abbasid control. From Egypt they would challenge the 'Abbasid caliphate itself. In 969 the Fatimid army conquered the Nile valley and advanced into Palestine and southern Syria as well.

EGYPT, SYRIA, AND THE HOLY CITIES

The Fatimid Dynasty

The Fatimids established a new and glorious city, Al-Qahirah ("The Victorious"; Cairo), to rival 'Abbasid Baghdad. They then adopted the title of caliph, laying claim to be the legitimate rulers of all Muslims as well as head of all Isma'ilis. Now three caliphs reigned in Islamdom, where there was supposed to be only one. In Cairo the Fatimids founded a great mosque-school complex, al-Azhar. They fostered local handicraft production and revitalized the Red Sea route from India to the Mediterranean. They built up a navy to trade as well as to challenge the Byzantines and underscore the 'Abbasid caliph's failure to defend and extend the frontiers. Fatimid occupation of the holy cities of Mecca and Medina, complete by the end of the 10th century, had economic as well as spiritual signifcance: it reinforced the caliph's claim to leadership of all Muslims, provided wealth, and helped him keep watch on the west Arabian coast, from the Hejaz to the Yemen, where a sympathetic Zaydi Shi'ite dynasty had ruled since 897. Fatimid presence in the Indian Ocean was even strong enough to establish an Isma'ili missionary in Sind. The Fatimids patronized the arts; Fatimid glass and ceramics were some of Islamdom's most brilliant. As in other regions, imported styles and tastes were transformed by or supplemented with local artistic impulses, especially in architecture, the most characteristic form of Islamicate art.

The reign of one of the most unusual Fatimid caliphs, al-Hakim, from 996 to 1021, again demonstrated the interregional character of the Isma'ili movement. Historians describe al-Hakim's personal habits as eccentric, mercurial, and unpredictable to the point of cruelty and his religious values as inconsistent with offcial Isma'ili teachings, tending toward some kind of accommodation with the Jama'i-Sunni majority. After he vanished under mysterious circumstances, his religious revisionism was not pursued by his successors or by the Isma'ili establishment in Egypt, but in Syria it inspired a peasant revolt that produced the Druze, who still await al-Hakim's return.

Al-Azhar University

Al-Azhar University (Arabic: Jami'at al-Azhar) is a chief locus of Islamic and Arabic learning centred on the mosque of that name in the medieval quarter of Cairo. It was founded by the Shi'ite (specifically, the Isma'ili sect) Fatimids in 970 CE and was formally organized by 988. Its name may allude to Fatimah, the Prophet's daughter, known as "al-Zahra'" ("the Luminous"), from whom the Fatimid dynasty derives its name. The format of education at al-Azhar remained relatively informal for much of its early history: initially there were no entrance requirements, no formal curriculum, and no degrees. The basic program of studies was—and still is—Islamic law, theology, and the Arabic langua

An Isma'ili centre of learning, al-Azhar fell into eclipse after Egypt's conquer by Saladin, founder of the Ayyubid dynasty and a Sunni, in the second half of the 12th century. It was revived under the Mam luks (1250- 1517), however, and continued to thrive thereafter as a centre of Sunni scholarship. It was damaged in an earthquake in the early 1300s and subsequently repaired, and additions, alterations, and renovations to its structures were undertaken at various points throughout the 14th and 15th centuries, particularly in the later Mamluk period, when it came under direct patronage.

With the defeat of the Mamluks in 1517, substantial architectural projects were few until the mid-18th century. In spite of this, al-Azhar's signifcance continued, and under Ottoman rule it held preeminent status among Egyptian institutions of learning. Opposition to the French in the late 18th century led to an uprising in 1798 centred on al-Azhar, and as a result it was bombarded by the French and temporarily closed. Nineteenth-century reform at al-Azhar owed in part to the involvement of a number of individuals. These included Jamal al-Din al-Afghani, who taught at al-Azhar in the 1870s and emphasized that modern science and other subjects were not incompatible with the Qur'an, and Muhammad 'Abduh, who was infuenced as a young intellectual by al-Afghani and later proposed, as a member of a government committee, a number of broad measures for reforming al-Azhar. In the late 19th century, procedures, including admission requirements and examinations, were formalized, and a number of modern subjects—some of them obligatory—were introduced.

Al-Azhar was nationalized and again underwent substantial reforms in the early 1960s. Since that time, faculties such as those of medicine and engineering have been established; women were first admitted in 1962. The modern university offers a number of faculties, some of them for women, as well as regional facilities.

The Hamdanid Dynasty

When the Fatimids expanded into southern Syria, another

Shi'ite dynasty, the Hamdanids, of Bedouin origin, had been ruling northern Syria from Mosul since 905. In 944 a branch of the family had taken Aleppo. Under the leadership of their most famous member, Sayf al-Dawlah (ruled *c.* 943– 967), the Hamdanids responded aggressively to renewed Byzantine expansionism in eastern Anatolia. They ruled from Aleppo until they were absorbed by the Fatimids after 1004; at their court some of Islamdom's most lastingly illustrious writers found patronage. Tw o notable examples are the poet al-Mutanabbi (915–965), who illustrated the importance of the poet as a premodern press agent of the court, and al-Farabi, who tried to reconcile reason and revelation. Al-Farabi contributed to the ongoing Islamization of Hellenistic thought. *Falsafah*, the Arabic cognate for the Greek *philosophia*, included metaphysics and logic, as well as the positive sciences, such as mathematics, music, astronomy, and anatomy. *Faylasufs* often earned their living as physicians, astrologers, or musicians. The *faylasuf*'s whole way of life, like that of the *adib*, reflected his studies. It was often competitive with that of more self-consciously observant Muslims because the *faylasuf* often questioned the relationship of revelation to real truth. The *faylasufs* felt free to explore inner truths not exposed to the view of ordinary people; they practiced prudent concealment (*taqiyyah*) of their deeper awareness wherever making it public might endanger the social order. The *faylasufs* shared the principle of concealment with the Shi'ites; both believed, for rather different reasons, that inner truth was accessible to only a very few. This esotericism had counterparts in all premodern societies, where learning and literacy were severely restricted.

IRAQ

Cultural Flowering in Iraq

By the late 9th and early 10th centuries the last remnant of the caliphal state was Iraq, under control of the Turkic soldiery. Political decline and instability did not preclude cultural creativity and productivity, however. In fact, Iraq's "generation of 870," loosely construed, contained some of the most striking and lastingly important fgures in all of early Islamicate civilization. Three of them illustrate well the range of culture in late 9th-and early 10th-century Iraq: the historian and Qur'anic exegete al-Tabari (*c.* 839–923), the theologian Abu al-Hasan al-Ash'ari (*c.* 873–*c.* 935), and the ecstatic mystic al-Hallaj (*c.* 858–922).

Al-Tabari was born in Tabaristan, south of the Caspian Sea, and as a young man he traveled to Baghdad. Rarely could a man earn his living from religious learning; unless he found patronage, he would probably engage in trade or a craft. All the more astounding was the productivity of scholars like al-Tabari, who said that he produced 40 leaves a day for 40 years. The size of his extant works, which include a commentary on the Qur'an and a universal history, testifes to the accuracy of his claim. His history is unique in sheer size and detail and especially in its long-term impact. His method involved the careful selection, organization, and juxtaposition of separate and often contradictory accounts cast in the form of Hadith. This technique celebrated the *ummah*'s collective memory and established a range of acceptable disagreement.

Al-Ash'ari, from Basra, made his contribution to systematic theological discourse (*kalam*). He had been attracted early to a leading Mu'tazilite teacher, but he broke away at the age of 40. He went on to use Mu'tazilite methods of reasoning to defend popular ideas such as the eternality and literal truth of the Qur'an and the centrality of Muhammad's Sunnah as conveyed by Hadith. Where his approach yielded objectionable results, such as an anthropomorphic rendering of God or a potentially polytheistic understanding of his attributes, al-Ash'ari resorted to the principle of *bila kayf* ("without regard to the how"), whereby a person of faith accepts that certain fundamentals are true without regard to how they are true and that divine intention is not always accessible to human intelligence. Al-Ash'ari's harmonization also produced a simple creed, which expressed faith in God, his angels, and his books, and affrmed belief in Muhammad as God's last messenger and in the reality of death, physical resurrection, the Last Judgment, and heaven and hell. Taken together, al-Tabari's historiography and al-Ash'ari's theology symbolize the consolidation of Jama'i-Sunni, Shari'ah-minded thought and piety.

The most visible and powerful 10th-century exponent of Sufsm was al-Hallaj. By his day, Sufsm had grown far beyond its early forms, which were represented by al-Hasan al-Basri (died 728), who practiced *zuhd*, or rejection of the world, and by Rabi'ah al-'Adawiyyah (died 801), who formulated the Suf ideal of a disinterested love of God. The mystics Abu Yazid Bistami (died 874) and Abu al-Qasim al-Junayd (died 910) had begun to pursue the experience of unity with God, first by being "drunk" with his love and with love of him and then by acquiring life-transforming self-possession and control. Masters (called sheikhs or *pirs*) were beginning to attract disciples (*murids*) to their way. Like other Muslims who tried to go "beyond" the Shari'ah to inner truth, the Sufs practiced concealment of inner awareness (*taqiyyah*). Al-Hallaj, one of al-Junayd's disciples, began to travel and preach publicly, however. His success was disturbing enough for the authorities in Baghdad to have him arrested and condemned to death; he was tortured and beheaded, and fnally his body was burned. Ye t his career had shown the power of Sufsm, which would by the 12th century become an institutionalized form of Islamic piety.

AL-TABARI

As a youth, Abu Ja'far Muhammad ibn Jarir al-Tabari (*c.* 839–923) demonstrated a precocious intellect and journeyed from his native town to study in the major centres of learning in Iraq, Syria, and Egypt. Over the course of many years he collected oral and written material from numerous scholars and libraries for his later work. Al-Tabari enjoyed suffcient fnancial independence to enable him to devote the latter part of his life to teaching and writing in Baghdad, the capital of the 'Abbasid caliphate, where he died in 923. The times in which he lived were marked by political disorder, social crisis, and philosophical-theological controversy. Discontent of diverse cause and circumstance brought open rebellion to the very heart of the caliph's empire, and, like all movements of socioeconomic origin in medieval Islam, sought legitimacy in religious expression directed against the offcial credo of Sunni orthodoxy.

Al-Tabari rejected out of hand the extreme theological positions of these opposition movements, but at the same time he also retreated from the embrace of the ultraorthodox Sunni faction, the Hanbali (a major school of Islamic law), which was represented most powerfully in the capital itself. An independent within orthodox ranks, he established his own school of jurisprudence, which did not long survive his own death. He nevertheless made a distinct contribution to the consolidation of Sunni thought during the 9th century. What al-Tabari accomplished for historical and Qur'anic studies consisted less in the discovery and initial recording of material than in the sifting and reorganization of it. His achievement was to condense the vast wealth of exegetical and historical erudition of the preceding generations of Muslim scholars (many of whose works are not extant in their original form) and to lay the foundations for both Qur'anic and historical sciences.

In his *Qur'an Commentary*, al-Tabari's method of composition was to follow the Qur'an text word by word, juxtaposing all of the juridical, lexicographical, and historical explanations transmitted in reports from the Prophet Muhammad, his companions, and their followers. To each report (hadith) was affxed a chain of "transmitters" (*isnad*) purporting to go back to the original informant. Divergent reports were seldom reconciled, the scholar's only critical tool being his judgment as to the soundness of the *isnad* and not of the content of the Hadith. Thus plurality of interpretation was admitted on principle.

The popular *History of Prophets and Kings* – which followed the *Commentary* – commenced with the Creation, followed by accounts regarding the patriarchs, prophets, and rulers of antiquity. The history of the Sasanian kings came next. For the period of the Prophet's life, al-Tabari drew upon the extensive researches of 8th-century Medinan scholars. Although pre-Islamic infuences are evident in their works, the Medinan perspective of Muslim history evolved as a theocentric (god-centred) universal history of prophecy culminating in the career of Muhammad and not as a continuum of tribal wars and values.

The sources for al-Tabari's *History* covering the years from the Prophet's death to the fall of the Umayyad dynasty (661–750 CE) were short monographs, each treating a major event or the circumstances attending the death of an important person. Al-Tabari supplemented this material with historical reports embodied in works on genealogy, poetry, and tribal affairs. Further, details of the early 'Abbasid period were available to him in a few histories of the caliphs that unfortunately have come down only in the fragments preserved by al-Tabari. Almost all of these accounts reflected an Iraqi perspective of the community; coupled with this is al-Tabari's scant attention to affairs in Egypt, North Africa, and Muslim Spain, so that his *History* does not have the secular "universal" outlook sometimes attributed to it. From the beginning of the Muslim era (dated from 622, the date of the Hijrah – the Prophet Muhammad's migration from Mecca to Medina), the *History* is arranged as a set of annals according to the years after the Hijrah. It terminates in the year 915. Obviously, al-Tabari could not sustain his preference for reports originating with the Prophet and the pious scholars of the early community known as *al-salaf*. His judgment of a report's reliability was now based upon the largely theoretical criterion that it should originate with either an eyewitness or a contemporary informant. This posed a problem for which al-Tabari had no practical solution. Oftentimes he placed separate accounts of an event side by side without editorial comment. He saw no relevance in searching for the nature and causes of events, for any ultimate explanation lay beyond history itself and was known to God alone. Prophetic tradition, like the Qur'an, provided positive commands and injunctions from God. History pointed to the consequences of heeding or ignoring him. For al-Tabari, therefore, history was the divine will teaching by example.

THE BUYID DYNASTY

Long before, however, a major political change occurred at Baghdad. In 945 control over the caliphs passed from their Turkish soldiery to a dynasty known as the Buyids or Buwayhids. The Buyids came from Daylam, near the southern coast of the Caspian Sea. Living beyond the reach of the caliphs in Baghdad, its residents had identifed with Imami Shi'ism. By about 930 three sons of a fsherman named Buyeh had emerged as leaders in Daylam. One of them conquered Baghdad, not replacing the caliph but ruling in his name. The fact that they were Shi'ite, as were the Idrisids, Fatimids, and Hamdanids, led scholars to refer to the period from the mid-10th to mid-11th century as the Shi'ite century.

Like other contemporary rulers, the Buyids were patrons of culture, especially of speculative thought (Shi'ism, Mu'tazilism, *kalam*, and *falsafah*). Jama'i-Sunni learning continued to be patronized by the caliphs and their families. The Buyids favoured no one party over another. However, their openness paradoxically invited a hardening in Jama'i-Sunni thought. Buyid attempts to maintain the cultural brilliance of the court at Baghdad were limited by a decline in revenue occasioned partly by a shift in trade routes to Fatimid Egypt, and partly by long-term neglect of Iraq's irrigation works. The caliphs had occasionally made land assignments (*t*) to soldiers in lieu of paying salaries; now the Buyids extended the practice to other individuals and thus removed an important source of revenue from central control. After 983, Buyid territories were split among various members of the family, and pressure was applied to their borders from both the west (by Hamdanids and Fatimids) and the east (by Samanids, Ghaznavids, and Seljuqs).

The economic diffculties of Buyid Iraq promoted urban unrest, accounts of which provide a rare glimpse into the lives of ordinary Muslim town dwellers. Numerous movements served as outlets for socioeconomic grievances, directed most often toward the wealthy or the military. The concentration of wealth in the cities had produced a bipolar stratifcation system conveyed in the sources by a pair of words, *khass* (special) and *'amm* (ordinary). In the environment of 10th-and 11th-century Iraq, an instance of rising food prices or offcial maltreatment could easily spark riots of varying size, duration, and intensity. Strategies for protest included raiding, looting, and assault. Some movements were more coherently ideological than others, and various forms of piety could reflect socioeco-nomic distinctions. Some movements were particularly attractive to artisans, servants, and soldiers, as was the case with the proponents of Hadith, whose mentor, Ahmad ibn Hanbal (died 855), was viewed as a martyr because of his suffering at the hands of the caliph. Other forms of piety, such as Shi'ism, could be associated with wealthier elements among the landowning and merchant classes.

Beneath the more organized forms of social action lay a more fuid kind of association, most often described by the labels *'ayyar* and *futuwwah*. These terms refer to individuals acting in concert, as needed, on the basis of certain rough-hewn concepts of proper male public behaviour. Such associations had counterparts in the late Hellenistic world, just as they have parallels in the voluntary protective associations formed in the 19th and 20th centuries whenever offcial institutions of protection were either chronically or temporarily defcient. For some of the Islamicate "gangs" or "clubs," thuggery may have been the norm; for others, the fgure of the fourth caliph and first imam, 'Ali, seems to have provided an exemplar. Even though Shi'ites had become a separate group with a distinctive interpretation of 'Ali's signifcance, a more generalized affection for the family of the Prophet and especially for 'Ali was widespread among Jama'i-Sunnis. 'Ali had come to be recognized as the archetypal young male (*fata*). A related word, *futuwwah*, signifed groups of young men who pursued such virtues as courage, aiding the weak, generosity, endurance of suffering, love of truth, and hospitality.

Premodern Islamicate societies were characterized by a high degree of fuidity, occasionalism, and voluntarism in the structuring of associations, organizations, loyalties, and occupations. Although all societies must develop ways to maintain social boundaries, ease interaction among groups, and buffer friction, the ways in which Muslim societies have fulflled these needs seem unusually diff-cult to delineate. For example, in Muslim cities of the period under discussion, the only offcial offceholders were appointees of the central government, such as the governor; the *muhtasib*, a transformed Byzantine *agorano-mos* who was monitor of public morality as well as of fair-market practice; or the *sahib al-shurtah*, head of the police. In the absence of an organized church or ordained clergy, those whose infuence derived from piety or learning were infuential because they were recognized as such, not because they were appointed, and men of very different degrees of learning might earn the designation of *'alim*. Although the ruler was expected to contribute to the maintenance of public services, neither he nor anyone else was obligated to do so. Though the ruler might maintain prisons for those whose behaviour he disapproved, the local *qadi*s had need of none, relying generally on persuasion or negotiation and borrowing the caliphal police on the relatively rare occasion on which someone needed to be brought before them by force. There was no formalized mode of succession for any of the dynasties of the time. Competition, sometimes armed, was relied upon to produce the most qualifed candidate.

Patronage was an important basis of social organization. The family served as a premodern welfare agency; where it was absent, minimal public institutions, such as hospitals, provided. One of the most important funding mechanisms for public services was a private one, the *waqf*. The *waqf* provided a legal way to circumvent the Shari'ah's requirement that an individual's estate be divided among many heirs. Through a *waqf*, an individual could endow an institution or group with all or part of his estate, in perpetuity, before his death. A *waqf* might provide books for a school, candles or mats for a mosque, salaries of religious functionaries, or land for a hospital or caravansary. *Waqf* money or lands were indivisible, although they might contribute to the welfare of a potential heir who happened to be involved in the *waqf*-supported activity. The *waqf*, like other forms of patronage, provided needed social services without offcial intervention. On other occasions, wealthy individuals, especially those connected with the ruling family, might simply patronize favourite activities. In addition to patronage, many other overlapping ties bound individual Muslims together: loyalties to an occupation— soldier, merchant, learned man, artisan, government worker—and loyalties to a town or neighbourhood, or to a form of piety, or to persons to whom one made an oath for a specifc purpose; and ties to patron or to family, especially foster-parentage (*istina'*), the counterpart of which was signifcant in medieval Christendom.

The Qur'an and Shari'ah discouraged corporate responsibility in favour of individual action; even the legal scope of partnership was limited. Ye t the unstable political realities that had militated against the emergence of broad-based institutions sometimes called for corporate action, as when a city came to terms with a new ruler or invader. In those cases, a vaguely defned group of notables, known usually as *a'yan*, might come together to represent their city in negotiations, only to cease corporate action when the more functional small-group loyalties could safely be resumed. Within this shifting frame of individuals and groups, the ruler was expected to maintain a workable, if not equitable, balance. More often than not the real ruler was a local *amir* of some sort. For this reason, the de facto system of rule that emerged during this period, despite the persistence of the central caliphate in Baghdad, has sometimes been referred to as the *a'yan-amir* system.

The city's physical and social organization reflected this complex relationship between public and private and between individual and group. It was marked by physically separated quarters; multiple markets and mosques; mazelike patterns of narrow streets and alleys with dwellings oriented toward an inner courtyard; an absence of public meeting places other than bath, market, and mosque; and the concentration of social life in private residences. The *qadi* and *adib* al-Tanukhi provides a lively and humorous picture of 10th-century Baghdad, of a society of individuals with overlapping affliations and shifting statuses: saints and scoundrels, heroes and rogues, rich men and poor. This mobility is illustrated by al-Tanukhi's boast to a rival, "My line begins with me while yours ends with you." The prose genre of *maqamah*, said to have been invented by al-Hamadhani (died 1008), recounted the exploits of a clever, articulate scoundrel dependent on his own wits for his survival and success.

IRAN, AFGHANISTAN, AND INDIA

In the middle of the "Shi'ite century" a major Sunni revival occurred in eastern Islamdom in connection with the emergence of the second major language of Islamicate high culture, New Persian. This double revival was accomplished by two Iranian dynasties, the Samanids and the Ghaznavids; Ghaznavid zeal even spilled over into India.

The Samanids

The Samanid dynasty (819–999) stemmed from a local family appointed by the 'Abbasids to govern at Bukhara and Samarkand. Gradually the Samanids had absorbed the domains of the rebellious Tahirids and Saffarids in northeastern Iran and reduced the Saffarids to a small state in Sistan. The Samanids, relying on Turkic slave troops, also managed to contain the migratory pastoralist Turkic tribes who continually pressed on Iran from across the Oxus River. In the 950s they even managed to convert some of these Turkic tribes to Islam.

The Samanid court at Bukhara attracted leading scholars, such as the philosophers Abu Bakr al-Razi (died 925 or 935) and Avicenna (Ibn Sina; 980–1037), who later worked for the Buyids; and the poet Ferdowsi (died *c.* 1020). Though not Shi'ites, the Samanids expressed an interest in Shi'ite thought, especially in its Isma'ili form, which was then the locus of so much intellectual vitality. The Samanids also fostered the development of a second Islamicate language of high culture, New Persian. It combined the grammatical structure and vocabulary of spoken Persian with vocabulary from Arabic, the existing language of high culture in Iran. A landmark of this "Persianizing" of Iran was Ferdowsi's epic poem, the *Shah-nameh* ("Book of Kings"), written entirely in New Persian in a long-couplet form (*masnavi*) derived from Arabic. Covering several thousand years of detailed mythic Iranian history, Ferdowsi brought Iran's ancient heroic lore, and its hero Rustam, into Islamicate literature and into the identity of self-consciously Iranian Muslims. He began to compose the poem under the rule of the Samanids; but he dedicated the fnished work to a dynasty that had meanwhile replaced them, the Ghaznavids.

The Ghaznavids

The Ghaznavid dynasty was born in a way that had become routine for Islamicate polities. Sebüktigin (ruled 977–997), a Samanid Turkic slave governor in Ghazna (now Ghazni), in the Afghan mountains, made himself independent of his masters as their central power declined. His eldest son, Mahmud, expanded into Buyid territory in western Iran, identifying himself staunchly with Sunni Islam. Presenting himself as a frontier warrior against the pagans, Mahmud invaded and plundered northwestern India, establishing a permanent rule in the Punjab, but it was through ruling Iran, which gave a Muslim ruler true prestige, that Mahmud sought to establish himself. He declared his loyalty to the 'Abbasid caliph, whose "investiture" he sought, and expressed his intention to defend Sunni Islam against the Shi'ite Buyids. Although he and his regime were proud of their Turkic descent, Mahmud encouraged the use of New Persian, with its echoes of pre-Islamic Iranian glory, for administration and for prose as well as poetry. This combination of Turkic identity and Persian language would characterize and empower many other Muslim rulers.

To Ghazna Mahmud brought, sometimes by force, writers and artisans who could adorn his court. Among these was al-Biruni (973–*c.* 1050), whose scholarly achievements no contemporary could rival. Before being brought to Ghazna, al-Biruni had served the Samanids and the Khwarazm-Shahs, a local dynasty situated just west of the Oxus River. Al-Biruni's works included studies of astronomy (he even suggested a heliocentric universe), gems, drugs, mathematics, and physics, but his most famous book, inspired by accompanying Mahmud on his Indian campaigns, was a survey of Indian life, language, religion, and culture.

Like most other rulers of the day, Mahmud styled himself an emir and emphasized his loyalty to the caliph in Baghdad, but he and later Ghaznavid rulers also called themselves by the Arabic word *sultan*. Over the next fvc centuries the offce of sultan would become an alternative to caliph. The Ghaznavid state presaged other changes as well, especially by stressing the cleavage between ruler and ruled and by drawing into the ruling class not only the military but also the bureaucracy and the learned establishment. So tied was the ruling establishment to the ruler that it even moved with him on campaign. Ghaznavid "political theory" shared with other states the concept of the circle of justice or circle of power – i.e., that justice is best preserved by an absolute monarch completely outside society; that such a ruler needs an absolutely loyal army; and that maintaining such an army requires prosperity, which in turn depends on the good management of an absolute ruler.

Abu al-Fadl Bayhaqi (995–1077) worked in the Ghaznavid chancery and wrote a remarkable history of the Ghaznavids, the first major prose work in New Persian. He exhibited the broad learning of even a relatively minor figure at court; in his history he combined the effective writing skills of the chancery employee, the special knowledge of Qur'an and Hadith, and the sophisticated and entertaining literature – history, poetry, and folklore – that characterized the *adib*.

He provided a vivid picture of life at court, graphically portraying the pitfalls of military absolutism – the dependence of the monarch on a fractious military and a large circle of assistants and advisors, who could mislead him and affect his decision making through internecine maneuvering and competition. In the reign of Mahmud's son, Mas'ud I, the weaknesses in the system had already become glaringly apparent. At the Battle of Dandanqan (1040), Mas'ud lost control of Khorasan, his main holding in Iran, to the pastoralist Seljuq Turks. He then decided to withdraw to Lahore in his Indian domains, from which his successors ruled until overtaken by the Ghurids in 1186.

By the end of Mas'ud's reign, government in Islamdom had become government by emir. Caliphal centralization had lasted 200 years; even after the caliphal empire became too large and complex to be ruled from a single centre, the separate emirates that replaced it all defned their legitimacy in relation to it, for or against. In fact, the caliphate's first systematic description and justifcation was undertaken just when its impracticality was being demonstrated.

As the Ghaznavids were ruling in Iran as "appointed" defenders of the caliph, a Baghdadi legal scholar named al-Mawardi (died 1058) retrospectively delineated the minimal requirements of the caliphate and tried to explain why it had become necessary for caliphal powers to be "delegated" in order for the *ummah*'s security to be maintained. Whereas earlier legists had tied the caliph's legitimacy to his defense of the borders, al-Mawardi separated the two, maintaining the caliph as the ultimate source of legitimacy and the guardian of pan-Islamic concerns and relegating day-to-day government to his "appointees." Al-Mawardi may have hoped that the Ghaznavids would expand far enough to be "invited" by the caliph to replace the uninvited Shi'ite Buyids. This replacement did occur, three years before al-Mawardi's death; however, it was not the Ghaznavids who appeared in Baghdad but rather the migratory pastoralist Turks who had meanwhile replaced them. The Seljuqs joined many other migrating groups to produce the next phase of Islamicate history.

5

Migration and Renewal (1041-1405)

During this period, migrating peoples once again played a major role, perhaps greater than that of the Arabs during the 7th and 8th centuries. No other civilization in premodern history experienced so much in-migration, especially of alien and disruptive peoples, or showed a greater ability to assimilate as well as to learn from outsiders. Nowhere has the capacity of a culture to redefine and incorporate the strange and the foreign been more evident. In this period, which ends with the death in 1405 of Timur (Tamerlane), the last great tribal conqueror, the tense yet creative relationship between sedentary and migratory peoples emerged as one of the great themes of Islamicate history, played out as it was in the centre of the great arid zone of Eurasia. Because this period can be seen as the history of peoples as well as of regions, and because the mobility of those peoples brought them to more than one cultural region, this period should be treated group by group rather than region by region.

As a general term, "migrating" peoples is preferable because it does not imply aimlessness, as "nomadic" does; or herding, as "pastoralist" does; or kin-related, as "tribal" does. "Migrating" focuses simply on movement from one home to another. Although the Franks, as the Crusaders are called in Muslim sources, differed from other migrating peoples, most of whom were pastoralists related by kinship, they too were migrating warriors organized to invade and occupy peoples to whom they were hostile and alien. Though not literally tribal, they appeared to behave like a tribe with a distinctive way of life and a solidarity based on common values, language, and objectives. Viewing them as alien immigrants comparable to, say, the Mongols helps to explain their reception: how they came to be assimilated into the local culture and drawn into the intra-Muslim factional competition and fghting that was under way in Syria when they arrived.

TURKS

For almost 400 years a succession of Turkic peoples entered eastern Islamdom from Central Asia. These nearly continuous migrations can be divided into three phases: Seljuqs (1055–92), Mongols (1256–1411), and neo-Mongols (1369–1405). Their long-term impact, more constructive than destructive on balance, can still be felt through the lingering heritage of the great Muslim empires they inspired. The addition of tribally organized warrior Turks to the already widely used Turkic slave soldiery gave a single ethnic group an extensive role in widening the gap between rulers and ruled.

SELJUQ TURKS

The Seljuqs were a family among the Oghuz Turks, a label applied to the migratory pastoralists of the Syr Darya–Oxus basin. Their name has come to stand for the group of Oghuz families led into Ghaznavid Khorasan after they had been converted to Sunni Islam, probably by Suf missionaries after the beginning of the 11th century. In 1040 the Seljuqs' defeat of the Ghaznavid sultan allowed them to proclaim themselves rulers of Khorasan. Having expanded into western Iran as well, Toghrïl Beg, also using the title "sultan," was able to occupy Baghdad (1055) after "petitioning" the 'Abbasid caliph for permission. The Seljuqs quickly took the remaining Buyid territory and began to occupy Syria, whereupon they encountered Byzantine resistance in the Armenian highlands. In 1071 a Seljuq army under Alp-Arslan defeated the Byzantines at Manzikert north of Lake Van; while the main Seljuq army replaced the Fatimids in Syria, large independent tribal bands occupied Anatolia, coming closer to the Byzantine capital than had any other Muslim force.

POLICIES OF NIZAM AL-MULK

The Seljuqs derived their legitimacy from investiture by the caliph, and from "helping" him reunite the *ummah;* yet their governing style prefgured the emergence of true alternatives to the caliphate. Some of their Iranian advisers urged them to restore centralized absolutism as it had existed in pre-Islamic times and in the period of Marwanid-'Abbasid strength. The best-known proponent was Nizam al-Mulk, chief minister to the second and third Seljuq sultans, Alp-Arslan and Malik-Shah. Nizam al-Mulk explained his plans in his *Seyasat-nameh* (*The Book of Government*), one of the best-known manuals of Islamicate political theory and administration. He was unable, however, to persuade the Seljuq sultans to assert enough power over other tribal leaders. Eventually the Seljuq sultans, like so many rulers before them, alienated their tribal supporters and resorted to the costly alternative of a Turkic slave core, whose leading members were appointed to tutor and train young princes of the Seljuq family to compete for rule on the death of the reigning sultan. The tutors were known as *atabegs*. More often than not, they became the actual rulers of the domains assigned to their young charges, cooperating with urban notables (*a'yan*) in day-today administration.

Although Nizam al-Mulk was not immediately successful, he did contribute to long-term change. He encouraged the establishment of state-supported schools (madrasahs); those he personally patronized were called Nizamiyyahs. The most important Nizamiyyah was founded in Baghdad in 1067. There Nizam al-Mulk gave government stipends to teachers and students whom he hoped he could subsequently not only appoint to the position of *qadi* but also recruit for the bureaucracy. Systematic and broad instruction in Jama'i-Sunni learning would counteract the disruptive infuences of non-Sunni or anti-Sunni thought and activity, particularly the continuing agitation of Isma'ili Muslims. In 1090 a group of Isma'ilis established themselves in a mountain fortress at Alamut in the mountains of Daylam. From there they began to coordinate revolts all over Seljuq domains. Nominally loyal to the Fatimid caliph in Cairo, the eastern Isma'ilis confrmed their growing independence and radicalism by supporting a failed contender for the Fatimid caliphate, Nizar. For that act they were known as the Nizari Isma'ilis. They were led by Hasan-e Sabbah and were dubbed by their detractors the *hashishiyyin* (assassins) because they practiced political murder while they were allegedly under the infuence of hashish.

Nizam al-Mulk's madrasah system enhanced the prestige and solidarity of the Jama'i-Sunni *ulama* without actually drawing them into the bureaucracy or combating anti-Sunni agitation, but it also undermined their autonomy. It established the connection between state-supported education and offce holding, and it subordinated the spiritual power and prestige of the *ulama* to the indispensable physical force of the military emirs. Nizam al-Mulk unintentionally encouraged the independence of these emirs by extending the *iqta'* system beyond Buyid practice. He regularly assigned land revenues to individual military offcers, assuming that he could keep them under bureaucratic control. When that failed, his system increased the emirs' independence and drained the central treasury.

The madrasah system had other unpredictable results that can be illustrated by al-Ghazali, who was born in 1058

Nizam al-Mulk

Abu 'Ali Hasan ibn 'Ali ibn Ishaq al-Tusi (1018/19–1092), known as Nizam al-Mulk (Arabic: "Order of the Kingdom"), was the son of a revenue offcial for the Ghaznavid dynasty. Through his father's position, he was born into the literate, cultured milieu of the Persian administrative class. His early years included a religious education, and he spent signifcant time with jurists and scholars of religion. In the years of confusion following the initial Seljuq Turk expansion, his father left Tu s for Ghazna (now in Afghanistan), where Nizam al-Mulk, too, in due course entered Ghaznavid service.

He soon returned to Khorasan, however, and joined the service of Alp-Arslan, who was then the Seljuq governor there. When Alp-Arslan's vizier died, Nizam al-Mulk was appointed to succeed him, and, when Alp-Arslan himself succeeded his father in 1059, Nizam al-Mulk had the entire administration of Khorasan in his hands. His abilities so pleased his master that, when Alp-Arslan became the supreme overlord of the Seljuq rulers in 1063, Nizam al-Mulk was made vizier.

For the next 30 years, under two remarkable rulers, he occupied this position in an empire that stretched from the Oxus River (now Amu Darya) in the east to Khwarezm and the southern Caucasus and westward into central Anatolia. During these decades, the Seljuq empire was at its zenith; Nizam al-Mulk's infuence guided the sultan's decisions, sometimes even military ones, and his frm control of the central and provincial administration, through his numerous dependents and relatives, implemented those decisions.

His infuence was especially felt in the rule of Sultan Malik-Shah, who succeeded to the Seljuq throne when he was only 18. Such was Nizam al-Mulk's reputation among contemporaries that he was compared to the Barmakids, viziers to the 8th-century caliph Harun al-Rashid.

Shortly before his assassination and at Malik-Shah's request, Nizam al-Mulk wrote down his views on government in the *Seyasat-nameh.* In this remarkable work, he barely refers to the organization of the *dewan* (administration) because he had been able, with the help of his well-chosen servants, to control and model it on traditional lines. But he never had the same power in the *dargah* (court) and found much to criticize in the sultan's careless disregard for protocol, the lack of magnifcence in his court, the decline in prestige of important offcials, and the neglect of the intelligence service. The most severe criticisms in the *Seyasat-nameh,* however, are of Shi'ite views in general and the Isma'ilis in particular, to whom he devotes his last 11 chapters. His support of "right religion," Sunni Islam, was not only for reasons of state but also a matter of passionate conviction.

Nizam al-Mulk expressed his religious devotion in ways that contributed to the Sunni revival. He founded Nizamiyyah madrasahs in many major towns throughout the empire to combat Shi'ite propaganda, as well as to provide reliable, competent administrators, schooled in his own branch of Islamic law. Less orthodox religious communities among the Suf orders also benefted from his generosity; hospices, pensions for the poor, and extensive public works related to the pilgrimage to Mecca and Medina were created or sustained by his patronage. Particularly in his last years, when the Isma'ili threat grew stronger and its partisans found a refuge in Alamut, the castle of the Assassins, he set himself the task of combating their infuence by every means possible.

On Alp-Arslan's death in 1073, Nizam al-Mulk was left with wider powers, since the late sultan's successor, Malik-Shah, was only a youth. By 1080, however, Malik-Shah had become less acquiescent. Nizam al-Mulk also antagonized the sultan's favourite courtier, Ta j al-Mulk, and he made an enemy of the sultan's wife Terken Khatun by preferring the son of another wife for the succession. Nizam al-Mulk was assassinated in 1092—a murder that was probably committed by an Isma'ili from Alamut, possibly with the complicity of Ta j al-Mulk and Terken Khatun, if not that of Malik-Shah himself. Within a month, however, the sultan too was dead, and the disintegration of the great Seljuq empire had begun.

at Tu s and in 1091 was made head of the Baghdad Nizamiyyah. For four years, to great admiration, he taught both *fqh* and *kalam* and delivered critiques of *falsafah* and Isma'ili thought. According to his autobiographical work *Al-Munqidh min al-dalal* (*The Deliverer from Error*), the more he taught, the more he doubted, until his will and voice became paralyzed. In 1095 he retreated from public life, attempting to arrive at a more satisfying faith. He undertook a radically skeptical reexamination of all of the paths available to the pious Muslim, culminating in an incorporation of the active, immediate, and inspired experience of the Sufs into the Shari'ah-ordered piety of the public cult. For his accomplishments, al-Ghazali was viewed as a renewer (*mujaddid*), a role expected by many Muslims to be flled by at least one fgure at the turn of every Muslim century.

Tariqah Fellowships

In the 12th century Muslims began to group themselves into *tariqah*, fellowships organized around and named for the *tariqah* ("way" or "path") of given masters. Al-Ghazali may have had such a following himself. One of the first large-scale orders, the Qadiriyah, formed around the teachings of 'Abd al-Qadir al-Jilani of Baghdad. Though rarely monastic in the European sense, the activities of a *tariqah* often centred around assembly halls (called *khanqah, zawiyah,* or *tekke*) that could serve as places of retreat or accommodate special spiritual exercises. The *dhikr*, for example, is a ceremony in which devotees meditated on the name of God to the accompaniment of breathing exercises, music, or movement, so as to attain a state of consciousness productive of a sense of union with God. Although shortcuts and excesses have often made Sufsm vulnerable to criticism, its most serious practitioners have conceived of it as a disciplined extension of Shari'ah-minded piety, not an escape. In fact, many Sufs have begun their path through supererogatory fulfllment of standard ritual requirements.

Thousands of *tariqahs* sprang up over the centuries, some associated with particular occupations, locales, or classes. It is possible that by the 18th century most adult Muslim males had some connection with one or more *tariqahs*. The structure of the *tariqah* ensued from the charismatic authority of the master, who, though not a prophet, replicated the direct intimacy that the prophets had shared with God. This quality he passed on to his disciples through a hierarchically ordered network that could extend over thousands of miles. The *tariqahs* thus became powerful centripetal forces among societies in which formal organizations were rare; but the role of the master became controversial because followers often made saints or intercessors of especially powerful Suf leaders and made shrines or pilgrimage sites of their tombs or birthplaces. Long before these developments could combine to produce stable alternatives to the caliphal system, Seljuq power had begun to decline, only to be replaced for a century and a half with a plethora of small military states. When the Frankish Crusaders arrived in the Holy Land in 1099, no one could prevent them from quickly establishing themselves along the eastern Mediterranean coast.

FRANKS

The Call for the Crusades

At the Council of Clermont in 1095 Pope Urban II responded to an appeal from the Byzantine emperor for help against the Seljuq Turks, who had expanded into western Anatolia just as the Kipchak Turks in the Ukraine had cut off newly Christian Russia from Byzantium. The First Crusade, begun the next year, brought about the conquest of Jerusalem in 1099. The Christian Reconquista (Reconquest) of Spain was already under way, having scored its first great victory at Toledo in 1085. Ironically, modern historiography has concentrated on the Crusades that failed and virtually ignored the ones that succeeded.

In the four centuries between the fall of Toledo and the fall of Granada (1492), Spanish Christians replaced Muslim rulers throughout the Iberian Peninsula, although Muslims remained as a minority under Christian rule until the early 17th century. In the 200 years from the fall of Jerusalem to the end of the Eighth Crusade (1291), western European Crusaders failed to halt the Turkish advance or to establish a permanent presence in the Holy Land. By 1187 local Muslims had managed to retake Jerusalem and thereby contain Christian ambitions permanently. By the time of the Fourth Crusade (1202–04) the Crusading movement had been turned inward against Christian heretics such as the Byzantines.

EFFECT OF THE CRUSADES IN SYRIA

The direct impact of the Crusades on Islamdom was limited largely to Syria. For the century during which western European Christians were a serious presence there, they were confned to their massive coastal fortifcations. The Crusaders had arrived in Syria at one of its most factional-ized periods prior to the 20th century. Seljuq control, never strong, was then insignifcant; local Muslim rule was anarchic; the Seljuq regime in Baghdad was competing with the Fatimid regime in Egypt; and all parties in Syria were the target of the Nizari Isma'ili movement at Alamut. The Crusaders soon found it diffcult to operate as more than just another faction. Ye t the signifcance of the Crusaders as a force against which to be rallied should not be underestimated any more than should the signifcance of Islamdom as a force against which Christendom could unite.

The Crusaders' situation encouraged interaction with the local population and even assimilation. They needed the food, supplies, and services available in the Muslim towns. Like their Christian counterparts in Spain, they took advantage of the enemy's superior skills, in medicine and hygiene, for example. Because warfare was seasonal and occasional, they spent much of their time in peaceful interaction with their non-Christian counterparts. Some early-generation Crusaders intermarried with Arab Muslims or Arab Christians and adopted their personal habits and tastes, much to the dismay of Christian latecomers. An intriguing account of life in Syria during the Crusades can be found in the *Kitab al-I'tibar* ("Book of Refection"), the memoirs of Usamah ibn Munqidh (1095–1188). Born in Syria, he was a small boy when the first generation of Franks controlled Jerusalem. As an adult, he fought with Saladin (Salah al-Din Yusuf ibn Ayyub) and lived to see him unite Egypt with Syria and restore Jerusalem to Muslim control. In this fne example of Islamicate autobiographical writing, Usamah draws a picture of the Crusades not easily found in European sources: Christians and Muslims observing, and sometimes admiring, each others' skills and habits, from the battlefeld to the bathhouse. Although the Franks in Syria were clearly infuenced by the Muslims, the Crusades seem to have contributed relatively little to the overall impact of Islamicate culture on Europe, even though they constituted the most prolonged direct contact.

Although the Crusaders never formed a united front against the Muslims, Syrian Muslims did eventually form a united front against them, largely through the efforts of the family of the emir Zangi, a Turkic slave offcer appointed Seljuq representative in Mosul in 1127. After Zangi had extended his control through northern Syria, one of his sons and successors, Nur al-Din (Nureddin), based at Aleppo, was able to tie Zangi's movement to the frontier warrior (*ghazi*) spirit. This he used to draw together urban and military support for a jihad against the Christians. After taking Damascus, he established a second base in Egypt. He offered help to the failing Fatimid regime in return for being allowed to place one of his own lieutenants, Saladin, as chief minister to the Fatimid caliph, thus warding off a Crusader alliance with the Fatimids. This action gave Nur al-Din two fronts from which to counteract the superior seaborne and naval support the Crusaders were receiving from western Europe and the Italian city-states.

SALAH-AL-DIN

Salah al-Din Yusuf ibn Ayyub (1137/38–1193)—known to many in the West as Saladin—was the founder of the Ayyubid dynasty and is among the most famous of Muslim heroes. In wars against the Christian Crusaders, he achieved great success with the capture of Jerusalem (Oct. 2, 1187), ending its nearly nine decades of occupation by the Franks.

Saladin was born into a prominent Kurdish family. His formal career began when he joined the staff of his uncle Asad al-Din Shirkuh, an important military commander under the emir Nur al-Din (the son and successor of 'Imad al-Din Zangi ibn Aq Sonqur, a powerful Turkish governor in northern Syria whom Saladin's father had served). In 1169 at the age of 31, Saladin was appointed both commander of the Syrian troops in Egypt and vizier of the Fatimid caliph there. As vizier of Egypt, he received the title "king" (*malik*), although he was generally known as the sultan.

Saladin's position was further enhanced when, in 1171, he abolished the weak and unpopular Shi'ite Fatimid caliphate, proclaiming a return to Sunni Islam in Egypt. Although he remained for a time theoretically a vassal of Nur al-Din, that relationship ended with the Syrian emir's death in 1174. From 1174 until 1186 he zealously pursued a goal of uniting, under his own standard, all the Muslim territories of Syria, northern Mesopotamia, Palestine, and Egypt. This he accomplished by skillful diplomacy backed when necessary by the swift and resolute use of military force. Gradually his reputation grew as a generous and virtuous but frm ruler, devoid of pretense, licentiousness, and cruelty.

Saladin was able to successfully turn the military balance of power with the Crusaders in his favour—more by uniting and disciplining a great number of unruly forces than by employing new or improved military techniques—and when at last, in 1187, he was able to throw his full strength into the struggle with the Latin Crusader kingdoms, his armies were their equals. On July 4, 1187, aided by his military good sense and by a remarkable lack of it on the part of his enemy, Saladin trapped and destroyed in one blow an exhausted and thirst-crazed army of Crusaders at Hattin, near Tiberias in northern Palestine. So great were the losses in the ranks of the Crusaders in this one battle that the Muslims were quickly able to overrun nearly the entire kingdom of Jerusalem. Acre, Toron, Beirut, Sidon, Nazareth, Caesarea, Nablus, Jaffa (Yafo), and Ascalon (Ashqelon) fell within three months. But Saladin's crowning achievement and the most disastrous blow to the whole Crusading movement came on Oct. 2, 1187, when the city of Jerusalem, holy to both Muslim and Christian alike, surrendered to Saladin's army after 88 years in the hands of the Franks. Saladin planned to avenge the slaughter of Muslims in Jerusalem in 1099 by killing all Christians in the city, but he agreed to let them purchase their freedom provided that the Christian defenders left the Muslim inhabitants unmolested.

His sudden success, which in 1189 saw the Crusaders reduced to the occupation of only three cities, was, however, marred by his failure to capture Tyre, an almost impregnable coastal fortress to which the scattered Christian survivors of the recent battles focked. It was to be the rallying point of the Latin counter attack. Most probably, Saladin did not anticipate the European reaction to his capture of Jerusalem, an event that deeply shocked the West and to which it responded with a new call for a Crusade. In addition to many great nobles and famous knights, this Crusade, the third, brought the kings of three countries into the struggle. The magnitude of the Christian effort and the lasting impression it made on contemporaries gave the name of Saladin, as their gallant and chivalrous enemy, an added lustre. The Crusade itself was long and exhausting in spite of the military genius of Richard I (the Lion-Heart). Therein lies the greatest—but often unrecognized—achievement of Saladin. With tired and unwilling feudal levies, committed to fght only a limited season each year, his indomitable will enabled him to fght the greatest champions of Christendom to a draw. The Crusaders retained little more than a precarious foothold on the Levantine coast, and when King Richard left the Middle East, in October 1192, the battle was over. Saladin withdrew to his capital at Damascus, where he died the following year.

Three years before Nur al-Din's death in 1174, Saladin substituted himself for the Fatimid caliph he theoretically served, thus ending more than 200 years of Fatimid rule in Egypt. When Nur al-Din died, Saladin succeeded him as head of the whole movement. When Saladin died in 1193, he had recaptured Jerusalem (1187) and begun the reunif-cation of Egypt and Syria; his successors were known, after his patronymic, as the Ayyubids. The efforts of a contemporary 'Abbasid caliph, al-Nasir, to revive the caliphate seem pale by comparison.

The Ayyubids ruled in Egypt and Syria until around 1250, when they were replaced first in Egypt and later in Syria by the leaders of their own slave-soldier corps, the Mamluks. It was they who expelled the remaining Crusaders from Syria, subdued the remaining Nizari Isma'ilis there, and consolidated Ayyubid holdings into a centralized state. That state became strong enough in its first decade to do what no other Muslim power could: in 1260 at 'Ayn Jalut, south of Damascus, the Mamluk army defeated the recently arrived Mongols and expelled them from Syria.

MONGOLS

The Mongols were pagan, horse-riding tribes of the northeastern steppes of Central Asia. In the early 13th century, under the leadership of Genghis Khan, they formed, led, and gave their name to a confederation of Turkic tribes that they channeled into a movement of global expansion, spreading east into China, north into Russia, and west into Islamdom. Like other migratory peoples before them, Arabs, Imazighen, and Turks, they had come to be involved in citied life through their role in the caravan trade. Unlike others, however, they did not convert to Islam before their arrival. Furthermore, they brought a greater hostility to sedentary civilization, a more ferocious military force, a more cumbersome material culture, a more complicated and hierarchical social structure, and a more coherent sense of tribal law. Their initial impact was physically more destructive than that of previous invaders, and their long-term impact perhaps more socially and politically creative.

GENGHIS KHAN

As far as can be judged from the disparate sources, the personality of the Mongolian warrior-ruler Genghis Khan (1162–1227)—one of the most famous conquerors of history, who consolidated tribes into a unifed Mongolia and then extended his empire across Asia to the Adriatic Sea—was a complex one. He had great physical strength, tenacity of purpose, and an unbreakable will. He was not obstinate and would listen to advice from others, including his wives and mother. He was fexible. He could deceive but was not petty. He had a sense of the value of loyalty: enemies guilty of treachery toward their lords could expect short shrift from him, but he would exploit their treachery at the same time. He was religiously minded, carried along by his sense of a divine mission, and in moments of crisis he would reverently worship the Eternal Blue Heaven, the supreme deity of the Mongols.

So much is true of his early life. The picture becomes less harmonious as he moves out of his familiar sphere and comes into contact with the strange, settled world beyond the steppe. At first he could not see beyond the immediate gains to be got from massacre and rapine and, at times, was consumed by a passion for revenge. Ye t all his life he could attract the loyalties of men willing to serve him, both fellow nomads and civilized men from the settled world. His fame could even persuade the aged Daoist sage Changchun (Qiu Chuji) to journey the length of Asia to discourse upon religious matters. He was above all adaptable, a man who could learn.

Organization, discipline, mobility, and ruthlessness of purpose were the fundamental factors in his military successes. Massacres of defeated populations, with the resultant terror, were weapons he regularly used. His practice of summoning cities to surrender and of organizing the methodical slaughter of those who did not submit has been described as psychological warfare; but, although it was undoubtedly policy to sap resistance by fostering terror, massacre was used for its own sake. Mongol practice, especially in the war against Khwarezm, was to send agents to demoralize and divide the garrison and populace of an enemy city, mixing threats with promises. The Mongols' reputation for frightfulness often paralyzed their captives, who allowed themselves to be killed when resistance or fight was not impossible. Indeed, the Mongols were unaccountable. Resistance brought certain destruction, but at Balkh, now in Afghanistan, the population was slaughtered in spite of a prompt surrender, for tactical reasons.

The achievements of Genghis Khan were grandiose. He united all the nomadic tribes, and with numerically inferior armies he defeated great empires, such as Khwarezm and the even more powerful Jin state. Ye t he did not exhaust his people. He chose his successor, his son Ögödei, with great care, ensured that his other sons would obey Ögödei, and passed on to him an army and a state in full vigour. At the time of his death, Genghis Khan had conquered the landmass extending from Beijing to the Caspian Sea, and his generals had raided Persia and Russia. His successors would extend their power over the whole of China, Persia, and most of Russia. They did what he did not achieve and perhaps never really intended—that is, to weld their conquests into a tightly organized empire. The destruction brought about by Genghis Khan survives in popular memory, but far more signifcant, these conquests were but the first stage of the Mongol Empire, the greatest continental empire of medieval and modern times.

FIRST MONGOL INCURSIONS

The first Mongol incursions into Islamdom in 1220 were a response to a challenge from the Khwarezm-Shah 'Ala' al-Din Muhammad, the aggressive reigning leader of a dynasty formed in the Oxus Delta by a local governor who had rebelled against the Seljuq regime in Khorasan. Under Genghis Khan's leadership, Mongol forces destroyed numerous cities in Transoxania and Khorasan in an unprecedented display of terror and annihilation. By the time of Genghis Khan's death in 1227, his empire stretched from the Caspian Sea to the Sea of Japan. A later successor, Möngke, decided to extend the empire in two new directions. From the Mongol capital of Karakorum, he simultaneously dispatched Kublai Khan to southern China (where Islam subsequently began to expand inland) and Hülegü to Iran (1256). Hülegü had already received Sunni ambassadors who encouraged him to destroy the Isma'ili state at Alamut. This he did and more, reaching Baghdad in 1258, where he terminated and replaced the caliphate. The 'Abbasid line continued, however, until 1517. The Mamluk sultan Baybars I, shortly after his defeat of the Mongols, invited a member of the 'Abbasid house to "invest" him and to live in Cairo as spiritual head of all Muslims.

The Mongol regimes in Islamdom quickly became rivals. The Il-Khans controlled the Tigris-Euphrates valley and Iran; the Chagatai dominated the Syr Darya and Oxus basins, the Kabul mountains, and eventually the Punjab; and the Golden Horde was concentrated in the Volga basin. The Il-Khans ruled in the territories where Islam was most frmly established. They patronized learning of all types and scholars from all parts of the vast Mongol empire, especially China. Evincing a special interest in nature, they built a major observatory at Maragheh. Just as enthusiastically as they had destroyed citied life, they now rebuilt it, relying as had all previous invaders of Iran on the administrative skills of indigenous Persian-speaking bureaucrats. The writings of one of these men, 'Ata Malek Joveyni, who was appointed governor in Baghdad after the Mongol capture of that city in 1258, described the type of rule the Mongols sought to impose. It has been called the military patronage state because it involved a reciprocal relationship between the foreign tribal military conquerors and their subjects. The entire state was defned as a single mobile military force connected to the household of the monarch; with no fxed capital, it moved with the monarch. All non-Turkic state workers, bureaucratic or religious, even though not military specialists, were defned as part of the army (*asker*); the rest of the subject population, as the herds (*ra'iyyah*). The leading tribal families could dispose of the wealth of the conquered populations as they wished, except that their natural superiority obligated them to reciprocate by patronizing whatever of excellence the cities could produce. What the Ghaznavids and Seljuqs had begun, the Mongols now accomplished. The self-confdence and superiority of the leading families were bolstered by a fairly elaborate set of tribal laws, inherited from Genghis Khan and known as the Yasa, which served to regulate personal status and criminal liability among the Mongol elite, as did the Shari'ah among Muslims. In Il-Khanid hands, this dynastic law merely coexisted but did not compete with Shari'ah; but in later Turkic regimes a reconciliation was achieved that extended the power of the rulers beyond the limitations of an autonomous Shari'ah.

CONVERSION OF MONGOLS TO ISLAM

For a time the Il-Khans tolerated and patronized all religious persuasions – Sunni, Shi'ite, Buddhist, Nestorian Christian, Jewish, and pagan. But in 1295 a Buddhist named Mahmud Ghazan became khan and declared himself Muslim, compelling other Mongol notables to follow suit. His patronage of Islamicate learning fostered such brilliant writers as Rashid al-Din, the physician and scholar who authored one of the most famous Persian universal histories of all time. The Mongols, like other Islamicate dynasties swept into power by a tribal confederation, were able to unify their domains for only a few generations. By the 1330s their rule had begun to be fragmented among myriad local leaders. Meanwhile, on both Mongol fanks, other Turkic Muslim powers were increasing in strength. To the east the Delhi Sultanate of Turkic slave-soldiers withstood Mongol pressure, benefted from the presence of scholars and administrators feeing Mongol destruction, and gradually began to extend Muslim control south into India, a feat that was virtually accomplished under Muhammad ibn Tughluq. Muslim Delhi was a culturally lively place that attracted a variety of unusual persons. Muhammad ibn Tughluq himself was, like many later Indian Muslim rulers, well-read in philosophy, science, and religion. Not possessing the kind of dynastic legitimacy the pastoralist Mongols had asserted, he tied his legitimacy to his support for the Shari'ah, and he even sought to have himself invested by the 'Abbasid "caliph" whom the Mamluks had taken to Cairo. His concern with the Shari'ah coincided with the growing popularity of Sufsm, especially as represented by the massive Suf Chishti *tariqah*. Its most famous leader, Nizam al-Din Awliya', had been a spiritual adviser to many fgures at court before Muhammad ibn Tughluq came to the throne, as well as to individual Hindus and Muslims alike. In India, Sufsm, which inherently undermined communalism, was bringing members of different religious communities together in ways very rare in the more westerly parts of Islamdom.

To the west the similarly constituted Mamluk state continued to resist Mongol expansion. Its sultans were chosen on a nonhereditary basis from among a group of freed slaves who acted as the leaders of the various slave corps. At the death of one sultan, the various military corps would compete to see whose leader would become the next sultan. The leaders of the various slave corps formed an oligarchy that exercised control over the sultan. Although political instability was the frequent and natural result of such a system, cultural forescence did occur. The sultans actively encouraged trade and building, and Mamluk Cairo became a place of splendour, flled with numerous architectural monuments. While the Persian language was becoming the language of administration and high culture over much of Islamdom, Arabic alone continued to be cultivated in Mamluk domains, to the beneft of a diversifed intellectual life. Ibn al-Nafs (died 1288), a physician, wrote about pulmonary circulation 300 years before it was "discovered" in Europe. For Mamluk administrative personnel, al-Qalqashandi composed an encyclopaedia in which he surveyed not only local practice but also all the information that a cultivated administrator should know. Ibn Khallikan composed one of the most important Islamicate biographical works, a dictionary of eminent men. Shari'ah-minded studies were elaborated: the *ulama* worked out a political theory that tried to make sense of the sultanate, and they also explored the possibility of enlarging on the Shari'ah by reference to *falsafah* and Sufsm.

However, in much the same way as al-Shaf'i had responded in the 9th century to what he viewed as dangerous legal diversity, another great legal and religious reformer, Ibn Taymiyyah, living in Mamluk Damascus in the late 13th and early 14th century, cautioned against such extralegal practices and pursuits. He insisted that the Shari'ah was complete in and of itself and could be adapted to every age by any *faqih* who could analogize according to the principle of human advantage (*maslahah*). A Hanbali himself, Ibn Taymiyyah became as popular as his school's founder, Ahmad ibn Hanbal. Like him, Ibn Taymiyyah attacked all practices that undermined what he felt to be the fundamentals of Islam, including all forms of Shi'ite thought as well as aspects of Jama'i-Sunni piety (often infuenced by the Sufs) that stressed knowledge of God over service to him. Most visible among such practices was the revering of saints' tombs, which was condoned by the Mamluk authorities. Ibn Taymiyyah's program and popularity so threatened the Mamluk authorities that they put him in prison, where he died.

His movement did not survive, but, when his ideas surfaced in the revolutionary movement of the Wahhabiyyah (Wahhabism) in the late 18th century, their lingering power became dramatically evident. Farther west, the Rum Seljuqs at Konya submitted to the Mongols in 1243 but survived intact. They continued to cultivate the Islamicate arts, architecture in particular. The most famous Muslim ever to live at Konya, Jalal al-Din Rumi, had emigrated from eastern Iran with his father before the arrival of the Mongols. In Konya, Jalal al-Din, attracted to Suf activities, attached himself to the master Shams al-Din. The poetry inspired by Jalal al-Din's association with Shams al-Din is unparalleled in Persian literature. Its recitation, along with music and movement, was a key element in the devotional activities of Jalal al-Din's followers, who came to be organized into a Suf *tariqah*—named the Mevleviyah (Mawlawiyyah) after their title of respect for him, Mevlana ("Our Master"). In his poetry Jalal al-Din explored all varieties of metaphors, including intoxication, to describe the ineffable ecstasy of union with God.

ASCENT OF THE OTTOMAN TURKS

It was not from the Rum Seljuqs, however, that lasting Muslim power in Anatolia was to come, but rather from one of the warrior states on the Byzantine frontier. The successive waves of Turkic migrations had driven unrelated individuals and groups across central Islamdom into Anatolia. Avoiding the Konya state, they gravitated toward an open frontier to the west, where they began to constitute themselves, often through fctitious kinship relationships, into quasi-tribal states that depended on raiding each other and Byzantine territory and shipping. One of these, the Osmanlis, or Ottomans, named for their founder, Osman I (ruled 1281–1324), was located not on the coast, where raiding had its limits, but in Bithynia just facing Constantinople. In the mid-1320s they won the town of Bursa and made it their first capital. From Anatolia they crossed over into Thrace in the service of rival factions at Constantinople, then began to occupy Byzantine territory, establishing their second capital at Edirne on the European side. Their sense of legitimacy was complex. They were militantly Muslim, bound by the *ghazi* spirit, spurred on in their intolerance of local Christians by Greek converts and traveling Sufs who gravitated to their domains. At the same time, *ulama* from more-settled Islamic lands to the east encouraged them to abide by the

Shari'ah and tolerate the Christians as protected non-Muslims. The Ottomans also cast themselves as deputies of the Rum Seljuqs, who were themselves originally "deputized" by the 'Abbasid caliph. Finally they claimed descent from the leading Oghuz Turk families, who were natural rulers over sedentary populations. Under Murad I (ruled *c.* 1360–89) the state began to downplay its warrior fervour in favour of more conventional Islamicate administration. Instead of relying on volunteer warriors, Murad established a regular cavalry, which he supported with land assignments, as well as a specially trained infantry force called the "New Troops," Janissaries, drawn from converted captives. Expanding first through western Anatolia and Thrace, the Ottomans under Bayezid I (ruled 1389– 1402) turned their eyes toward eastern and southern Anatolia. Just as they had incorporated the whole, they encountered a neo-Mongol conqueror expanding into Anatolia from the east who utterly defeated their entire army in a single campaign (1402).

TIMUR'S EFFORTS TO RESTORE MONGOL POWER

Timur (Tamerlane) was a Turk, not a Mongol, but he aimed to restore Mongol power. He was born a Muslim in the Syr Darya valley and served local pagan Mongol warriors and fnally the Chagatai heir apparent, but he rebelled and made himself ruler in Khwarezm in 1380. He planned to restore Mongol supremacy under a thoroughly Islamic program. He surpassed the Mongols in terror, constructing towers out of the heads of his victims. Having established himself in Iran, he moved first on India and then on Ottoman Anatolia and Mamluk Syria, but he died before he could consolidate his realm. His impact was twofold: his defeat of the Ottomans inspired a comeback that would produce one of the greatest Islamicate empires of all time, and one of the Central Asian heirs to his tradition of conquest would found another great Islamicate empire in India. These later empires managed to fnd the combination of Turkic and Islamic legitimacy that could produce the stable centralized absolutism that had eluded all previous Turkic conquerors.

TIMUR

The Turkic conqueror Timur (1336–1405), remembered for the barbarity of his conquests from India and Russia to the Mediterranean Sea and for the cultural achievements of his dynasty, began his rise as the leader of a small nomad band. By guile and force of arms, he established dominion over the lands between the Oxus and Jaxartes rivers (Transoxania) by the 1360s. He then, for three decades, led his mounted archers to subdue each state from Mongolia to the Mediterranean. He was the last of the mighty conquerors of Central Asia to achieve such military successes as leader of the nomad warrior lords, ruling both agricultural and pastoral peoples on an imperial scale. The poverty, bloodshed, and desolation caused by his campaigns gave rise to many legends, which in turn inspired such works as Christopher Marlowe's *Tamburlaine the Great*.

The name Timur Lenk (Turkish: "Timur the Lame"), as Timur was known, was a title of contempt used by his Persian enemies, which became Tamburlaine, or Tamerlane, in Europe. Timur was heir to a political, economic, and cultural heritage rooted in the pastoral peoples and nomad traditions of Central Asia. He and his compatriots cultivated the military arts and discipline of Genghis Khan and, as mounted archers and swordsmen, scorned the settled peasants. Timur never took up a permanent abode. He personally led his almost constantly campaigning forces, enduring extremes of desert heat and lacerating cold. When not campaigning he moved with his army according to season and grazing facilities. His court traveled with him, including his household of one or more of his nine wives and concubines. He strove to make his capital, Samarkand, the most splendid city in Asia, but when he visited it he stayed only a few days and then moved back to the pavilions of his encampment in the plains beyond the city.

Timur was, above all, master of the military techniques developed by Genghis Khan, using every weapon in the military and diplomatic armory of the day. He never missed an opportunity to exploit the weakness (political, economic, or military) of the adversary or to use intrigue, treachery, and alliance to serve his purposes. The seeds of victory were sown among the ranks of the enemy by his agents before an engagement. He conducted sophisticated negotiations with both neighbouring and distant powers, which are recorded in diplomatic archives from England to China. In battle, the nomadic tactics of mobility and surprise were his major weapons of attack.

Timur's most lasting memorials are the Timurid architectural monuments of Samarkand, covered in azure, turquoise, gold, and alabaster mosaics; these are dominated by the great cathedral mosque, ruined by an earthquake but still soaring to an immense fragment of dome. His mausoleum, the Gur-e Amir, is one of the gems of Islamic art. Within the sepulchre he lies under a huge, broken slab of jade. The tomb was opened in 1941, having remained intact for half a millennium. The Soviet Archae ological Com mission found the skeleton of a man who, though lame in both right limbs, must have been of powerful physique and above-average height.

Timur's sons and grandsons fought over the succession when the Chinese expedition d banded, but his dynas survived in Central Asi for a century in spite of fratricidal strife. Samarkand became a centre of scholarship and science. It was here that Ulugh Beg, his grandson, set up an observatory and drew up the astronomical tables that were later used by the English royal astronomer in the 17th century. During the Timurid renaissance of the 15th century, Herat, southeast of Samarkand, became the home of the brilliant school of Persian miniaturists. At the beginning of the 16th century, when the dynasty ended in Central Asia, his descendant Babur established himself in Kabul and then conquered Delhi, to found the Muslim line of Indian emperors known as the Great Mughals.

ARABS

When the Fatimids conquered Egypt in 969, they left a governor named Ziri in the Maghrib. In the 1040s the dynasty founded by Ziri declared its independence from the Fatimids, but it too was challenged by breakaways such as the Zanatah in Morocco and the Hammadids in Algeria. Gradually the Zirids were restricted to the eastern Maghrib. There they were invaded from Egypt by two Bedouin Arab tribes, the Banu Halil and the Banu Sulaym, at the instigation (1052) of the Fatimid ruler in Cairo. This mass migration of warriors as well as wives and children is known as the Hilalian invasion. Though initially disruptive, the Hilalian invasion had an important cultural impact: it resulted in a much greater spread of the Arabic language than had occurred in the 7th century and inaugurated the real Arabization of the Maghrib.

IMAZIGHEN

When the Arab conquerors arrived in the Maghrib in the 7th century, the indigenous peoples they met were the Imazighen (Berbers; singular Amazigh), a group of predominantly but not entirely migratory tribes who spoke a recognizably common Afro-Asiatic language with signif-cant dialectal variations. Amazigh tribes could be found from present-day Morocco to present-day Algeria and from the Mediterranean to the Sahara. As among the Arabs, small tribal groupings of Imazighen occasionally formed short-lived confederations or became involved in caravan trade. No previous conqueror had tried to assimilate the Imazighen, but the Arabs quickly converted them and enlisted their aid in further conquests. Without their help, for example, Andalusia could never have been incorporated into the Islamicate state. At first only Imazighen nearer the coast were involved, but by the 11th century Muslim affliation had begun to spread far into the Sahara.

The Sanhajah Confederation

One particular western Saharan Amazigh confederation, the Sanhajah, was responsible for the first Amazigh-directed effort to control the Maghrib. The Sanhajah were camel herders who traded mined salt for gold with the black kingdoms of the south. By the 11th century their power in the western Sahara was being threatened by expansion both from other Amazigh tribes, centred at Sijilmassa, and from the Soninke state at Ghana to the south, which had actually captured their capital of Audaghost in 990. The subsequent revival of their fortunes parallels Muhammad's revitalization of the Arabs 500 years earlier, in that Muslim ideology reinforced their efforts to unify several smaller groups. The Sanhajah had been in contact with Islam since the 9th century, but their distance from major centres of Muslim life had kept their knowledge of the faith minimal. In 1035, however, Yahya ibn Ibrahim, a chief from one of their tribes, the Gudalah, went on *hajj*. For the Maghribi pilgrim, the cultural impact of the *hajj* was experienced not only in Mecca and Medina but also on the many stops along the 3,000-mile (4,828 km) overland route. When Yahya returned, he was accompanied by a teacher from Nafs (in present-day Libya), 'Abd Allah ibn Yasin, who would instruct the Imazighen in Islam as teachers under 'Umar I had instructed the Arab fghters in the first Muslim garrisons. Having met with little initial success, the two are said to have retired to a *ribat*, a fortifed place of seclusion, perhaps as far south as an island in the Sénégal River, to pursue a purer religious life. The followers they attracted to that *ribat* were known, by derivation, as *al-murabitun* (Arabic:

"those who are garrisoned"). The dynasty they founded came to be known by the same name, or Almoravids in its Anglicized form. In 1042 Ibn Yasin declared a jihad against the Sanhajah tribes, including his own, as people who had embraced Islam but then failed to practice it properly. By his death in 1059, the Sanhajah confederation had been restored under an Islamic ideology, and the conquest of Morocco, which lacked strong leadership, was under way.

The Almoravid Dynasty

A consultative body of *ulama* took over Ibn Yasin's spiritual role. His successor as military commander was Abu Bakr ibn 'Umar. While pursuing the campaign against Morocco, Abu Bakr had to go south, leaving his cousin Yusuf ibn Tashufn as his deputy. When Abu Bakr tried to return, Ibn Tashufn turned him back to the south, where he remained until his death in 1087. Under Ibn Tashufn's leadership, by 1082, Almoravid control extended as far as Algiers. In 1086 Ibn Tashufn responded to a request for help from the Andalusian party kings, unable to defend themselves against the Christian kingdoms in the north, such as Castile. By 1110 all Muslim states in Andalusia had come under Almoravid control.

Like most other Jama'i-Sunni rulers of his time, Ibn Tashufn had himself "appointed" deputy by the caliph in Baghdad. He also based his authority on the claim to bring correct Islam to peoples who had strayed from it. For him, "correct" Islam meant the Shari'ah as developed by the Maliki *faqihs,* who played a key role in the Almoravid state by working out the application of the Shari'ah to everyday problems. Like their contemporaries elsewhere, they received stipends from the government, sat in the ruler's council, went on campaign with him, and gave him recommendations (fatwas) on important decisions. This was an approach to Islam far more current than the one it had replaced but still out of touch with the liveliest intellectual developments. During the next phase of Amazigh activism, newer trends from the east reached the Maghrib.

A second major Amazigh movement originated in a revolt begun against Almoravid rule in 1125 by Ibn Tumart, a settled Masmudah Amazigh from the Atlas Mountains. Like Ibn Yasin, Ibn Tumart had been inspired by the *hajj,* which he used as an opportunity to study in Baghdad, Cairo, and Jerusalem, acquainting himself with all current schools of Islamic thought and becoming a disciple of the ideas of the recently deceased al-Ghazali. Emulating his social activism, Ibn Tumart was inspired to act on the familiar Muslim dictum, "Command the good and forbid the reprehensible." His early attempts took two forms, disputations with the scholars of the Almoravid court and public chastisement of Muslims who in his view contradicted the rules of Islam. He went so far as to throw the Almoravid ruler's sister off her horse because she was unveiled in public. His activities aroused hostility, and he fed to the safety of his own people. There, like Muhammad, he grew from teacher of a personal following to leader of a social movement.

Like many subsequent reformers, especially in Africa and other outlying Muslim lands, Ibn Tumart used Muhammad's career as a model. He interpreted the Prophet's rejection and retreat as an emigration (*hijrah*) that enabled him to build a community, and he divided his followers into *muhajirun* ("fellow emigrants") and *ansar* ("helpers"). He preached the idea of surrender to God to a people who had strayed from it.

Thus could Muhammad's ability to bring about radical change through renewal be invoked without actually claiming the prophethood that he had sealed forever. Ibn Tumart further based his legitimacy on his claim to be a sharif (descendant of Muhammad) and the *mahdi,* not in the Shi'ite sense but in the more general sense of a human sent to restore pure faith. In his view Almoravid students of legal knowledge were so concerned with pursuing the technicalities of the law that they had lost the purifying fervour of their own founder, Ibn Yasin.

They even failed to maintain proper Muslim behaviour, be it the veiling of women in public or the condemning of the use of wine, musical instruments, and other unacceptable, if not strictly illegal, forms of pleasure. Like many Muslim revitalizers before and since, Ibn Tumart decried the way in which the law had taken on a life of its own, and he called upon Muslims to rely on the original and only reliable sources, the Qur'an and Hadith. Although he opposed irresponsible rationalism in the law, in matters of theological discourse he leaned toward the limited rationalism of the Ash'arite school, which was becoming so popular in the eastern

Muslim lands. Like the Ash'arites, he viewed the unity of God as one of Islam's fundamentals and denounced any reading of the Qur'an that led to anthropomorphism. Because he focused on attesting the unity of God (*tawhid*), he called his followers al-Muwahhidun (Almohads), "Those Who Attest the Unity of God." Ibn Tumart's movement signifes the degree to which Maghribis could participate in the intellectual life of Islamdom as a whole, but his need to use the Tamazight language for his many followers who did not know Arabic also illustrates the limits of interregional discourse.

The Almohad Dynasty

By 1147, 17 years after Ibn Tumart's death, Almohads had replaced Almoravids in all their Maghribi and Andalusian territories. In Andalusia their arrival slowed the progress of the Christian Reconquista. There, as in the Maghrib, arts and letters were encouraged. An example is an important movement of *falsafah* that included Ibn Tufayl, Ibn al-'Arabi, and Ibn Rushd (Latin Averroës), the Andalusian *qadi* and physician whose interpretations of Aristotle became so important for medieval European Christianity.

During the late Almohad period in Andalusia the inter-communal nature of Islamicate civilization became especially noticeable in the work of non-Muslim thinkers, such as Moses Maimonides, who participated in trends outside their own communities even at the expense of criticism from within. By the early 13th century, Almohad power began to decline; a defeat in 1212 at Las Navas de Tolosa by the Christian kings of the north forced a retreat to the Maghrib.

But the impact of Almohad cultural patronage on Andalusia long outlasted Almohad political power. Successor dynasties in surviving Muslim states were responsible for some of the highest cultural achievements of Andalusian Muslims, among them the Alhambra palace in Granada. Furthermore, the 400-year southward movement of the Christian-Muslim frontier resulted, ironically, in some of the most intense Christian-Muslim interaction in Andalusian history. The Cid could fght for both sides; Muslims, as Mudejars, could live under Christian rule and contribute to its culture; Jews could translate Arabic and Hebrew texts into Castilian. Almohads were replaced in the Maghrib as well, through a revolt by their own governors—the Hafsids in Tunis and the Marinid Amazigh dynasty in Fès. There too, however, Almohad infuence outlasted their political presence: both towns became centres, in distinctively Maghribi form, of Islamicate culture and Islamic piety.

Continued Spread of Islamic Influence

As the Maghrib became frmly and distinctively Muslim, Islam moved south. The spread of Muslim identity into the Sahara and the involvement of Muslim peoples, especially the Tuareg, in trans-Saharan trade provided several natural channels of infuence. By the time of the Marinids, Hafsids, and Mamluks, several major trade routes had established crisscrossing lines of communication: from Cairo to Timbuktu, from Tripoli to Bornu and Lake Chad, from Tunis to Timbuktu at the bend of the Niger River, and from Fès and Taflalt through major Saharan entrepôts into Ghana and Mali.

The rise at Timbuktu of Mali, the first great western Sudanic empire with a Muslim ruler, attested the growing incorporation of sub-Saharan Africa into the North African orbit. The reign of Mansa Musa, who even went on pilgrimage, demonstrated the infu-ence of Islam on at least the upper echelons of African society.

The best picture of Islamdom in the 14th century appears in the work of a remarkable Maghribi *qadi* and traveler, Ibn Battutah (1304–1368/69 or 1377). In 1325, the year that Mansa Musa went on pilgrimage, Ibn Battutah also left for Mecca, from his hometown of Tangiers. He was away for almost 30 years, visiting most of Islamdom, including Andalusia, all of the Maghrib, Mali, Syria, Arabia, Iran, India, the Maldive Islands, and, he claimed, China. He described the unity within diversity that was one of Islamdom's most prominent features. Although local customs often seemed at variance with his notion of pure Islamic practice, he felt at home everywhere. Despite the divisions that had occurred during Islam's 700-year history, a Muslim could attend the Friday worship session in any Muslim town in the world and feel comfortable, a claim that is diffcult if not impossible to make for any other major religious tradition at any time in its history. By the time of Ibn Battutah's death, Islamdom comprised the most far-fung yet interconnected set of societies in the world. As one author has pointed out, Thomas Aquinas (*c.* 1224–74) might have been read from Spain to Hungary and from Sicily to Norway, but Ibn al-'Arabi (1165–1240) was read from Spain to Sumatra and from the Swahili coast to Kazan on the Volga River. By the end of the period of migration and renewal, Islam had begun to spread not only into sub-Saharan Africa but also into the southern seas with the establishment of a Muslim presence in the Straits of Malacca. Conversion to Islam across its newer frontiers was at first limited to a small elite, who supplemented local religious practices with Muslim ones. Islam could offer not only a unifying religious system but also social techniques, including alphabetic literacy, a legal system applicable to daily life, a set of administrative institutions, and a body of science and technology – all capable of enhancing the power of ruling elements and of tying them into a vast and lucrative trading network.

The period of migration and renewal exposed both the potentiality and the limitations of government by tribal peoples. This great problem of Islamicate history received its most sophisticated analysis from a Maghribi Muslim named Ibn Khaldun (1332–1406), a contemporary of Petrarch. His family had migrated from Andalusia to the Maghrib, and he himself was born in Hafsid territory. He was both a *faylasuf* and a *qadi*, a combination more common in Andalusia and the Maghrib than anywhere else in Islamdom. His *falsafah* was activist; he strove to use his political wisdom to the beneft of one of the actual rulers of the day. To this end he moved from one court to another before becoming disillusioned and retiring to Mamluk Cairo as a *qadi*. His life thus demonstrated the importance and the constraints of royal patronage as a stimulant to intellectual creativity. In his *Muqaddimah* (the introduction to his multivolume world history) he used his training in *falsafah* to discern patterns in history. Transcending the critiques of historical method made by historians of the Buyid period, such as al-Mas'udi, Ibn Miskawayh, and al-Suli, Ibn Khaldun established careful standards of evidence.

Whereas Muslim historians conventionally subscribed to the view that God passed sovereignty and hegemony (*dawlah*) from one dynasty to another through his divine wisdom, Ibn Khaldun explained it in terms of a cycle of natural and inevitable stages. By his day it had become apparent that tribally organized migratory peoples, so favoured by much of the ecology of the Maghrib and the Nile-to-Oxus region, could easily acquire military superiority over settled peoples if they could capitalize on the inherently stronger group feeling (*'asabiyyah*) that kinship provides. Once in power, according to Ibn Khaldun, conquering groups pass through a phase in which a small number of "builders" among them bring renewed vitality to their conquered lands. As the family disperses itself among sedentary peoples and ceases to live the hard life of migration, it becomes soft from the prosperity it has brought and begins to degenerate. Then internal rivalries and jealousies force one member of the family to become a king who must rely on mercenary troops and undermine his own prosperity by paying for them. In the end, the ruling dynasty falls prey to a new tribal group with fresh group feeling. Thus did Ibn Khaldun call attention to the unavoidable instability of all premodern Muslim dynasties, caused by their lack of the regularized patterns of succession that were beginning to develop in European dynasties.

6

Consolidation and Expansion (1405-1683)

After the death of Timur in 1405, power began to shift from migrating peoples to sedentary populations living in large centralized empires. After about 1683, when the last Ottoman campaign against Vienna failed, the great empires for which this period is so famous began to shrink and weaken, just as western Europeans first began to show their potential for worldwide expansion and domination. When the period began, Muslim lands had begun to recover from the devastating effects of the Black Death (1346-48), and many were prospering. Muslims had the best opportunity in history to unite the settled world, but by the end of the period they had been replaced by Europeans as the leading contenders for this role. Muslims were now forced into direct and repeated contact with Europeans, through armed hostilities as well as through commercial interactions, and often the Europeans competed well.

Yet Muslim power was so extensive and the western Europeans such an unexpected source of competition that Muslims were able to realize that their situation had changed only after they no longer had the strength to resist. Furthermore, the existence of several strong competitive Muslim states militated against a united response to the Europeans and could even encourage some Muslims to align themselves with the European enemies of others. In this period, long after Islamdom was once thought to have peaked, centralized absolutism reached its height, aided in part by the exploitation of gunpowder warfare and in part by new ways to fuse spiritual and military authority. Never before had Islamicate ideals and institutions better demonstrated their ability to encourage political centralization or to support a Muslim style of life where there was no organized state, be it in areas where Islam had been long established or in areas where it was newly arrived. The major states of this period impressed contemporary Europeans; in them some of the greatest Islamicate artistic achievements were made. In this period Muslims formed the cultural patterns that they brought into modern times, and adherence to Islam expanded to approximately its current distribution. As adherence to Islam expanded, far-f ung cultural regions began to take on a life of their own. The unity of several of these regions was expressed through empire—the Ottomans in southeastern Europe, Anatolia, the eastern Maghrib, Egypt, and Syria; the Safavids in Iran and Iraq; the Indo-Timurids (Mughals) in India.

In these empires, Sunni and Shi'ite became identities on a much larger scale than ever before, expressing competition between large populations. Simultaneously Shi'ism acquired a permanent base from which to generate international opposition. Elsewhere, less formal and often commercial ties bound Muslims from distant locales. Growing commercial and political links between Morocco and the western Sudan produced a trans-Saharan Maghribi Islam. Egyptian Islam inf uenced the central and eastern Sudan. And steady contacts between East Africa, South Arabia, southern Iran, southwest India, and the southern seas promoted a recognizable Indian Ocean Islam, with Persian as its lingua franca. In fact, Persian became the closest yet to an international language; but the expansion and naturalization of Islam also fostered a number of local languages into vehicles for Islamicate administration and high culture—Ottoman, Chagatai, Swahili, Urdu, and Malay. Everywhere Muslims were confronting adherents of other religions, and new converts often practiced Islam without abandoning their previous practices. The various ways in which Muslims responded to religious syncretism and plurality continue to be elaborated to the present day.

This was a period of major realignments and expansion. The extent of Muslim presence in the Eastern Hemisphere in the early 15th century was easily discernible, but only with diffculty could one have imagined that it could soon produce three of the greatest empires in world history. From the Atlantic to the Pacifc, from the Balkans to Sumatra, Muslim rulers presided over relatively small kingdoms; but nowhere could the emergence of a world-class dynasty be predicted. In Andalusia only one Muslim state, Granada, remained to resist Christian domination of the Iberian Peninsula. The Maghrib, isolated between an almost all-Christian Iberia and an eastward-looking Mamluk Egypt and Syria, was divided between the Marinids and Hafsids. Where the Sahara shades off into the Sudanic belt, the empire of Mali at Gao was ruled by a Muslim and included several Saharan "port" cities, such as Timbuktu, that were centres of Muslim learning. On the Swahili coast, oriented as always more toward the Indian Ocean than toward its own hinterland, several small Muslim polities centred on key ports such as Kilwa. In western Anatolia and the Balkan Peninsula the Ottoman state under Sultan Mehmed I was recovering from its defeat by Timur.

Iraq and western Iran were the domains of Turkic tribal dynasties known as the Black Sheep (Kara Koyunlu) and the White Sheep (Ak Koyunlu). They shared a border in Iran with myriad princelings of the Timurid line and the neo-Mongol, neo-Timurid Uzbek state ruled in Transoxania. North of the Caspian Sea, several Muslim khanates ruled as far north as Moscow and Kazan. In India, even though Muslims constituted a minority, they were beginning to assert their power everywhere except the south, which was ruled by Vijayanagar. In Islamdom's far southeast, the Muslim state of Samudra held sway in Sumatra, and the rulers of the Moluccas had recently converted to Islam and begun to expand into the southern Malay Peninsula. Even where no organized state existed, as in the outer reaches of Central Asia and into southern China, scattered small Muslim communities persisted, often centred on oases. By the end of this period, Islamdom's borders had retreated only in Russia and Iberia, but these losses were more than compensated by continuing expansion in Europe, Africa, Central Asia, and South and Southeast Asia. Almost everywhere this plethora of states had undergone realignment and consolidation, based on experimentation with forms of legitimation and structure.

OTTOMANS

Continuation of Ottoman Rule

After the Ottoman state's devastating defeat by Timur, its leaders had to retain the vitality of the warrior spirit (without its unruliness and intolerance) and the validation of the Shari'ah (without its confning independence). In 1453 Mehmed II (the Conqueror) fulflled the warrior ideal by conquering Constantinople (soon to be known as Istanbul), putting an end to the Byzantine Empire, and subjugating the local Christian and Jewish populations. Even by then, however, a new form of legitimation was taking shape. The Ottomans continued to wage war against Christians on the frontier and to levy and convert (through the *devsirme*) young male Christians to serve in the sultan's household and army, but warriors were being pensioned off with land grants and replaced by troops more beholden to the sultan. Except for those forcibly converted, the rest of the non-Muslim population was protected for payment according to the Shari'ah and the preference of the *ulema* (the Turkish spelling of *ulama*), and organized into self-governing communities known as *millets*. Furthermore, the sultans began to claim the caliphate because they met two of its traditional qualifcations: they ruled justly, in principle according to the Shari'ah, and they defended and extended the frontiers, as in their conquest of Mamluk Egypt, Syria, and the holy cities in 1516–17. Meanwhile, they began to undercut the traditional oppositional stance of the *ulema* by building on Seljuq and Mongol practice in three ways: they promoted state-supported training of *ulema*; they defned and paid holders of religious offces as part of the military; and they aggressively asserted the validity of dynastic law alongside Shari'ah. Simultaneously, they emphasized their inheritance of Byzantine legitimacy by transforming Byzantine symbols, such as Hagia Sophia (Church of the Divine Wisdom), into symbols for Islam, and by favouring their empire's European part, called, signifcantly, Rum.

Reign of Süleyman I

The classical Ottoman system crystallized during the reign of Süleyman I (the Lawgiver; ruled 1520–66). He also pushed the empire's borders almost to their farthest limits—to the walls of Vienna in the northwest, throughout the Maghrib up to Morocco in the southwest, into Iraq to the east, and to the Yemen in the southeast. During Süleyman's reign the Ottomans even sent an expedition into the southern seas to help Aceh against the Portuguese colonizers. In theory, Süleyman presided over a balanced four-part structure: the palace household, which contained all of the sultan's wives, concubines, children, and servants; the bureaucracy (chancery and treasury); the armed forces;

and the religious establishment. Important positions in the army and bureaucracy went to the cream of the *devsirme,* Christian youths converted to Islam and put through special training at the capital to be the sultan's personal "slaves." *Ulema* who acquired government posts had undergone systematic training at the major *medreses* (madrasahs) and so in the Ottoman state were more integrated than were their counterparts in other states. Ye t they were freeborn Muslims, not brought into the system as slaves of the sultan. The ruling class communicated in a language developed for their use only, Ottoman, which combined Turkic syntax with largely Arabic and Persian vocabulary. It was in this new language that so many important fgures demonstrated the range and sophistication of Ottoman interests, such as the historian Mustafa Naima, the encyclopaedist Kâtip Çelebi, and the traveler Evliya Çelebi. The splendour of the Ottoman capital owed not a little to Süleyman's chief architect, the Greek *devsirme* recruit Sinan, who transformed the city's skyline with magnifcent mosques and *medreses.*

Süleyman I

The only son of Sultan Selim I, Süleyman I (1494/95–1566) succeeded his father in September 1520 and began his reign with campaigns against the Christian powers in central Europe and the Mediterranean. Belgrade fell to him in 1521 and Rhodes, long under the rule of the Knights of St. John, in 1522. At Mohács, in August 1526, Süleyman broke the military strength of Hungary, the Hungarian king, Louis II, losing his life in the battle.

The vacant throne of Hungary was now claimed by Ferdinand I, the Habsburg archduke of Austria, and by John (János Zápolya), who was *voivode* (lord) of Transylvania, and the candidates of the "native" party opposed to the prospect of Habsburg rule. Süleyman agreed to recognize John as a vassal king of Hungary, and in 1529, hoping to remove at one blow all further intervention by the Habsburgs, he laid siege to Vienna. Diffculties of time and distance and of bad weather and lack of supplies, no less than the resistance of the Christians, forced the sultan to raise the siege.

The campaign was successful, however, in a more immediate sense, for John was to rule thereafter over most of Hungary until his death, in 1540. A second great campaign in 1532, notable for the brilliant Christian defense of Güns, ended as a mere foray into

Austrian border territories. The sultan, preoccupied with affairs in the East and convinced that Austria was not to be overcome at one stroke, granted a truce to the archduke Ferdinand in 1533.

The death of John in 1540 and the prompt advance of Austrian forces once more into central Hungary drove Süleyman to modify profoundly the solution that he had imposed in the time of John. His campaigns of 1541 and 1543 led to the emergence of three distinct Hungarys—Habsburg Hungary in the extreme north and west; Ottoman Hungary along the middle Danube, a region under direct and permanent military occupation by the Ottomans and with its main centre at Buda; and Transylvania, a vassal state dependent on the Porte and in the hands of John Sigismund, the son of John Zápolya.

Between 1543 and 1562 the war in Hungary continued, broken by truces and with few notable changes on either side; the most important was the Ottoman capture of the Banat of Temesvár (Timisoara) in 1532. After long negotiations a peace recognizing the status quo in Hungary was signed in 1562.

During the course of his rule, Süleyman waged three major campaigns against Persia. The first (1534–35) gave the Ottomans control over the region of Erzurum in eastern Asia Minor and also witnessed the Ottoman conquest of Iraq, a success that rounded off the achievements of Selim I. The second campaign (1548–49) brought much of the area around Lake Va n under Ottoman rule, but the third (1554–55) served rather as a warning to the Ottomans of the diffculty of subduing the Safavid state in Persia. The first formal peace between the Ottomans and the Safavids was signed in 1555, but it offered no clear solution to the problems confronting the Ottoman sultan on his eastern frontier.

The naval strength of the Ottomans became formidable in the reign of Süleyman. Khayr al-Din, known in the West as Barbarossa, became *kapudan* (admiral) of the Ottoman feet and won a sea fght off Preveza, Greece (1538), against the combined feets of Venice and Spain, which gave to the Ottomans the naval initiative in the Mediterranean until the Battle of Lepanto in 1571. Tripoli in North Africa fell to the Ottomans in 1551. A strong Spanish expedition against Tripoli was crushed at Jarbah (Djerba) in 1560, but the Ottomans failed to capture Malta from the Knights of St. John in 1565. Ottoman naval power was felt at this time even as far afeld as India, where a feet sent out from Egypt made an unsuccessful attempt in 1538 to take the town of Diu from the Portuguese.

Süleyman's later years were troubled by conflict between his sons. Mustafa had become by 1553 a focus of disaffection in Asia Minor and was executed in that year on the order of the sultan. There followed during 1559–61 a conflict between the princes Selim and Bayezid over the succession to the throne, which ended with the defeat and execution of Bayezid. Süleyman himself died while besieging the fortress of Szigetvár in Hungary.

The Extent of Ottoman Administration

Even in North Africa and the Fertile Crescent, where Ottoman rule was indirect, the effect of its administration, especially its land surveys and *millet* and tax systems, could be felt. Remnants of the Ottoman system continue to play a role in the political life of modern states such as Israel and Lebanon, despite the fact that Ottoman control had already begun to relax by the first quarter of the 17th century. By then control of the state treasury was passing, through land grants, into the hands of local *a'yan,* and they gradually became the real rulers, serving local rather than imperial interests. Meanwhile discontinuance of the *dev-sirme* and the rise of hereditary succession to imperial offces shut off new sources of vitality. Monarchs, confned to the palace during their youth, became weaker and participated less in military affairs and government councils.

As early as 1630, Sultan Murad IV was presented by one of his advisers with a memorandum explaining the causes of the perceived decline and urging a restoration of the system as it had existed under Süleyman. Murad IV tried to restore Ottoman effciency and central control, and his efforts were continued by subsequent sultans aided by a talented family of ministers known as the Köprülüs. However, during a war with the Holy League (Austria, Russia, Venice, and Poland) from 1683 to 1699, in which a major attack on Vienna failed (1683), the Ottomans suffered their first serious losses to an enemy and exposed the weakness of their system to their European neighbours. They signed two treaties, at Carlowitz in 1699 and at Passarowitz in 1718, that confrmed their losses in southeastern Europe, signifed their inferiority to the Habsburg coalition, and established the defensive posture they would maintain into the 20th century.

Safavids

The Safavid state began not from a band of *ghazi* warriors but from a local Suf *tariqah* of Ardabil in the Azerbaijan region of Iran. The *tariqah* was named after its founder, Shaykh Saf al-Din (1252/53–1334), a local holy man. As for many *tariqah*s and other voluntary associations, Sunni and Shi'ite alike, affection for the family of 'Ali was a channel for popular support. During the 15th century Shaykh Saf's successors transformed their local *tariqah* into an interregional movement by translating 'Alid loyalism into full-fedged Imami Shi'ism. By asserting that they were the Suf "perfect men" of their time as well as descendants and representatives of the last imam, they strengthened the support of their Turkic tribal disciples (known as the Kizilbash, or "Red Heads," because of their symbolic 12-fold red headgear). They also attracted support outside Iran, especially in eastern Anatolia (where the anti-Ottoman Imami Bektashi *tariqah* was strong), in Syria, the Caucasus, and Transoxania. The ability of the Iranian Shi'ite state to serve as a source of widespread local opposition outside of Iran was again to become dramatically apparent many years later, with the rise of the ayatollah Ruhollah Khomeini's Islamic republic in the late 1970s.

Expansion in Iran and Beyond

By 1501 the Safavids were able to defeat the Ak Koyunlu rulers of northern Iran, whereupon their teenage leader Isma'il I (ruled 1501–24) had himself proclaimed shah, using that pre-Islamic title for the first time in almost 900 years and thereby invoking the glory of ancient Iran. The Safavids thus asserted a multivalent legitimacy that few in the face of Ottoman claims to have restored caliphal authority for all Muslims. Eventually, irritant became threat: by 1510, when Isma'il had conquered all of Iran (to approximately its present frontiers) as well as the Fertile Crescent, he began pushing against the Uzbeks in the east and the Ottomans in the west, both of whom already suffered from signifcant Shi'ite opposition that could easily be aroused by Safavid successes.

Having to fight on two fronts was the most diffcult military problem any Muslim empire could face. According to the persisting Mongol pattern, the army was a single force attached to the household of the ruler and moving with him at all times; so the size of an area under effective central control was limited to the farthest points that could be reached in a single campaign season. After dealing with his eastern front, Isma'il turned west. At Chaldiran (1514) in northwestern Iraq, having refused to use gunpowder weapons, Isma'il suffered the kind of defeat at Ottoman hands that the Ottomans had suffered from Timur. Ye t through the war of words waged in a body of correspondence between Shah Isma'il and the Ottoman sultan Selim I, and through the many invasions from both fronts that occurred during the next 60 years, the Safavid state survived and prospered. Still living off its position at the crossroads of the trans-Asian trade that had supported all previous empires in Iraq and Iran, it was not yet undermined by the gradual emergence of more signifcant sea routes to the south.

The first requirement for the survival of the Safavid state was the conversion of its predominantly Jama'i-Sunni population to Imami Shi'ism. This was accomplished by a government-run effort supervised by the state-appointed leader of the religious community, the *sadr*. Gradually forms of piety emerged that were specifc to Safavid Shi'ism; they centred on pilgrimage to key sites connected with the imams, as well as on the annual remembering and reenacting of the key event in Shi'ite history, the caliph Yazid I's destruction of Imam al-Husayn at Karbala' on the 10th of Muharram, AH 61 (680 CE). The 10th of Muharram, or 'Ashura', already marked throughout Islamdom with fasting, became for Iranian Shi'ites the centre of the religious calendar. The first 10 days of Muharram became a period of communal mourning, during which the pious imposed suffering on themselves to identify with their martyrs of old, listened to sermons, and recited appropriate elegiac poetry. In later Safavid times the name for this mourning, *ta'ziyyeh,* also came to be applied to passion plays performed to reenact events surrounding al-Husayn's martyrdom. Through the depths of their empathetic suffering, Shi'ites could help to overturn the injustice of al-Husayn's martyrdom at the end of time, when all wrongs would be righted, all wrongdoers punished, and all true followers of the imams rewarded.

Shah 'Abbas I

The state also survived because Isma'il's successors moved, like the Ottomans, toward a type of legitimation different from the one that had brought them to power. This development began in the reign of Tahmasp (1524–76) and culminated in the reign of the greatest Safavid shah, 'Abbas I (ruled 1588–1629). Since Isma'il's time, the tribes had begun to lose faith in the Safavid monarch as spiritual leader. Now 'Abbas appealed for support more as absolute monarch and less as the charismatic Suf master or incarnated imam. At the same time, he freed himself from his unruly tribal emirs by depending more and more on a paid army of converted Circassian, Georgian, and Armenian Christian captives. Meanwhile, he continued to rely on a large bureaucracy headed by a chief minister with limited responsibilities, but, unlike his Ottoman contemporaries, he distanced members of the religious community from state involvement while allowing them an independent source of support in their administration of the *waqf* system. Because the Shi'ite *ulama* had a tradition of independence that made them resist incorporation into the military "household" of the shah, 'Abbas's policies were probably not unpopular, but they eventually undermined his state's legitimacy. By the end of the period under discussion, it was the religious leaders, the *mujtahids*, who would claim to be the spokesmen for the hidden imam. Having shared the ideals of the military patronage state, the Ottoman state became more frmly militarized and religious, as the Safavid became more civilianized and secular.

The long-term consequences of this breach between government and the religious institution were extensive, culminating in the establishment of the Islamic republic of Iran in 1978.

'Abbas expressed his new role by moving his capital about 1597–98 to Esfahan in Fars, the central province of the ancient pre-Islamic Iranian empires and symbolically more Persian than Turkic. Esfahan, favoured by a high and scenic setting, became one of the most beautiful cities in the world, leading its boosters to say that "Esfahan is half the world." It came to contain, often thanks to royal patronage, myriad palaces, gardens, parks, mosques, *medreses*, caravansaries, workshops, and public baths. Many of these still stand, including the famed Masjed-e Shah, a mosque that shares the great central mall with an enormous covered bazaar and many other structures. It was there that 'Abbas received diplomatic and commercial visits from Europeans, including a Carmelite mission from Pope Clement XIII (1604) and the adventuring Sherley brothers from Elizabethan England. Just as his visitors hoped to use him to their own advantage, 'Abbas hoped to use them to his, as sources of frearms and military technology, or as pawns in his economic warfare against the Ottomans, in which he was willing to seek help from apparently anyone, including the Russians, Portuguese, and Habsburgs.

Under Safavid rule, Iran in the 16th and 17th centuries became the centre of a major cultural fowering expressed through the Persian language and through the visual arts. This fowering extended to Safavid neighbour states as well—Ottomans, Uzbeks, and Indo-Timurids. Like other Shi'ite dynasties before them, the Safavids encouraged the development of *falsafah* as a companion to Shi'ite eso-tericism and cosmology. Tw o major thinkers, Mir Damad and his disciple Mulla Sadra, members of the Ishraqi, or illuminationist, school, explored the realm of images or symbolic imagination as a way to understand issues of human meaningfulness. The Safavid period was also important for the development of Shi'ite Shari'ah-minded studies, and it produced a major historian, Iskandar Beg Munshi, chronicler of 'Abbas's reign.

Decline of Central Authority

None of 'Abbas's successors was his equal, though his state, ever weaker, survived for a century. The last effective shah, Husayn I (1694–1722), could defend himself neither from tribal raiding in the capital nor from interfering *mujtahids* led by Muhammad Baqir Majlisi (whose writings later would be important in the Islamic republic of Iran). In 1722, when Mahmud of Qandahar led an Afghan tribal raid into Iran from the east, he easily took Esfahan and destroyed what was left of central authority.

INDO-TIMURIDS (MUGHALS)

Foundation by Babur

Although the Mongol-Timurid legacy infuenced the Ottoman and Safavid states, it had its most direct impact on Babur (1483–1530), the adventurer's adventurer and founder of the third major empire of the period. Babur's father, 'Umar Shaykh Mirza (died 1494) of Fergana, was one among many Timurid "princes" who continued to rule small pieces of the lands their great ancestor had conquered. After his father's death the 11-year-old Babur, who claimed descent not only from Timur but also from Genghis Khan (on his mother's side), quickly faced one of the harshest realities of his time and place—too many princes for too few kingdoms. In his youth he dreamed of capturing Samarkand as a base for reconstructing Timur's empire. For a year after the Safavid defeat of the Uzbek Muhammad Shaybani Khan, Babur and his Chagatai followers did hold Samarkand, as Safavid vassals. But, when the Safavids were in turn defeated, Babur lost not only Samarkand but his native Fergana as well. He was forced to retreat to Kabul, which he had occupied in 1504. From there he never restored Timur's empire. Rather, barred from moving north or west, he took the Timurid legacy south, to a land on which Timur had made only the slightest impression.

When Babur turned toward northern India, it was ruled from Delhi by the Lodi sultans, one of many local Turkic dynasties scattered through the subcontinent. In 1526 at Panipat, Babur met and defeated the much larger Lodi army In his victory he was aided, like the Ottomans at Chaldiran, by his artillery. By his death just four years later, he had laid the foundation for a remarkable empire, known most commonly as the Mughal (i.e., Mongol) Empire. It is more properly called Indo-Timurid because the Chagatai Turks were distinct from the surviving Mongols of the time and because Babur and his successors acknowledge Timur as the founder of their power.

Babur is also remembered for his memoirs, the *Babur-nameh.* Written in Chagatai, then an emerging Islamicate literary language, his work gives a lively and compelling account of the wide range of interests, tastes, and sensibilities that made him so much a counterpart of his contemporary, the Italian Niccolò Machiavelli (1469–1527).

Reign of Akbar

Süleyman's and 'Abbas's counterpart in the Indo-Timurid dynasty was their contemporary, Akbar (ruled 1556–1605), the grandson of Babur. At the time of his death, he ruled all of present-day India north of the Deccan plateau and Gondwana and more: one diagonal of his empire extended from the Hindu Kush to the Bay of Bengal; the other, from the Himalayas to the Arabian Sea. Like its contemporaries to the west, particularly the Ottomans, this state endured because of a regularized and equitable tax system that provided the central treasury with funds to support the ruler's extensive building projects as well as his *mansabdars*, the military and bureaucratic offcers of the imperial service. For these key servants, Akbar, again like his counter parts to the west, relied largely on foreigners who were trained especially for his service. Like the Janissaries, the *mansabdar*s were not supposed to inherit their offces, and, although they were assigned lands to supervise, they themselves were paid through the central treasury to assure their loyalty to the interests of the ruler.

Although Akbar's empire was, like Süleyman's and 'Abbas's, a variation on the theme of the military patronage state, his situation, and consequently many of his problems, differed from theirs in important ways. Islam was much more recently established in most of his empire than in either of the other two, and Muslims were not in the majority. Although the other two states were not religiously or ethnically homogeneous, the extent of their internal diversity could not compare with Akbar's, where Muslims and non-Muslims of every stripe alternately coexisted and came into conflict—Jacobites (members of the monophysite Syrian church), Sufs, Isma'ili Shi'ites, Zoroastrians, Jains, Jesuits, Jews, and Hindus. Consequently, Akbar was forced even more than the Ottomans to confront and address the issue of religious plurality. The option of aggressive conversion was virtually impossible in such a vast area, as was any version of the Ottoman *millet* system in a setting in which hundreds if not thousands of *millets* could be defned.

In some ways, Akbar faced in exaggerated form the situation that the Arab Muslims faced when they were a minority in the Nile-to-Oxus region in the 7th–9th centuries. Granting protected status to non-Muslims was legally and administratively justifable, but, unless they could be kept from interacting too much with the Muslim population, Islam itself could be affected. The power of Suf *tariqahs* like the infuential Chishtis, and of the Hindu mystical movement of Guru Nanak, were already promoting intercommunal interaction and cross-fertilization. Akbar's response was different from that of the 'Abbasid caliph al-Mahdi. Instead of institutionalizing intolerance of non-Muslim infuences and instead of hardening communal lines, Akbar banned intolerance and even the special tax on non-Muslims. To keep the *ulama* from objecting, he tried, for different reasons than had the Ottomans and Safavids, to tie them to the state fnancially. His personal curiosity about other religions was exemplary; with the help of Abu al-Fadl, his

Suf adviser and biographer, he established a kind of salon for religious discussion. A very small circle of personal disciples seems to have emulated Akbar's own brand of *tawhid-i ilahi* ("divine oneness"). This appears to have been a general monotheism akin to what the *hanifs* of Mecca, and Muhammad himself, had once practiced, as well as to the boundary-breaking pantheistic awareness of great Sufs like Rumi and Ibn al-'Arabi, who was very popular in South and Southeast Asia. Akbar combined toleration for all religions with condemnation of practices that seemed to him humanly objectionable, such as enslavement and the immolation of widows.

CONTINUATION OF THE EMPIRE

For half a century, Akbar's first two successors, Jahangir and Shah Jahan, continued his policies. A rebuilt capital at Delhi was added to the old capitals of Fatehpur Sikri and Agra, site of Shah Jahan's most famous building, the Ta j Mahal. The mingling of Hindu and Muslim traditions was expressed in all the arts, especially in naturalistic and sensuous painting; extremely refned and sophisticated design in ceramics, inlay work, and textiles; and in delicate yet monumental architecture. Shah Jahan's son, Dara Shikoh (1615–59), was a Suf thinker and writer who tried to establish a common ground for Muslims and Hindus. In response to such attempts, a Shari'ah-minded movement of strict communalism arose, connected with a leader of the Naqshbandi *tariqah* named Shaykh Ahmad Sirhindi. With the accession of Aurangzeb (ruled 1658–1707), the tradition of ardent ecumenicism, which would reemerge several centuries later in a non-Muslim named Mohandas K. (Mahatma) Gandhi, was replaced with a stricter communalism that imposed penalties on protected non-Muslims and stressed the shah's role as leader of the Muslim community, by virtue of his enforcing the Shari'ah. Unlike the Ottoman and Safavid domains, the Indo-Timurid empire was still expanding right up to the beginning of the 18th century, but the empire began to disintegrate shortly after the end of Aurangzeb's reign, when Safavid and Ottoman power were also declining rapidly.

Shah Jahan

Shah Jahan (1592–1666; known until 1628 as Prince Khurram) was the third son of the Mughal emperor Jahangir and the Rajput princess Manmati. In 1612 he married Arjumand Banu Begum, niece of Jahangir's wife Nur Jahan, and became one of the infuential Nur Jahan clique of the middle period of Jahangir's reign. In 1622 Shah Jahan, ambitious to win the succession, rebelled, ineffectually roaming the empire until reconciled to Jahangir in 1625. After Jahangir's death in 1627, the support of Asaf Khan, Nur Jahan's brother, enabled Shah Jahan to proclaim himself emperor at Agra (February 1628).

Shah Jahan's reign was notable for successes against the Deccan states: by 1636 Ahmadnagar had been annexed and Golconda and Bijapur forced to become tributaries. Mughal power was also temporarily extended in the northwest. In 1638 the Persian governor of Kandahar, 'Ali Mardan Khan, surrendered that fortress to the Mughals. In 1646 Mughal forces occupied Badakhshan and Balkh, but in 1647 Balkh was relinquished, and attempts to reconquer it in 1649, 1652, and 1653 failed. The Persians reconquered Kandahar in 1649. Shah Jahan transferred his capital from Agra to Delhi in 1648, creating the new city of Shahjahanabad (now Old Delhi) there.

Shah Jahan had an almost insatiable passion for building. At his first capital, Agra, he undertook the building of two great mosques, the Pearl Mosque and the Great Mosque, as well as the superb mausoleum known as the Ta j Mahal. The Ta j Mahal is the masterpiece of his reign and was erected in memory of the favourite of his three queens, Mumtaz Mahal (the mother of Aurangzeb). At Delhi, Shah Jahan built a huge fortress-palace complex called the Red Fort as well as another Great Mosque, which is among the fnest mosques in India. Shah Jahan's reign was also a period of great literary activity, and the arts of painting and calligraphy were not neglected. His court was one of great pomp and splendour, and his collection of jewels was probably the most magnifcent in the world.

Indian writers have generally characterized Shah Jahan as the very ideal of a Muslim monarch. But though the splendour of the Mughal court reached its zenith under him, he also set in motion infuences that fnally led to the decline of the empire. His expeditions against Balkh and Badakhshan and his attempts to recover Kandahar brought the empire to the verge of bankruptcy. In religion, Shah Jahan was a more orthodox Muslim than Jahangir or his grandfather Akbar but a less orthodox one than Aurangzeb. He proved a relatively tolerant ruler toward his Hindu subjects.

In September 1657 Shah Jahan fell ill, precipitating a struggle for succession between his four sons, Dara Shikoh, Murad Bakhsh, Shah Shuja', and Aurangzeb. The victor, Aurangzeb, declared himself emperor in 1658 and strictly confned Shah Jahan in the fort at Agra until his death.

Between the 15th and the 18th century the use of coffee, tea, and tobacco, despite the objections of the *ulama,* became common in all three empires. Teahouses became important new centres for male socializing, in addition to the home, the mosque, the marketplace, and the public bath. (Female socializing was restricted largely to the home and the bath.) In the teahouses men could practice the already well-developed art of storytelling and take delight in the clever use of language. *The Thousand and One Nights* (*Alf laylah wa laylah*), the earliest extant manuscripts of which date from this period, and the stories of the Arabian hero 'Antar must have been popular, as were the tales of a wise fool known as Mullah Nasr al-Din in Persian (Nasreddin), Hoca in Turkish, and Juha in Arabic. The exploits of Nasr al-Din, sometimes in the guise of a Suf dervish or royal adviser, often humorously portray centralized absolutism and mysticism:

Nasr al-Din was sent by the king to investigate the lore of various kinds of Eastern mystical teachers. They all recounted to him tales of the miracles and the sayings of the founders and great teachers, all long dead, of their schools. When he returned home, he submitted his report, which contained the single word "Carrots." He was called upon to explain himself. Nasr al-Din told the king: "The best part is buried; few know – except the farmer – by the green that there is orange underground; if you don't work for it, it will deteriorate; there are a great many donkeys associated with it."

TRANS-SAHARAN ISLAM

When the Ottomans expanded through the southern Mediterranean coast in the early 16th century, they were unable to incorporate Morocco, where a new state had been formed in reaction to the appearance of the Portuguese. The Portuguese were riding the momentum generated by their own seaborne expansion as well as by the fulfllment of the Reconquista and the establishment of an aggressively intolerant Christian regime in the centre of the Iberian Peninsula. In Morocco it was neither the fervour of warriors nor Shi'ite solidarity nor Timurid restoration that motivated the formation of a state; rather, it was a very old form of legitimacy that had proved to be especially powerful in Africa—that of the sharifs, descendants of Muhammad. It had last been relied on with the Idrisids; now the sharifs were often associated with Suf holy men, known as *marabouts*. It was one such Suf, Sidi Barakat, who legitimated the Sa'di family of sharifs as leaders of a jihad that expelled the Portuguese and established an independent state (1511-1603) strong enough to expand far to the south. Meanwhile, the greatest Muslim kingdom of the Sudan, Songhai, was expanding northward, and its growing control of major trade routes into Morocco provoked Moroccan interference. Invaded in 1591, Songhai was ruled as a Moroccan vassal for 40 years, during which time Morocco itself was experiencing political confusion and instability. Morocco was reunited under Isma'il (ruled 1672–1727), an 'Alawite sharif. A holy family of Sijilmassa, the 'Alawites were brought to power by Arab tribal support, which they eventually had to replace with a costly army of black slaves. Like the Sa'dis, they were legitimated in two ways: by the recognition of leading Sufs and by the special spiritual quality (*barakah*) presumed to have passed to them by virtue of their descent from the Prophet through 'Ali. Although they were not Shi'ites, they cultivated charismatic leadership that undermined the power of the *ulama* to use the Shari'ah against them. They also recognized the limits of their authority as absolute monarchs, dividing their realm into the area of authority and the area of no authority (where many of the Amazigh tribes lived). Thus, the Moroccan sharifs solved the universal problems of legitimacy, loyalty, and control in a way tailored to their own situation.

While the Sa'di dynasty was ruling in Morocco but long before its incursions into the Sahara, a number of small Islamic states were strung from one end of the Sudanic region to the other: Senegambia, Songhai, Aïr, Mossi, Nupe, Hausa, Kanem-Bornu, Darfur, and Funj. Islam had come to these areas along trade and pilgrimage routes, especially through the efforts of a number of learned teaching-trading families such as the Kunta. Ordinarily the ruling elites became Muslim first, employing the skills of Arab immigrants, traders, or travelers, and taking political and commercial advantage of the Arabic language and the Shari'ah without displacing indigenous religious practices or legitimating principles. By the 16th century the Muslim states of the Sudanic belt were in contact not only with the major Muslim centres of the Maghrib and Egypt but also with each other through an emerging trans-Sudanic pilgrimage route. Furthermore, Islam had by then become well enough established to provoke efforts at purifcation comparable to the Almoravid movement of the 11th century. Sometimes these efforts were gradualist and primarily educational, as was the case with the enormously infuential Egyptian scholar al-Suyuti (1445–1505). His works, read by many West African Muslims for centuries after his death, dealt with numerous subjects, including the coming of the *mahdi* to restore justice and strengthen Islam. He also wrote letters to Muslim scholars and rulers in West Africa more than 2,000 miles (3,200 km) away, explaining the Shari'ah and encouraging its careful observance.

Other efforts to improve the observance of Islam were more militant. Rulers might forcibly insist on an end to certain non-Muslim practices, as did Muhammad Rumfa (ruled 1463–99) in the Hausa city-state of Kano, or Muhammad I Askia, the greatest ruler of Songhai (ruled 1493–1528). Often, as in the case of both of these rulers, militance was encouraged by an aggressive reformist scholar like al-Maghili (fourished 1492), whose writings detailed the conditions that would justify a jihad against Muslims who practiced their faith inadequately. Like many reformers, al-Maghili identifed himself as a *mujaddid*, a fgure expected to appear around the turn of each Muslim century. (The 10th century AH began in 1494 CE.) To the east in Ethiopia, an actual jihad was carried out by Ahmad Grañ (*c.* 1506–43), in the name of opposition to the Christian regime and purifcation of "compromised" Islam. Farther to the east, a conquest of Christian Nubia by Arab tribes of Upper Egypt resulted in the conversion of the pagan Funj to Islam and the creation of a major Muslim kingdom there. Although most indigenous West African scholars looked to foreigners for inspiration, a few began to chart their own course. In Timbuktu, where a rich array of Muslim learning was available, one local scholar and member of a Tukulor learned family, Ahmad Baba, was writing works that were of interest to North African Muslims. Local histories written in Arabic also survive, such as the *Ta'rikh al-fattash* (written by several generations of the Kati family, from 1519 to 1665), a chronological history of Songhai, or al-Sa'di's *Ta'rikh al-Sudan* (completed in 1655). By the end of the period of consolidation and expansion, Muslims in the Sudanic belt were being steadily infuenced by North African Islam but were also developing distinctive traditions of their own.

Indian Ocean Islam

A similar relationship was simultaneously developing across another "sea," the Indian Ocean, which tied South and Southeast Asian Muslims to East African and south Arabian Muslims the way the Sahara linked North African and Sudanic Muslims. Several similarities are clear: the alternation of advance and retreat, the movement of outside infuences along trade routes, and the emergence of signifcant local scholarship. There were differences too: Indian Ocean Muslims had to cope with the Portuguese threat and to face Hindus and Buddhists more than pagans, so that Islam had to struggle against sophisticated and refned religious traditions that possessed written literature and considerable political power.

The first major Muslim state in Southeast Asia, Aceh, was established around 1524 in northern and western Sumatra in response to more than a decade of Portuguese advance. Under Sultan Iskandar Muda (ruled 1607–37), Aceh reached the height of its prosperity and importance in the Indian Ocean trade, encouraging Muslim learning and expanding Muslim adherence. By the end of the 17th century, Aceh's Muslims were in touch with major intellectual centres to the west, particularly in India and Arabia, just as West African Muslims were tied to centres across *The Great Mosque, Palembang, Sumatra, Indon.* Richard Allen Thompson the Sahara. Because they could draw on many sources, often f ltered through India, Sumatran Muslims may have been exposed to a wider corpus of Muslim learning than Muslims in many parts of the heartland. Aceh's scholarly disputes over Ibn al-'Arabi were even signif cant enough to attract the attention of a leading Medinan, Ibrahim al-Kurani, who in 1640 wrote a response. The same kind of naturalization and indigenization of Islam that was taking place in Africa was also taking place elsewhere; for example, 'Abd al-Ra'uf of Singkel, after studying in Arabia from about 1640 to 1661, returned home, where he made the f rst "translation" of the Qur'an into Malay, a language that was much enriched during this period by Arabic script and vocabulary. This phenomenon extended even to China. Liu Zhi, a scholar born around 1650 in Nanjing, created serious Islamicate literature in Chinese, including works of philosophy and law.

In the early 17th century another Muslim commercial power emerged when its ruler, the prince of Tallo, converted. Macassar (now Makassar) became an active centre for Muslim competition with the Dutch into the third quarter of the 17th century, when its greatest monarch, Hasan al-Din (ruled 1631–70), was forced to cede his independence. Meanwhile, however, a serious Islamic presence was developing in Java, inland as well as on the coasts; by the early 17th century the first inland Muslim state in Southeast Asia, Mataram, was established. There Suf holy men performed a missionary function similar to that being performed in Africa. Unlike the more seriously Islamized states in Sumatra, Mataram suffered, as did its counterparts in West Africa, from its inability to suppress indigenous beliefs to the satisfaction of the more conservative *ulama*. Javanese Muslims, unlike those in Sumatra, would have to struggle for centuries to negotiate the confrontation between Hindu and Muslim cultures. Their situation underscores a major theme of Islamicate history through the period of consolidation and expansion – that is, the repeatedly demonstrated absorptive capacity of Muslim societies, a capacity that was soon to be challenged in unprecedented ways.

7

Reform, Dependency and Recovery

The history of modern Islam has often been explained in terms of the impact of "the West." From this perspective, the 18th century was a period of degeneration and a prelude to European domination, symbolized by Napoleon's conquest of Egypt in 1798. Yet it is also possible to argue that the period of Western domination was merely an interlude in the ongoing development of indigenous styles of modernization. In order to resolve this question, it is necessary to begin the "modern" period with the 18th century, when activism and revival were present throughout Islamdom. The three major Muslim empires did experience a decline during the 18th century, as compared with their own earlier power and with the rising powers in Europe, but most Muslims were not yet aware that Europe was partly to blame.

Similar decline had occurred many times before, a product of the inevitable weaknesses of the military conquest state turned into centralized absolutism, overdependence on continuous expansion, weakening of training for rule, the difficulty of maintaining efficiency and loyalty in a large and complex royal household and army, and the diff culty of maintaining suff cient revenues for an increasingly lavish court life. Furthermore, population increased, as it did almost everywhere in the 18th-century world, just as inf ation and expensive reform reduced income to central governments. Given the insights of Ibn Khaldun, however, one might have expected a new group with a fresh sense of cohesiveness to restore political strength.

Had Muslims remained on a par with all other societies, they might have revived. But by the 18th century one particular set of societies in western Europe had developed an economic and social system capable of transcending the 5,000-year-old limitations of the agrarian-based settled world as def ned by the Greeks (who called it *Oikoumene*). Unlike most of the lands of Islamdom, those societies were rich in natural resources (especially the fossil fuels that could supplement human and animal power) and poor in space for expansion.

Cut off by Muslims from controlling land routes from the East, European explorers had built on and surpassed Muslim seafaring technology to compete in the southern seas and discover new sea routes—and, accidentally, a new source of wealth in the Americas. In Europe, centralized absolutism, though an ideal, had not been the success it was in Islamdom.

Emerging from the landed classes rather than from the cities, it had benef ted from and been constrained by independent urban commercial classes. In Islamdom, the power of merchants had been inhibited by imperial overtaxation of local private enterprise, appropriation of the benef ts of trade, and the privileging of foreign traders through agreements known as the Capitulations.

In Europe independent f nancial and social resources promoted an unusual freedom for technological experimentation and, consequently, the technicalization of other areas of society as well. Unlike previous innovations in the *Oikoumene*, Europe's technology could not easily be diffused to societies that had not undergone the prerequisite fundamental social and economic changes. Outside Europe, gradual assimilation of the "new," which had characterized change and cultural diffusion for 5,000 years, had to be replaced by hurried imitation, which proved enormously disorienting.

This combination of innovation and imitation produced an unprecedented and persisting imbalance among various parts of the *Oikoumene*.

Muslims' responses paralleled those of other "non-Western" peoples but were often fltered through and expressed in peculiarly Islamic or Islamicate symbols and motifs. The power of Islam as a source of public values had already waxed and waned many times; it intensifed in the 18th and 19th centuries, receded in the early 20th century, and surged again after the mid-20th century. Thus European colonizers appeared in the midst of an ongoing process that they greatly affected but did not completely transform.

PRE-COLONIAL REFORM AND EXPERIMENTATION (1683 TO 1818)

From the mid-17th century through the 18th and early 19th centuries certain Muslims expressed an awareness of internal weakness in their societies. In some areas, Muslims were largely unaware of the rise of Europe; in others, such as India, Sumatra, and Java, the 18th century actually brought European control. Responses to decline, sometimes offcial and sometimes unoffcial, sometimes Islamizing and sometimes Europeanizing, fell into two categories, as the following examples demonstrate.

In some areas leaders attempted to revive existing political systems. In Iran, for example, attempts at restoration combined military and religious reform. About 1730 a Turk from Khorasan named Nadr Qoli Beg reorganized the Safavid army in the name of the Safavid shah, whom he replaced with himself in 1736. Taking the title Nadir Shah, he extended the borders of the Safavid state farther than ever; he even defeated the Ottomans and may have aspired to be the leader of all Muslims. To this end he made overtures to neighbouring rulers, seeking their recognition by trying to represent Iranian Shi'ism as a *madhhab* (school of Islamic law) alongside the Sunni *madhhabs*. After he was killed in 1747, however, his reforms did not survive and his house disintegrated. Karim Khan Zand, a general from Shiraz, ruled in the name of the Safavids but did not restore real power to the shah. By the time the Qajars (1779–1925) managed to resecure Iran's borders, reviving Safavid legitimacy was impossible.

In the Ottoman Empire restoration involved selective imitation of things European. Its first phase, from 1718 to 1730, is known as the Tulip Period because of the cultivation by the wealthy of a Perso-Turkish fower then popular in Europe. Experimentation with European manners and tastes was matched by experimentation with European military technology. Restoration depended on reinvigo-rating the military, the key to earlier Ottoman success, and Christian Europeans were hired for the task. After Nadir Shah's defeat of the Ottoman army, this first phase of absolutist restoration ended, but the pursuit of European fashion had become a permanent element in Ottoman life. Meanwhile, central power continued to weaken, especially in the area of international commerce. The certifcates of protection that had accompanied the Capitulations arrangements for foreign nationals were extended to non-Muslim Ottoman subjects, who gradually oriented themselves toward their foreign associates. The Ottoman state was further weakened by the recognition, in the disastrous Treaty of Kücük Kaynarca (1774), of the Russian tsar as protector of the Ottoman's Greek Orthodox *millet*. A second stage of absolutist restoration occurred under Selim III, who became sultan in the first year of the French Revolution and ruled until 1807. His military and political reforms, referred to as the new order *(jiizam-t cedid)*, went beyond the Tulip Period in making use of things European; for example, the enlightened monarch, as exemplifed by Napoleon himself, became an Ottoman ideal. There, as in Egypt under Muhammad 'Ali (reigned 1805-48), the famed corps of Janissaries, the elite troops that had been a source of Ottoman strength was destroyed and replaced with European-trained troops.

In other areas, leaders envisioned or created new social orders that were self-consciously Islamic. The growing popularity of Westernization and a decreasing reliance on Islam as a source of public values was counterbalanced in many parts of Islamdom by all sorts of Islamic activism, ranging from educational reform to jihad. "Islamic" politics were often marked by an oppositional quality that drew on long-standing traditions of skepticism about government. Sufsm could play very different roles. In the form of renovated *tariqahs,* communities of followers gathered around sheikhs *(or pirs,* "teachers"), it could support reform and stimulate a consciousness marked by Pan-Islamism (the idea that Islam can be the basis of a unifed political and cultural order). Sufs often encouraged the study of Hadith, which they used to establish a model for spiritual and moral reconstruction and to invalidate many unacceptable traditional or customary Islamic practices. Suf *tariqahs* provided interregional communication and contact and an indigenous form of social organization that in some cases led to the founding of a dynasty, as with the Libyan monarchy

Sufsm could also be condemned as a source of degeneracy. The most famous and infuential militant anti-Sufi movement arose in the Arabian Peninsula and called itself *al-Muwahhidun* ("the Unitarians"), although it came to be known as Wahhabism, after its founder, Muhammad ibn 'Abd al-Wahhab (1703–92). Inspired by Ibn Taymiyyah, Ibn al-Wahhab argued that the Qur'an and Sunnah could provide the basis for a reconstruction of Islamic society out of the degenerate form in which it had come to be practiced. Islam itself was not an inhibiting force; "traditional" Islam was. Far from advocating the traditional, the Wahhabis argued that what had become traditional had strayed very far from the fundamental, which can always be found in the Qur'an and Sunnah. The traditional they associated with blind imitation (*taqlid*); reform, with making the pious personal effort (*ijtihad*) necessary to understand the fundamentals. Within an Islamic context this type of movement was not conservative because it sought not to conserve what had been passed down but to renew what had been abandoned. The Wahhabi movement attracted the support of a tribe in the Najd led by Muhammad ibn Sa'ud. Although the first state produced by this alliance did not last, it laid the foundations for the existing Saudi state in Arabia and inspired similar activism elsewhere down to the present day.

In West Africa a series of activist movements appeared from the 18th century into the 19th. There as in Arabia, Islamic activism was directed less at non-Muslims than at Muslims who had gone astray. As in many of Islamdom's outlying areas, emergent groups of indigenous educated, observant Muslims, such as the Tukulor, were fnding the casual, syncretistic, opportunistic nature of offcial Islam to be increasingly intolerable. Such Muslims were inspired by reformist scholars from numerous times and places (including al-Ghazali, al-Suyuti, and al-Maghili), by a theory of jihad comparable to that of the Wahhabis, and by expectations of a *mujaddid* at the turn of the Islamic century in AH 1200 (1785 CE). In what is now northern Nigeria, the discontent of the 1780s and 1790s erupted in 1804, when the Fulani mystic, philosopher, and revolutionary reformer Usman dan Fodio (1754–1817) declared a jihad against the Hausa rulers. Others followed, among them Muhammad al-Jaylani in Aïr, Shehuh Ahmadu Lobbo in Macina, al-Hajj 'Umar Ta l (a member of the reformist Tijani *tariqah*) in Fouta Djallon, and Samory in the Malinke (Mandingo) states. Jihad activity continued for a century; it again became millennial near the turn of the next Muslim century in AH 1300 (1882 CE), as the need to resist European occupation became more urgent. For example, Muhammad Ahmad declared himself to be the *mahdi* in the Sudan in 1881.

In the Indian Ocean area, Islamic activism was more often intellectual and educational. Its best exemplar was Shah Wali Allah of Delhi (1702/3–62), the spiritual ancestor of many later

Indian Muslim reform movements. During his lifetime the collapse of Muslim political power was painfully evident. He tried to unite the Muslims of India, not around Sufsm as Akbar had tried to do, but around the Shari'ah. Like Ibn Taymiyyah, he understood the Shari'ah to be based on frm sources—the Qur'an and Sunnah—that could with pious effort be applied to present circumstances. Once again the study of Hadith provided a rich array of precedents and inspired a positive spirit of social reconstruction akin to that of the Prophet Muhammad.

THE RISE OF BRITISH COLONIALISM TO THE END OF THE OTTOMAN EMPIRE

The many efforts to revive and resist were largely unsuccessful. By 1818 British hegemony over India was complete, and many other colonies and mandates followed between then and the aftermath of World Wa r I. Not all Muslim territories were colonized, but nearly all experienced some kind of dependency, be it psychological, political, technological, cultural, or economic. Perhaps only the Saudi regime in the central parts of the Arabian Peninsula could be said to have escaped any kind of dependency; but even there oil exploration, begun in the 1930s, brought European interference. In the 19th century Westernization and Islamic activism coexisted and competed. By the turn of the 20th century secular ethnic nationalism had become the most common mode of protest in Islamdom, but the spirit of Islamic reconstruction was also kept alive, either in conjunction with secular nationalism or in opposition to it.

In the 19th-century Ottoman Empire, selective Westernization coexisted with a reconsideration of Islam. The program of reform known as the Tanzimat, which was in effect from 1839 to 1876, aimed to emulate European law and administration by giving all Ottoman subjects, regardless of religious confession, equal legal standing and by limiting the powers of the monarch. In the 1860s a group known as the Young Ottomans tried to identify the basic principles of European liberalism—and even love of nation—with Islam itself. In Iran the Qajar shahs brought in a special "Cossack Brigade," trained and led by Russians, while at the same time the Shi'ite *mujtahids* viewed the decisions of their spiritual leader as binding on all Iranian Shi'ites and declared themselves to be independent of the shah. (One Shi'ite revolt, that of the Bab [died

1850], led to a whole new religion, the Baha'i faith.) Like the Young Ottomans, Shi'ite religious leaders came to identify with constitutionalism in opposition to the ruler.

Islamic protest often took the form of jihad against Europeans: by Southeast Asians against the Dutch; by the Sanusi *tariqah* over Italian control in Libya; by the Mahdist movement in the Sudan; or by the Salihi *tariqah* in Somalia, led by Sayyid Muhammad ibn 'Abd Allah Hasan, who was nicknamed the Mad Mullah by Europeans. Sometimes religious leaders, such as those of the Shi'ites in Iran (1905–11), took part in constitutional revolutions. Underlying much of this activity was a Pan-Islamic sentiment that drew on very old conceptions of the *ummah* as the ultimate solidarity group for Muslims. Three of the most prominent Islamic reconstructionists were Jamal al-Din al-Afghani, his Egyptian disciple Muhammad 'Abduh, and the Indian poet Sir Muhammad Iqbal. All warned against the blind pursuit of Westernization, arguing that blame for the weaknesses of Muslims lay not with Islam but rather with Muslims themselves, because they had lost touch with the progressive spirit of social, moral, and intellectual reconstruction that had made early Islamicate civilization one of the greatest in human history. Although al-Afghani, who taught and preached in many parts of Islamdom, acknowledged that organization by nationality might be necessary, he viewed it as inferior to Muslim identity. He further argued that Western technology could advance Muslims only if they retained and cultivated their own spiritual and cultural heritage. He pointed out that at one time Muslims had been intellectual and scientifc leaders in the world, identifying a golden age under the 'Abbasid caliphate and pointing to the many contributions Muslims had made to the West. Like al-Afghani, Iqbal assumed that without Islam Muslims could never regain the strength they had possessed when they were a vital force in the world, united in a single international community and unaffected by differences of language or ethnos. This aggressive recovery of the past became a permanent theme of Islamic reconstruction. In many regions of Islamdom the movement known as Salafyyah also identifed with an ideal time in history, that of the "pious ancestors" (*salaf*) in the early Muslim state of Muhammad and his companions, and advocated past-oriented change to bring present-day Muslims up to the progressive standards of an earlier ideal. In addition to clearly Islamic thinkers, there were others, such as the Egyptian Mustafa Kamil, whose nationalism was not simply secular. Kamil saw Egypt as simultaneously European, Ottoman, and Muslim. The Young Turk Revolution of 1908 was followed by a period in which similarly complex views of national identity were discussed in the Ottoman Empire.

ISLAM AND NATIONALISM IN THE AGE OF GLOBALIZATION (THE EARLY 20TH CENTURY TO THE PRESENT)

Reform and Revival in the Colonial Period

The tension between Islamic and national identifcation remained crucial for Muslims at the start of the 20th century. In countries under Western colonial rule, the struggle for national independence often went hand in hand with an effort by reformist intellectuals to recover the authentic message of the original Muslim community. Between the two World Wars, two distinct interpretations of Islam emerged from the Salafyyah movement.

One interpretation, drawing upon Pan-Islamism, politicized Islam by taking its scriptures to be the proper foundation of the social and political order. The writings of the Syrian Egyptian scholar Muhammad Rashid Rida (1865–1935) provided a basis for such an interpretation. Like earlier reformers, Rashid Rida viewed the cult of saints (the veneration of holy fgures) as a corruption of Islam, and he sought a renovated religion that would be grounded in and faithful to the religion's early scriptures. He insisted, however, that such a renovation entailed the implementation of Islamic precepts in social and political life. Rashid Rida considered the 1924 dissolution of the Ottoman caliphate to be a traumatic event because it marked the end (in his eyes) of a religious and political entity that had existed since the death of the Prophet. Ye t he hailed the seizure of Mecca by the Arabian tribal leader 'Abd al-'Aziz ibn Sa'ud that same year. This led to the founding in 1932 of the modern state of Saudi Arabia, which Rashid Rida considered a model Islamic state.

Rashid Rida was widely infuential among Muslims who were hoping for a wholly Islamic society. For example, his thought inspired Hasan al-Banna' (1906–49), who founded the militant organization the Muslim Brotherhood in Egypt in 1928. The Brotherhood later infuenced other militant Islamic groups.

In contrast to these thinkers, the Egyptian reformer 'Ali 'Abd al-Raziq (1888–1966) claimed that Islam could not be the basis of a society's political system because Muhammad was the last of the prophets. After direct revelation from God ended with Muhammad, al-Raziq maintained, Islam could have only a spiritual function; the use of religion for political aims could not be legitimate. The caliphate was merely a political construction and not an essential aspect of Islam. Its disappearance with the end of the Ottoman Empire, therefore, was not a matter of concern. Henceforward, each predominantly Muslim country would be free to determine its own political system. Although the great majority of the *ulama* rejected 'Abd al-Raziq's view, secular elites blended it with a liberal conception of society that regarded religion as only one of several cultural elements rather than as a comprehensive code of life. In the countries of the Maghrib (the North African Mediterranean), this understanding of Islam inspired visions of uniting the religion with Amazigh,

Rashid Rida

Muhammad Rashid Rida (1865–1935) was a Syrian scholar who helped formulate an intellectual response to the problem of reconciling Islamic heritage with the modern world.

Rashid Rida was educated according to traditional forms of Muslim learning—the sciences of the Islamic religion and the Arabic language. He was profoundly infuenced in his early years by the writings of Muhammad 'Abduh and Jamal al-Din al-Afghani, Muslim reformist and nationalist thinkers, and he became 'Abduh's biographer and the leading exponent and defender of his ideas. Rashid Rida founded the newspaper *al-Manar* in 1898 and published it throughout his life. To a limited extent, he also participated in the political affairs of Syria and Egypt.

He was concerned with the backwardness of the Muslim countries, which he believed resulted from a neglect of the true principles of Islam. He believed that these principles could be found in the teachings of the Prophet Muhammad and in the practices of the first generation of Muslims, before corruptions began to spread among the religious practices of the faithful (*c.* 655). He was convinced that Islam, as a body of teachings correctly understood, contained all the principles necessary for happiness in this world and the hereafter, and that positive effort to improve the material basis of the community was of the essence of Islam.

Rashid Rida urged Arabs to emulate the scientifc and technological progress made by the West. In the political affairs of the Muslim community, he wanted rulers to respect the authority of the men of religion and to consult with them in the formulation of governmental policies. Here he showed his tendency to assimilate practices of traditional Islam into the forms of modern societies. Consultation had never been institutionalized in traditional Islam, but he equated it with modern parliamentary government. He sanctioned the bending of Islam to ft the demands of modern times in other important respects; for example, the Prophet had forbidden the taking of interest, but Rashid Rida believed that, to combat effectively the penetration of Western capitalism, Muslims had to accept the policy of taking interest.

To realize a political and cultural revival, Rashid Rida saw the need to unify the Muslim community. He advocated the establishment of a true caliph, who would be the supreme interpreter of Islam and whose prestige would enable him to guide Muslim governments in the directions demanded by an Islam adapted to the needs of modern society.

Arab, and Mediterranean cultures to create a single cultural identity. Similarly, in Egypt liberal intellectuals such as Taha Husayn (1889–1973) viewed their national culture as incorporating Islamic, Arabic, ancient Egyptian, and European elements.

The question of whether Islam should be the foundation of a national culture and politics dominated political discourse in Islamic countries throughout the 20th century and beyond. In particular, the political interpretation of Islam inspired resistance to Western acculturation. Religious scholars and intellectuals such as 'Abd al-Hamid ben Badis (1899–1940), founder in 1931 of the Association of Algerian Muslim Ulama, and Muhammad 'Allal al-Fasi (1910–74) in Morocco reconceived the identity of their countries in Islamic terms and played signifcant roles in nationalist movements until independence was achieved. Between the two World Wars, these scholars established several Islamic private schools offering Arabic-language instruction for boys and girls. Islamic intellectuals and movements often put their educational endeavours at the centre of their projects to bring Islam into agreement with their times. Thus, the question of the transmission of Islamic knowledge versus secular and Westernized education became crucial. Yet not all Islamic thinkers viewed the two systems of education as incompatible. Some argued that they should be integrated and could complement each other. The Indonesian Nahdatul Ulama, for instance, favoured a system of Islamic schooling along modernized lines that would integrate religious and secular knowledge.

Nationalism: Postcolonial States and Islam

Later in the 20th century, colonized Muslim societies (except Palestine) gradually achieved political independence and built new states. Many of these states adopted a "Muslim" identity that they interpreted in various ways and implemented within such domains as law, education, and moral conduct. Tw o states, though established in societies that had not been colonized, exemplifed contrasting paradigms. In 1924 the Turkish military off-cer Mustafa Kemal, taking the name Atatürk ("Father of the Turks"), brought a formal end to the Ottoman caliphate. Maintaining that Islam had contributed to the backwardness of Turkish society and that a modern country must be founded upon science and reason rather than religion, Atatürk claimed to relegate Islam to the private sphere. This brand of secularist government also controlled the public expression of Islam and did not separate state and religion. In Saudi Arabia, on the other hand, the state regulated public life according to Islamic norms, using a rigorous interpretation of Shari'ah.

In Egypt, which became a constitutional monarchy after 1922 (though it was under colonial control until 1952), the question of the relation between state and Islam generated ferce political controversies between secularists and those who interpreted Islam as a system of government. Among the latter, the Muslim Brotherhood grew from a grassroots organization into a mass movement that provided key popular support for the 1952 Revolution of the Free Offcers, a military coup led by Col. Gamal Abdel Nasser that ousted the monarchy. Similar movements in Palestine, Syria, Jordan, and North Africa, the politicized heirs of earlier reformist intellectual trends, later emerged as signifcant actors in their respective political scenes. It was not until the end of the 1960s, however, that they became strong enough to pose a serious political challenge to their countries' authoritarian regimes.

Muslim Brotherhood

The Muslim Brotherhood (Arabic: al-Ikhwan al-Muslimun) is a religio-political organization founded in 1928 at Ismailia, Egypt, by Hasan al-Banna'. It advocated a return to the Qur'an and the Hadith as guidelines fcr a healthy, modern Islamic society. The Brotherhood spread rapidly throughout Egypt, the Sudan, Syria, Palestine, Lebanon, and North Africa. Although fgures of Brotherhood membership are variable, it is estimated that at its height in the late 1940s it may have had some 500,000 members.

Initially centred on religious and educational programs, the Muslim Brotherhood was seen as providing much-needed social services, and in the 1930s its membership grew swiftly. In the late 1930s the Brotherhood began to politicize its outlook, and, as an opponent of Egypt's ruling Wafd party, during World War II it organized popular protests against the government. An armed branch organized in the early 1940s was subsequently linked to a number of violent acts, including bombings and political assassinations, and it appears that the armed element of the group began to escape Hasan al-Banna''s control. The Brotherhood responded to the government's attempts to dissolve the group by assassinating Prime Minister Mahmud Fahmi al-Nuqrashi in December 1948. Hasan al-Banna' himself was assassinated shortly thereafter; many believe his death was at the behest of the government.

With the advent of the revolutionary regime in Egypt in 1952, the Brotherhood retreated underground. An attempt to assassinate Egyptian Pres. Gamal Abdel Nasser in Alexandria on Oct. 26, 1954, led to the Muslim Brotherhood's forcible suppression. Six of its leaders were tried and executed for treason, and many others were imprisoned. Among those imprisoned was writer Sayyid Qutb, who authored a number of books during the course of his imprisonment; among these works was *Signposts in the Road*, which would become a template for modern Sunni militancy. Although he was released from prison in 1964, he was arrested again the following year and executed shortly thereafter. In the 1960s and 1970s the Brotherhood's activities remained largely clandestine.

In the 1980s the Muslim Brotherhood experienced a renewal as part of the general upsurge of religious activity in Islamic countries. The Brotherhood's new adherents aimed to reorganize society and government according to Islamic doctrines, and they were vehemently anti-Western. An uprising by the Brotherhood in the Syrian city of Hamah in February 1982 was crushed by the government of Hafz al-Assad at a cost of perhaps 25,000 lives. The Brotherhood revived in Egypt and Jordan in the same period, and beginning in the late 1980s it emerged to compete in legislative elections in those countries.

In Egypt the participation of the Muslim Brotherhood in parliamentary elections there in the 1980s was followed by its boycott of the elections of 1990, when it joined most of the country's opposition in protesting electoral strictures. Although the group itself remained formally banned, in the 2000 elections Brotherhood supporters running as independent candidates were able to win 17 seats, making it the largest opposition bloc in the parliament. In 2005, again running as independents, the Brotherhood and its supporters captured 88 seats in spite of efforts by Pres. Hosni Mubarak's administration to restrict voting in the group's strongholds. Its unexpected success in 2005 was met with additional restrictions and arrests, and the Brotherhood opted to boycott the 2008 elections.

Islamist Movements from the 1960s

With the defeat in June 1967 of the Arab states by Israel in the Six-Day (June) War, socialist and Pan-Arab ideologies declined in the Islamic world while political Islam emerged as a public force. Egypt, which had been under the infu-ence of the Soviet Union since the mid-1950s, withdrew from military and other treaties with the Soviets in the 1970s under Pres. Anwar el-Sadat. A new alliance between Egypt and Saudi Arabia, fostered by economic assistance to Egypt from Saudi Arabia and other oil-producing Persian Gulf states, altered the geopolitical map of Islam and led to new religious dynamics. In 1962 the Saudi regime established the Muslim World League in Mecca with the participation of Muslim scholars and intellectuals from all over the world. The league, whose mission was to unify Muslims and promote the spread of Islam, opened offces in the Islamic world in the 1960s and in the West in subsequent decades. With fnancial assistance as well as religious guidance from the league, new Islamic organizations were created by revivalist movements in the Islamic world and by immigrant Muslim communities in Europe and America. During this period Islamist movements, which insisted that society and government should conform to Islamic values, began to openly criticize state control of Islam in their countries and condemned their governments' minimalist interpretations of Islamic norms. These movements were diverse from the start and did not reach public prominence until 1979, when an Islamic state was founded in Iran through revolution. The Iranian Revolution was infu-enced by Third Worldism (a political ideology emphasizing the economic gap between developed Western states and countries in other parts of the world) and by Marxism. Particularly important were the vehement critique of Western infuence developed by Jalal Al-e Ahmad (1923–69) and the Marxist-oriented Islamic reformism promoted by 'Ali Shari'ati (1933–77). The revolution's leader, Ayatollah Ruhollah Khomeini (1900–89), emphasized the themes of defending the disinherited (referred to by the Qur'anic word *mustadh'af n)* and resisting "Westoxif cation" (Farsi: *gharbzadegi)*, a concept he borrowed from Al-e Ahmad and Shari'ati. He also coined and implemented in the new Islamic republic the concept of *velayat-e faqih,* or government by the Muslim jurist. The Iranian Revolution gave hope to many Islamist movements with similar programs by demonstrating the potential of Islam as a foundation for political mobilization and resistance. It further provided them with a blueprint for political action against governments that they believed had betrayed authentic Islam and grown corrupt and authoritarian. The Islamic republic of Iran also competed with Saudi Arabia at the international level for influence in the Middle East.

Ruhollah Khomeini

Ruhollah Khomeini (1900?–1989) was an Iranian Shi'ite cleric who led the revolution that overthrew Mohammad Reza Shah Pahlavi in 1979 and who was Iran's ultimate political and religious authority for the next 10 years.

Little is known of Khomeini's early life. There are various dates given for his birth, the most common being May 17, 1900, and Sept. 24, 1902. He was the grandson and son of mullahs, or Shi'ite religious leaders. When he was fve months old, his father was killed on the orders of a local landlord. The young Khomeini was raised by his mother and aunt and then by his older brother. He was educated in various Islamic schools, and he settled in the city of Qom about 1922. About 1930 he adopted the name of his home town, Khomayn (also spelled Khomeyn or Khomen), as his surname. As a Shi'ite scholar and teacher, Khomeini produced numerous writings on Islamic philosophy, law, and ethics, but it was his outspoken opposition to Iran's ruler, Mohammad Reza Shah Pahlavi, his denunciations of Western infuences, and his uncompromising advocacy of Islamic purity that won him his initial following in Iran. In the 1950s he was acclaimed as an ayatollah, or major religious leader, and by the early 1960s he had received the title of grand ayatollah, thereby making him one of the supreme religious leaders of the Shi'ite community in Iran.

In 1962–63 Khomeini spoke out against the shah's reduction of religious estates in a land-reform program and against the emancipation of women. His ensuing arrest sparked antigovernment riots, and, after a year's imprisonment, Khomeini was forcibly exiled from Iran on Nov. 4, 1964. He eventually settled in the Shi'ite holy city of Al-Najaf, Iraq, from where he continued to call for the shah's overthrow and the establishment of an Islamic republic in Iran.

From the mid-1970s Khomeini's infuence inside Iran grew dramatically owing to mounting public dissatisfaction with the shah's regime. Iraq's ruler, Saddam Hussein, forced Khomeini to leave Iraq on Oct. 6, 1978. Khomeini then settled in Neauphle-le-Château, a suburb of Paris. From there his supporters relayed his tape-recorded messages to an increasingly aroused Iranian populace, and massive demonstrations, strikes, and civil unrest in late 1978 forced the departure of the shah from the country on Jan. 16, 1979. Khomeini arrived in Tehran in triumph on Feb. 1, 1979, and was acclaimed as the religious leader of Iran's revolution. He appointed a government four days later and on March 1 again took up residence in Qom. In December a referendum on a new constitution created an Islamic republic in Iran, with Khomeini named Iran's political and religious leader for life.

Khomeini himself proved unwavering in his determination to transform Iran into a theocratically ruled Islamic state. Iran's Shi'ite clerics largely took over the formulation of governmental policy, while Khomeini arbitrated between the various revolutionary factions and made fnal decisions on important matters requiring his personal authority. First his regime took political vengeance, with hundreds of people who had worked for the shah's regime reportedly executed. The remaining domestic opposition was then suppressed, its members being systematically imprisoned or killed. Iranian women were required to wear the veil, Western music and alcohol were banned, and the punishments prescribed by Islamic law were reinstated.

The main thrust of Khomeini's foreign policy was the complete abandonment of the shah's pro-Western orientation and the adoption of an attitude of unrelenting hostility toward both superpowers, the United States and the Soviet Union. In addition, Iran tried to export its brand of Islamic revivalism to neighbouring Muslim countries. Khomeini sanctioned Iranian militants' seizure of the U.S. embassy in Tehran (Nov. 4, 1979) and their holding of American diplomatic personnel as hostages for more than a year. He also refused to countenance a peaceful solution to the Iran-Iraq War, which had begun in 1980 and which he insisted on prolonging in the hope of overthrowing Saddam. Khomeini fnally approved a cease-fre in 1988 that effectively ended the war.

Iran's course of economic development foundered under Khomeini's rule, and his pursuit of victory in the Iran-Iraq Wa r ultimately proved futile. Khomeini, however, was able to retain his charismatic hold over Iran's Shi'ite masses, and he remained the supreme political and religious arbiter in the country until his death. His gold-domed tomb in Tehran's Behesht-e Zahra' cemetery has since become a shrine for his supporters. Ideologically, he is best remembered for having developed the concept of *velayat-e faqih* ("guardianship of the jurist") in a series of lectures and tracts first promulgated during exile in Iraq in the late 1960s and 1970s. Khomeini argued therein for the establishment of a theocratic government administered by Islamic jurists in place of corrupt secular regimes. The Iranian constitution of 1979 embodies articles upholding this concept of juristic authority.

Even before the Iranian Revolution, however, offshoots of the Muslim Brotherhood were radicalizing political Islam in other parts of the Islamic world. The most infuential fgure in this trend was the Egyptian author and Muslim Brotherhood member Sayyid Qutb. Qutb was a prolifc writer while in prison and became an infuential voice among Islamists until his execution by the regime of Nasser, then premier, in 1966. In his writings Qutb declared that the infuence of Western-inspired secularism had caused his society to become un-Islamic and that a new vanguard of Muslims must bring it back to Islam. He saw this as the "solution" to the two failed secular ideologies, capitalism and communism, that had relegated religion to the periphery of government throughout the Islamic world. Thus, a new *ummah* under the sole sovereignty of Allah and his revealed word needed to be constituted, because secular nation-states—exemplifed by Nasserist Egypt—had led only to barbarity. Qutb's ideology was also infuenced by Abu al-A'la al-Mawdudi (1903–79), founder of the Islamic Assembly in British India in 1941, the first Islamic political party. The Islamic Assembly was reconfgured after the partition of Pakistan and India in 1947 in order to support the establishment of an Islamic state in Pakistan.

Beginning in the 1970s, a new generation of political activists who used violence and had no thorough Islamic education declared that their national leaders were "apostates" who had to be eliminated by force. In 1981 the radical group Egyptian Islamic Jihad assassinated el-Sadat for the 1979 peace treaty he had made with Israel, among other things. This trend was also present in North Africa and South Asia. In many cases these activists were violently repressed. In some instances conflicts with government authorities led to bloody civil wars, as in Algeria between 1992 and 2002, or to protracted armed struggles between military forces and Islamist groups, as in Egypt from the 1970s to the mid-1990s. This repression resulted in the exile of many Islamist activists to Europe and the Americas and led many others to join such military fronts as the Afghan Jihad.

The Mainstreaming of Islamist Movements

From the late 1970s, Islamist groups were the object of sustained worldwide media attention. Ye t nonviolent groups received signifcantly less attention than the few groups that advocated the use of violence. Nonviolent Islamists often expressed their will to participate in legal electoral politics. This became possible in the 1990s, when authoritarian regimes—faced with serious socioeconomic crises and seeking to legitimize themselves in the eyes of the public— implemented policies of limited political liberalization, which in turn led to the participation of some Islamist movements in electoral politics and even to the co-optation of Islamist ideas by some governments.

The Muslim Brotherhood first engaged in electoral politics in Egypt in the 1980s and in Jordan as early as 1989. In Morocco the Party of Justice and Development elected its first parliamentary representatives in 1997. In Indonesia the Prosperous Justice Party took part in legislative elections in 2004. Turkey allowed Islamists not only to participate in elections but also to govern at the national level. In 2002, Recep Tayyip Erdogan, chairman of the Justice and Development Party, which won a majority of seats in that year's general elections, formed a pragmatic Islamist government that cultivated diplomatic relations with Western powers.

In all these cases, mainstream opposition Islamist movements demonstrated their power to mobilize voters, a consequence of their social and charitable activism and their programs of good governance, especially their fght against government corruption. In contrast, such secular regimes as Fatah in the Palestinian territories and the government of Hosni Mubarak in Egypt were criticized by some segments of the citizenry as corrupt and repressive.

In spite of their tendencies to speak about the universality of the Muslim community, Islamists remained nationalistic. Holding a conservative view of politics, they abandoned the revolutionary and utopian aspects of radical activism and instead struggled to moralize public and political life—e.g., by protesting "indecent" forms of entertainment and public behaviour and by insisting on accountability for political authorities. When they were allowed to govern, they rarely imposed Shari'ah-based legislation. Laws inspired by the Islamic legal tradition were implemented, however, in various forms in Iran after the 1979 revolution and in northern Sudan after 1983.In countries that did not practice electoral politics, movements of opposition devised other means of protest and participation. In Saudi Arabia in 1993, a "Memorandum of Advice" was signed by more than 100 *ulama* and Islamists and was sent to Sheikh 'Abd al-'Aziz ibn Baz, the head of the Board of Senior Ulama and grand mufti of the state, to be passed on to the king. They requested an even greater role for the *ulama,* a comprehensive implementation of Shari'ah in Saudi society, social-welfare programs, respect for human rights, and a reorientation of Saudi foreign policy along "Islamic" lines.

Contemporary Islamist movements are polarized between two main trends. On the one hand, most movements are mainstream and pragmatic, seeking eventually to govern through participation in the political system and public debate. On the other hand, more-radical opposition groups reject electoral politics and seek revolutionary change, sometimes violently. Some groups alternate between these poles, choosing electoral participation or violence depending upon political circumstances, as in the case of Hamas in the West Bank and Gaza Strip and Hezbollah in Lebanon. In the first decade of the 21st century, some groups disconnected themselves from national politics in order to join transnational movements.

Dimensions of the Islamic Revival

Various scholars have argued that Islamist movements emerged in reaction to the failure of state-led modernization projects and to general socioeconomic problems such as youth unemployment and poverty. Ye t Islamist movements are not limited to poor countries or to disadvantaged, marginalized groups. In fact, members of these movements are generally highly educated, predominantly in secular felds, as a result of state-led modernization projects. In particular, mainstream Islamist parties are typically led by young men and women who are successful professionals with college or university degrees.

Scholars have also attempted to explain Islamism's rise as the direct result of the failure of Pan-Arabism in the Arab Middle East and of secular nationalism in the Islamic world. As their Arab or national self-identifcations break down, according to this view, people living in those countries turn to Islamism as a replacement. This is a misconception for two reasons. First, earlier forms of nationalism in Islamic countries were not devoid of religious ideas. Second, state institutions in those countries regulated the legal and public manifestations of Islam, in particular through their systems of public education.

In addition to becoming politicized in the hands of opposition movements and governments in the second half of the 20th century, Islam also followed a dynamic of revival that was deeply linked to sweeping educational, demographic, and social transformations. A young generation came of age in the 1960s, a time of rural exodus and urbanization, without having experienced colonial times. General access to education and the availability of printed Islamic literature also gave these young people an opportunity to build their own interpretations of Islam. Muslims could now study the Qur'an and the Sunnah without the mediation of the *ulama*, who represented a more institutionalized interpretation of Islam. Technological innovations allowed some Islamic preachers to be heard or read, and even to develop follow-ings, across the world. In the 1970s both the Ayatollah Khomeini and the Egyptian preacher Sheikh Kishk disseminated their speeches and sermons on audiocassettes. In the 1990s such new media as satellite television and the Internet began to offer faster means of access to ideas about Islam. In the late 1990s the Egyptian 'Amr Khalid became one of many popular preachers who reached a global audience. Through his We b site he disseminated advice on understanding and living Islam as a general ethics and on specifc disciplines for achieving success and happiness in this world and in the afterlife.

Modernization in the Islamic world also encouraged Muslims to reevaluate gender relations. As Muslim women gained signifcant access to higher education and the job market, they became integral to public life in Muslim countries. In many instances, they sought to express their piety in the public sphere by drawing from and adapting Islamic tradition. One of the most widespread and (since the late 20th century) controversial expressions of piety among Muslim women was *hijab*, or the wearing of the veil.Veiling was never a uniform practice: elite women of earlier generations had unveiled, and the veils themselves ranged from a simple scarf to a full-body covering, depending upon country, culture, and economic class. In some Muslim countries—notably Iran and Saudi Arabia—veiling was required by law. Ye t in many other countries and in the Muslim minority communities of Europe, Australia, and the United States, veiling was a massive voluntary phenomenon beginning in the 1970s. The veil remains a subject of political controversy in Western countries with large Muslim minorities, and throughout the Islamic world there is continuing debate about whether women should be veiled in public.

ISLAM AND GLOBALIZATION: THE AGE OF MOBILITY

Emigration of Muslims from the Middle East and South Asia accelerated after World Wa r II and eventually produced large Muslim communities in the United States, Canada, and the countries of western Europe. While Islam was becoming politicized in the Islamic world, Western Muslims pondered how they could live and practice their religion in a non-Muslim context and whether full participation in Western culture and political life was possible, let alone desirable. These issues prompted the formation of numerous Muslim religious and cultural organizations in the West in the 1980s and '90s, including the Islamic Society of North

America, the Union of Islamic Organizations in France, and the European Council for Fatwa and Research. These groups attempted to provide guidance to Muslims who wished to preserve their Islamic identity while contributing to the political and social life of their adoptive countries.

In the first decade of the 21st century, Western Muslims were still not fully integrated into their societies, and many suffered various forms of discrimination. Many also retained important links with their countries of origin through frequent travel and modern means of communication (e.g., the Internet). Second-and third-generation immigrants often had the opportunity to redefne Islamic practices and beliefs in opposition to their parents and grandparents, whose interpretations they considered too parochial, too strongly infuenced by the culture of origin, or not close enough to a more abstract and universal type of Islam. While thus articulating a more personal religious identity, young Western Muslims (like young Muslims in other parts of the world) came to rely on religious authorities who were not associated with traditional Islamic institutions of learning. For this young generation, the fatwas (formal opinions on questions of Islamic doctrine) issued by such authorities became a crucially important source of answers to political and ethical questions. These fatwas, moreover, tended to represent Islam as a moral rather than a political community.

It was in this context of the Western institutionaliza-tion cf Islam, and more generally of the transformation of Islam from a blueprint for a political and legal system into an ethics of conduct, that the September 11, 2001, attacks against the United States occurred. The attacks were staged by al-Qaeda, a radical Islamist organization founded in the late 1980s by Osama bin Laden, a Saudi national. Bin Laden viewed the world as divided in a war between Muslims and "Crusaders and Zionists." Although the so-called "clash of civilizations" between Islam and the West was largely f ctional, the term itself (coined in 1991 by the historian Bernard Lewis and popularized from 1993 by the political scientist Samuel P. Huntington) had a tremendously real power to mobilize public perceptions. The notion was reinforced both in the West and in the Islamic world by the September 11 attacks and the U.S.-led invasion of Afghanistan in 2001, the Iraq Wa r in 2003, and the protracted inability of the international community to solve the conflict between the Palestinians and Israel.

Amid the ubiquitous language of global religious warfare, there were internal debates among Muslims about how the religious tradition should be interpreted, particularly as it concerned the use of violence, women's rights, and interfaith relations. Intellectuals such as Nurcholis Majid in Indonesia and Amina Wadud in the United States attempted to reclaim Islamic traditions by showing how Islam could accommodate liberal-democratic societies and ideas. Their visions of Islam also recognized full gender equality and individual freedom of expression. Meanwhile, such controversies as the banning of the veil in public schools in France and the publication in Denmark of cartoons caricaturing the Islamic faith (and particularly the Prophet Muhammad) became instantly global, transforming intellectual and political debates between Islam and other faiths and within Islam itself, challenging the modes of regulation of Islam in Muslim and non-Muslim countries alike.

Today, one-third of the world's Muslims live within minority communities. The rapid movement of Muslim immigrants to non-Muslim countries in modern times has meant a blurring of the distinction between Islam and the West. And although Islam has met with globalization before through migration, conquest, pilgrimage, and the use of Arabic language among far-fung learned classes, modern globalized Islam is altogether unique. It is a mass movement, not an elite one, and as emigration continues, the homeland left behind is not static but is itself greatly changed. The ummah, the community of believers, must be considered in abstract terms. As Islam is deterritorialized – increasingly belonging not to a particular geographic place, culture, or society – the faith must now be redefned outside the context of a particular culture, and identities must be recast. Thus, the relationship between believers and their religion, and between Islam and society, continues to evolve. And as Muslims continue to face questions such as integration, exclusion, religious expression, and the relationship between religion and politics, such issues become ever increasingly global – and yet at the same time, local – in scope.

8

Islamist Groups in India

Contemporary India is a Hindu-majority Country, governed under a secular democratic constitution since 1947, when it achieved independence from British rule. At first glance India's pluralism appears to protect it from falling under the spell of extremist ideologies, including Islamism. Muslim influence—cultural, political, economic, religious and linguistic—has been an integral part of the Indian ethos since the seventh century, and for the most part this influence has been benign. But India has been home to some significant thinkers of political Islam, and militant Islamist groups continue to operate in, and even target, India today.

Islam was first introduced to India's coastal regions by Arab Muslim traders soon after its advent. In 711, a young general commanding an Arab army captured the kingdom of Sindh and established Muslim political power on the Indian subcontinent. Parts of India, now in Pakistan, were ruled by governors or tributaries of the Umayyad and Abbasid dynasties that ruled from Damascus and Baghdad respectively.

Muslim traders, mystics, preachers and invaders have shaped and influenced India for thirteen centuries. Muslim sultanates ruling from Delhi, beginning in the eleventh century, and the great Mughal Empire (1526-1857) that followed created a substantive Islamic legacy before India fell under British colonial rule. Decolonization resulted in the partition of India along religious lines, but the birth of Pakistan in 1947 did not sever India's linkages with Islam. At least one-third of pre-partition India's Muslims stayed in India. Today almost 12 percent of modern India's population is Muslim, and with an estimated Muslim population of 170 million, India has one of the largest concentrations of Islamic believers. Islam in India has historically been represented by both its esoteric form of Sufism as well as its various exoteric, traditional forms.

Even after ruling large parts of India for eight centuries, Muslims overall remained a minority on the subcontinent. The ruling Muslim minority was generally tolerant toward the majority. This coexistence resulted in an Indo-Muslim syncretism exemplified in art, architecture, and culture throughout the subcontinent. However, the decline in Muslim political power in India from the late eighteenth century onward changed Muslim attitudes significantly. After the demise of the Mughal Empire, Islamic fundamentalism increased. Muslim elites, seeing a decline in their power, prestige and influence, focused on ways to revive their ascendancy. This generated in India's Muslim elites a preoccupation with the "revival of Islam's lost glory," which has been an important factor in the rise and spread of Islamist ideology the world over.

One of political Islam's most significant thinkers, Syed Abul Ala Maududi, explains the concept of Islamic revivalism in the context of an eternal struggle between "Islam and un-Islam." According to him, *Islamic Revival is neither striking compromises with un-Islam, nor preparing new blends of Islam and un-Islam, but it is cleansing Islam of all the un-Godly elements and presenting it and making it flourish more or less in its original pure form. Considered from this viewpoint, a mujaddid [Islamic revivalist] is a most uncompromising person with regard to un-Islam and one least tolerant as to the presence of even a tinge of un-Islam in the Islamic system.*

From the point of view of Islamists, the syncretism emerging under Muslim rule in India amounted to blending Islam with un-Islam. The foremost task for Islamic revival, as they saw it, was to purify Islam by purging it of outside influences. In Maududi's words, any program for Islamic revival must also include a scheme "to wrest authority from the hands of un-Islam and practically reestablish government on the pattern described as 'Caliphate after the pattern of Prophethood' by the Holy Prophet." Furthermore, Muslim revivalists must not "rest content with establishing the Islamic system in one or more countries already inhabited by the Muslims." They must "initiate such a strong universal movement as may spread the reformative and revolutionary message of Islam among mankind at large." The final aim of Islamic revivalism is to "enable Islam to become a predominant cultural force in the world and capture the moral, intellectual and political leadership of mankind."

Most South Asian Muslims recognize Shaykh Ahmad of Sirhind (1563-1624) as the subcontinent's first Islamic revivalist. Shaykh Ahmad questioned the Mughal emperor Akbar's efforts to create a formal Indian religion (Deene-Ilahi, or "religion of God") and insisted instead on strict adherence to sharia (Islamic law). Although Shaykh Ahmad's intellectual efforts did not result in sharia-based government throughout the subcontinent, they did ensure that Islam retained its separate identity. Shaykh Ahmad did not demand an end to Sufi traditions, and he managed only to circumscribe the influence of other faiths over Muslims rather than ending that influence completely. For that reason, the scholarly Shaykh Ahmad does not serve as a model for modern day Islamist militants. That mantle is conferred on Shah Waliullah of Delhi (1703-1753), who combined religious scholarship with an active role in political matters.

Shah Waliullah's birth coincided with the slow decline of Mughal influence and the corresponding rise of Hindu political power under the Marathas, a fighting force from India's southwestern Maharashtra region. Shah Waliullah wrote to the Afghan chieftain Ahmed Shah Abdali (1722-1772) asking him to attack the Maratha chieftains and save the Mughal empire from losing territory. In his writings Shah Waliullah emphasized the importance of Muslim political power and ascribed Muslim decline to the rise of secular monarchy at the expense of the religiously guided caliphate. Shah Waliullah's critique of Muslim history and his linking political decline with spiritual decline have significantly influenced subsequent Islamist movements throughout the subcontinent.

MUSLIMS UNDER BRITISH COLONIAL RULE

Shah Waliullah's efforts had a profound impact on India's Muslims, but were in themselves not sufficient to revitalize the declining Mughal Empire. The Mughals, as well as other autonomous indigenous rulers that emerged during the period of Mughal decline, gradually lost power, and by 1857 all of South Asia—including contemporary India, Pakistan and Bangladesh—had fallen under British colonial rule. The British brought new ideas and technology, as well as other far-reaching changes, into the lives of South Asia's peoples. The nineteenth and twentieth centuries in India witnessed, on the one hand, the rise of the Indian national movement and, on the other, the growth of religious revivalist organizations among both Hindus and Muslims. In 1875 the Arya Samaj (Aryan Society) was established to promote Hindu reformation and to reconvert Hindus who had been "lost" to Islam. Calls for *shuddhi* (purification) and *sangathan* (organization) among the Hindus prompted Muslim organizations to call for *tanzim* (organization) and *tabligh* (evangelism). Muslims were also influenced by the Mujahidin Movement initiated by Sayyid Ahmed Bareili in northwest India (discussed in "The Ideologies of South Asian Jihadi Groups," *Current Trends in Islamist Ideology, Volume 1*) and the Faraizi Movement in Bengal.

The Mujahidin Movement's founder Sayyid Ahmed Bareili had been influenced by the teachings of Shaykh Muhammad bin Abdel Wahhab during a pilgrimage to Mecca and had returned to India with the belief that there was a need to purify Islam as it was practiced in India and to reestablish Muslim power. Sayyid Ahmed Bareili designated regions of India under British or Sikh (i.e., non-Muslim) rule as a Land of War (Dar al-Harb) and declared that it was the duty of every Muslim to leave these regions and migrate to the Land of Islam, or Dar al-Islam. He described the northwestern region of India, along the Afghan border, as Dar al-Islam because Muslim Afghan tribes held sway there. Sayyid Ahmed set up cells throughout India that supplied men and money to his base in the northwestern region and continued his jihad until his death in 1831.

Around the same period Haji Shariatullah (1781-1840) initiated a movement to bring the Muslims of Bengal back to the true path of Islam. Like Sayyid Ahmed he, too, had been influenced by Wahhabi teachings during his pilgrimage to Mecca. Shariatullah emphasized a return to the five pillars of Islam and called any deviation from them a *bida* (sinful innovation). As such, his followers were called the "Faraizis" which derives from the word *farz*, meaning obligation. The influence of the Mujahidin and Faraizi movements receded as the British gradually dispersed the fruits of modernity and introduced representative institutions among Indians, while simultaneously repressing their militant opponents. The beginning of the twentieth century witnessed the flowering of Indian nationalism, however. When Muslim leaders Muhammad

Ali Jauhar and Shaukat Ali launched the Committee for the Defense of the Caliphate to show support for the Ottoman Empire during World War I, the Indian nationalist leader Mohandas Karamchand Gandhi (1869-1948) joined hands with them in an effort to undermine British authority in India. Hindu-Muslim cooperation against the British kept radical Islam at bay for some time and also contained the influence of Hindu religious extremism. But individuals and groups espousing the view that Hindus and Muslims could not be part of one nation persisted, challenging the supporters of secular Indian nationalism.

Fears of being swamped by the Hindu majority in an independent India and the inability of the Indian National Congress led by Gandhi to reassure the Muslim elite about its future gave impetus to the demand for a separate Muslim homeland as a precondition of independence. Indian scholars have also cited the long-term impact of Britain's "divide-and-rule" policy as a key factor leading to the partition of the subcontinent and the birth of Pakistan in 1947. Although Pakistan itself was later divided by the creation of Bangladesh in 1971, the partition of 1947 was final in terms of taking two-thirds of British India's Muslims out of postcolonial independent India.

Indian Secularism and Radical Islam

Modern India's twin founders, Gandhi and Jawaharlal Nehru (1889-1964) espoused a secular ideology that called on the state not to favor any religion, to extend equal rights to all religious communities, and to grant minorities special protections and privileges. Serving as India's prime minister from independence in 1947 until his death in 1964, Nehru attempted to translate these secular ideals into the state's political philosophy. But Indian secularism was frowned upon by both radical Muslims and Hindu nationalists. For radical Muslims, the ideal remained an Islamic state and universal Islamic revolution. Hindu nationalists, on the other hand, embraced the ideology of Hindutva, which insists that India's identity be defined in terms of its Hindu origins and that religions of foreign origin, such as Islam and Christianity, be reduced to a subordinate position in India's national life.

The preamble to the Indian Constitution declares India to be a secular state and guarantees religious freedom to all minorities, which includes the right to set up and manage cultural and educational institutions. India's Muslims have lived in a functioning democracy for almost sixty years, while Muslim-majority states have been mostly governed by authoritarian regimes. Three of India's eleven presidents, including its current president, have been Muslim, and Muslims have regularly enjoyed representation in parliament and ministerial cabinets. The inclusion of Muslims within the democratic process has, by and large, kept radicalism among Muslims in check. But communal riots, involving Hindus and Muslims, have erupted on several occasions sparked by issues such as the slaughter of cows near a Hindu temple or the playing of music in front of mosques.

The post-partition era has also seen the steady presence of Hindu fundamentalist groups in India's polity, highlighted since the 1990s by the rise of the Hindu nationalist Bharatiya Janata Party (BJP, or Indian People's Party). The BJP was formed in 1980 but traces its origins to the Hindu Maha Sabha (Hindu Grand Assembly), which was founded in 1915 to defend Hindus against Muslim influence. The BJP rose to prominence in the early 1990s when it started a campaign to rebuild Hindu temples on sites where India's Muslim rulers had allegedly constructed mosques after demolishing temples. This campaign provoked a violent dispute at Ayodhya in northern India on December 6, 1992, when thousands of Hindutva volunteers tore down the sixteenth-century Babri Masjid (Babar's mosque, named after the first Mughal emperor).

Militant Islamist groups gained some ground as Muslims rioted across India to protest the destruction of the Babri Masjid. The riots were followed by bomb blasts in the Bombay Stock Exchange, an attack Indian officials attributed to collusion among organized crime groups that involved Muslims and Islamist organizations. Ten years later in 2002, large-scale communal riots in the western state of Gujarat also resulted in the death of thousands of Muslims and Hindus.

Contemporary India's encounter with radical Islam has been complicated by India's relationship with its predominantly Muslim neighbor, Pakistan. The two countries have fought three wars since partition, and their dispute over the Himalayan territories of Jammu and Kashmir has been particularly bitter. Since 1989, Islamist groups supported by Pakistan have fought Indian control over Kashmir with a guerilla insurgency and terrorism. Most of the militant Islamist groups currently believed to be operating in India are linked to the conflict in Kashmir. But radical ideological groups beholden to the global Islamist agenda also exist.

Each of India's radical Islamist groups, whether in Kashmir or elsewhere, traces its ideological origins to one or more of three principal sources. The first source is the Darul Uloom Deoband, a conservative *madrasa* established in 1867 to train Muslim reformers and to combat Western influences. The second is the Jamaat-e-Islami (Islamic Society), which was founded by Abul Ala Maulana in 1941 to serve as the vanguard of global Islamic revolution. And the third is the Wahhabi movement originating in Saudi Arabia.

Darul Uloom Deoband and Its Offshoots

Founded in 1867 by Maulana Muhammad Qasim Nanautawi, the Darul Uloom (Center of Learning) at Deoband spearheaded a traditionalist reform movement among South Asia's Muslims. The Deobandis, as the seminary's graduates and followers of the movement it inspired are known, attribute the decline of Islamic societies in all spheres of endeavor to Muslims being seduced by an amoral and materialist Western culture, and from assorted Hindu practices believed to have crept into and corrupted the Islamic religion. The basic goal of the Deoband School is purifying Islam of such un-Islamic beliefs and practices. In the training of *ulama*, or religious scholars, the Deobandis emphasize the teachings of the Quran and the practices of Prophet Muhammad as reported in the Hadith. Within a couple of years of its establishment, the Darul Uloom spawned several branches in different parts of India, the most prominent of which was a sister school called Mazahirul Uloom at Saharanpur. After modernist Muslims set up Aligarh University in 1875 to pursue Western learning, the *madrasa* at Deoband and its offshoots were increasingly defined as traditionalist centers of learning to rival Western education.

To occupy some of the ground between these antagonists, the Nadwatul Ulama (Congress of Ulama) was set up in 1893 at Kanpur. This institution, which moved to Lucknow in 1898 and still exists today, sought to create a corps of ulama who would be conversant with conditions and events occurring around the world. It offered both a challenge to the Aligarh movement and an updated version of Deoband. The curriculum at Nadwatul

Ulama was an amalgamation of traditional Islamic curricula, as taught at Deoband, along with modern sciences, vocational training and some paramilitary training. Deobandi religious scholars have historically been opposed to the West, and this tradition endures today. A statement titled "What Is Terrorism?" on the website of Darul Uloom Deoband argues that the label of "terrorist" has been unfairly applied to Islam and Muslims because the latter are weak and the Zionists and the West are strong:

> The powerful commits the destruction and brutal massacre of innocent persons, yet claims to be a defender of freedom, mankind and torchbearer of justice and civilization. The struggle or resistance of the weak for securing their legitimate rights against suppression or aggression is branded as terrorism. The barbarous bombing of several countries by USA, Israeli aggression against Palestinians, Russian atrocities in Chechnya and Chinese brutalities against Muslims in Sinkiang (Xinjiang) are glaring examples of double standards being applied for defining terrorism. According to the de.nition of terrorism by intellectuals, and thinkers of the West, the conduct of the governments of USA, Israel, Russia, the Philippines and Burma may be regarded as brazen acts of state terrorism. Unfortunately, the organs of (the) United Nations and the media have been utterly unsuccessful in restraining the tyrants and aggressors... The struggle waged by Muslims of Palestine, Chechnya and Sinkiang cannot be called 'terrorism'. That is a legitimate resistance against aggressors and oppressors for securing their just rights.

In an interview in May 2003, the deputy rector of the Deoband seminary, Maulana Abdul Khaliq Madrasi, blamed Zionist and Christian forces for waging a "crusade to realize their dream of greater Israel." He quoted extensively from the speeches and writings of organizations like the Southern Baptist Convention, the Touch Ministries and Franklin Graham to state that the war in Iraq is a war "between forces that believe in one God and forces upholding Trinity." In what can be seen as a definitive enunciation of the Deobandi worldview, Madrasi explained:

> It is the sacred duty of every Muslim to defend the territory for the defence of the Faith. They must continue their efforts till all threats to Islam are dismissed. In view of the presence of the forces of US and allies in Saudi Arabia, Kuwait and Iraq, it is obligatory for the Islamic World and every Muslim, individually

and collectively, to ensure that the resistance against the enemy is continued till each and every member of anti-Islam Christian forces is expelled from Muslim countries....There are various verses at several places in the Holy Quran which state that if a Muslim country is attacked, or if Muslims are subjected to atrocities, if they are deprived of their rights, or if their religious beliefs are attacked or if Muslims are deprived of their power and suppressed; in every case it is obligatory for Muslims to fight the enemy. All that is being done by US forces in Iraq; for that reason it is mandatory for Muslims of the world, particularly of Muslims of adjoining countries that they should rise in an organized manner against the USA for defense of the nation and the country....[The] Islamic world should form a united defense instead of taking recourse to verbal rhetoric. They should mobilize all their material and martial resources with unflinching faith to defeat Zionist forces. If that is done, the time is not far off when Muslims will emerge from the life of humiliation and degradation to lead life of success and dignity.

The rhetoric of jihad notwithstanding, the Darul Uloom has not been charged so far with direct involvement in violence or militant training. The only significant Deobandi groups known to be involved in acts of terrorism have operated primarily in Kashmir. These Kashmiri groups—including Harakatul Mujahidin (Movement of Holy Warriors), Harakatul Ansar (Movement of Enablers) and Harakatul Jihad al-Islami (Movement for Islamic Holy War)—are the main Deobandi militant groups. They emerged during the anti-Soviet Afghan jihad and turned their attention to Kashmir after 1989 under the influence of Pakistan's Inter-Services Intelligence (ISI).

Jamaat-e-Islami and Its Jihadi Offshoots

The Jamaat-e-Islami, founded in 1941 by Abu Ala Maududi, divided itself into three distinct organizations after partition, one each for India, Pakistan and Kashmir. Maududi moved to Pakistan in 1947, leaving Jamaat-e-Islami India in the hands of his followers. Like the Arab Muslim Brotherhood founded by Hasan al-Banna, which originated in Egypt but spread to other Arab countries, the Jamaat-e-Islami considered itself the "vanguard of the Islamic Revolution" in South Asia. While the organization in Pakistan, and subsequently Bangladesh, embraced electoral politics in addition to organization and training of cadres, the Jamaat-e-Islami in India stayed away from the electoral fray. Rather, the Indian Jamaat emulated more closely the Eyptian Muslim Brotherhood in seeking to expand its influence through social and charitable work. Maududi can be described as the first complete theoretician of the modern Islamic state. He argued that Western civilization was leading the world to doom and only Islam could rescue humanity. For him Islam was not just a religion but an ideology, a way of life. He put forth the concept of "theo-democracy," which meant a theologically circumscribed democracy or, as Frederic Grare puts it, "limited people's sovereignty under the suzerainty of God."

Maududi's main ideas focused on the notion of a single law (i.e., sharia), divine sovereignty and the belief that the struggle between Islam and un-Islam would lead to an Islamic revolution that would bring about the creation of an Islamic state. But Maududi realized that the Islamic state he envisaged would not be able to uphold the rigid demands of Islamic law in democratic conditions unless the population willingly abided by such demands. For that reason, he insisted, it was necessary to Islamize society before creating the Islamic state.

Although the Jamaat-e-Islami agreed to reorder its priorities in Pakistan by demanding an Islamic state before society had been Islamized, no similar revision occurred in India. Pakistan had an overwhelming Muslim majority, and the Pakistani establishment embraced Islam as a national ideology; this encouraged Maududi to believe that he and the Jamaat-e-Islami could secure political power and carry forward the task of the Islamization of society in stages. In India, however, where Muslims remained a minority, the situation was quite different, and the Indian wing of the movement continued to adhere to a purer version of its original ideological agenda.

The Jamaat-e-Islami of India, named "Jamaat-e-Islami Hind," was organized in 1948, soon after partition, at Allahabad with Abul Lais Nadvi as its head. In 1960 its headquarters were moved to Delhi. The Indian organization's literature and constitution assert that Jamaat-e-Islami in India has been involved in promoting communal harmony, and emphasizes *dawa* (call to faith) and social work among Muslims. But the Indian section of the movement continues to espouse Maududi's fundamental worldview. Jamaat-e-Islami still expects to show Muslims where they went wrong and to make them good Muslims, as well as to convert non-Muslims whenever possible. While the movement does not eschew politics, it is waiting for "the basic tenets of the Jamaat's ideology that the Divine Guidance should form the basis of our entire activity, expressed in political language as the Sovereignty of God, the Viceregency of Man and the Supremacy of His Law" to be appreciated by the majority of Indians. Jamaat-e-Islami Hind does not, in other words, consider the conditions in India to be ripe for it to assume an overt political role.

A radical offshoot of this movement is the Students Islamic Movement of India (SIMI), which was banned by the Indian government in 2001 for having links with terrorism. Founded at Aligarh in 1977 by students tied to Jamaate-Islami Hind, SIMI is a radical Islamist organization dedicated to converting India to an Islamic land. Indian officials believe that the rationale for setting up SIMI as a separate militant organization was to insulate Jamaat-e-Islami Hind from a direct political role and to avoid a confrontation between the parent organization and India's secular state. But SIMI's open admiration of jihadi and radical views has led—at least on the surface—to serious differences with Jamaat-e-Islami Hind, which has now established a separate student front called the Student's Islamic Organisation (SIO). Before 1987 all of SIMI's presidents were senior members of Jamaat-e-Islami Hind, but the organization publicly disowned SIMI in 1986 after it called for the "liberation" of India through Islam. This slogan greatly embarrassed the Jamaat-e-Islami Hind leadership, which had consistently tried not to do or say anything openly that would cause the Indian government to brand Jamaat a terrorist or jihadi organization. Covert links between SIMI and Jamaat are alleged to have continued, however, even after their public discord.

SIMI's expressed goal is to convert India into Dar al-Islam by converting everyone there to Islam, and the group has declared jihad against the secular Indian state. SIMI seeks inspiration from the views of Maudụdi and Jamaate-Islami: According to SIMI, Islam is not just a religion but an ideology, the Quran is the only basis for governing human life, and it is the duty of every Muslim to propagate Islam and wage jihad to establish an Islamic state. SIMI is against not only the Western culture and modernization that Maududi critiqued at length, but also the prevalent Hindu

Brahmanical culture and idol worship. In other words, the mere existence of other faiths and beliefs is unacceptable, and religious tolerance amounts to diluting Islam's purity. Jihad, the *Umma*, and the Caliphate are core concepts in the ideology of SIMI, which stridently asserts pan-Islamic ideals.

According to Safdar Nagori, a prominent SIMI leader, Osama bin Laden is "not a terrorist" but rather, an "outstanding example of a true *Mujahid*" who has undertaken jihad on behalf of the entire community of believers, the *Umma*. For Nagori other inspiring personalities include Shaykh Ahmed Yassin of Hamas and Masood Azhar of Jaish-e-Muhammad, the hardline Pakistani jihadi group most known for beheading the Wall Street Journal reporter Daniel Pearl. SIMI held a conference in 1999 under the slogan "Allah's Party Shall Indeed Prevail" (Allah Ki Jamaat He Ghalib Rahne Wali Hai). The conference logo depicted the Quran with the superimposed image of a hand holding a gun against a globe. The conference heard an address in Arabic by Shaykh Yasin, which was primarily an exhortation to jihad. Conference participants were issued certificates declaring the "Quran is our constitution; Jihad is our path; and Martyrdom is our desire."

SIMI targets Muslim youth between the ages of fifteen and thirty for membership, and demands that members retire after the age of thirty. Several former members of SIMI have moved to different parts of India and set up such local radical Islamist groups as the National Democratic Front and the Islamic Youth Center (IYC), based in the southern state of Kerala; Darsgah Jihado-Shahadat (School for Jihad and Martyrdom), based in Andhra Pradesh; and the Muslim Munnetra Kazhagam (Muslim National Movement—TMMK) in Tamil Nadu. SIMI and its associated groups publish several magazines in various Indian languages, including Vivekam in Malayalam, Sedhi Madal in Tamil, Rupantar in Bengali, Iqraa in Gujarati, Tahreek in Hindi, Al Harkah in Urdu and the Shaheen Times in English and Urdu. In its 2000 annual report, the year before it was banned, SIMI explained its ideological agenda:

> It is the responsibility of this (Muslim) 'last community', the 'best community', the 'middle community', to rise up and face the challenges that surround it, to revive Deen, to lead and guide not only the Islamic world, but all of humanity along the 'Straight Path' and rescue it from the clutches of Satanic power. It is the

demand of the time that Muslim youth should struggle for the superiority and establishment of Deen and revival of Islam in the light of Holy Quraan [sic] and Sunnah...The end of the Khilafah (Caliphate) led to our (Muslim) disintegration into different countries on the basis of nationalism, language and other sectarian prejudices. Naturally therefore, our main responsibility is to strive in those areas, which are directly related to the reinstating of Khilafah...It is essential to emphasize that no political party or organization can bring about a solid and constructive change through secularism in the light of their erratic ideologies. The only way to bring about real change [is] through ...establishing an Islamic system of life."

THE WAHHABI MOVEMENT AND ITS INDIAN OFFSHOOTS

Although the nineteenth-century Bareili and Faraizi movements, originally inspired by the Wahhabis of the Arabian peninsula, fizzled out against the might of the British Empire, some Indian Muslims adopted their puritanical doctrine. The Wahhabis of India describe themselves as "Ahle Hadith" or "Followers of Hadith." Their numbers have generally remained small, however, due to their limited cultural appeal.

South Asian Islam has been very different from the Islam practiced in Saudi Arabia's Nejd desert. Sufi influence has been widespread in India, affecting not only Muslims but also the lives of Hindus and Sikhs, who often participate in Sufi rituals and visit Sufi shrines. Wahhabism's strong dislike of local practices and condemnation of Sufism has prevented its influence in India from being very strong. For years Indian Muslims used "Wahhabi" as a term of denigration for someone who does not respect saints and traditions. It is for this reason that the Deobandis and members of the Jamaat-e-Islami have always avoided the appellation of Wahhabi even when their political cause has been inspired by such ideas.

The global spread of Wahhabi Islam, backed by modern Saudi Arabia's petro-dollars, has not spared India, however. India's small Ahle Hadith and Wahhabi communities have expanded with the construction of new madrasas and mosques funded by Gulf Arab governments and individuals. The Afghan jihad of the 1980s and the Kashmir jihad of the 1990s served as opportunities for militant training for radical Muslims, and India's Wahhabis have won converts from existing Muslim sects, as well as among non-Muslims.

The most prominent Ahle Hadith or Wahhabi-jihadi group operating in India is the Lashkar-e-Taiba ("Army of the Pure.") It is the armed wing of the Pakistan-based religious organization Markaz Dawa-wal-Irshad (Center for the Call to Righteousness,) which was set up in 1989 by Hazrat Muhammad Sayeed (and subsequently renamed Jamaat-ud-Dawa (Party for the Call to Righteousness). The group has been illegal in India and Indian-controlled parts of Kashmir since its inception, and was renamed Jamaat-ud-Dawa in Pakistan to circumvent a U.S.-inspired ban on the group as a terrorist organization. Lashkar-e-Taiba is closely linked to the Saudi religious establishment, as well as to Pakistan's Inter-Services Intelligence, and its ambitions lie beyond Kashmir.

A smaller and not yet well-known organization with Wahhabi roots is the Lashkar-e-Jabbar (LJ—Army of the Compelling God). LJ activists reportedly threw acid on two women in Srinagar on August 7, 2000, on the grounds that their dress did not conform to the Islamic code. Furthermore, several other jihadi organizations with obscure ideological orientations have surfaced in other parts of India. The Muslim United Liberation Tigers of Assam (MULTA) was reportedly founded in 1996 and, along with the Muslim United Liberation Front of Assam (MULFA), is part of the All Muslim United Liberation Forum of Assam (AMULFA). These groups have engaged in random acts of violence in the northeast region of India, claiming that their ultimate aim is to set up a "greater independent Islamistan" for the Muslims of Assam.

9

Unity and Diversity in Islam

No one can claim to speak with final authority concerning the diversity found among the more than five hundred million Muslims who seek to follow the straight path of Islam. One can only record some observations concerning the variations in practices among the Muslims from Morocco and the Balkans to China and Indonesia. It is possible, however, to be much more explicit about the basic unity of Islam, for throughout the Muslim world there is general agreement concerning the sources of Islam, the fundamentals of the faith, and the particular requirements which are the obligations of all believers.

THE SOURCES OF ISLAM

There is general agreement that the sources of Islam are the Quran, the Sunnah, and reasoning about them. Of these, the primary source is the Quran. Concerning matters not explicitly clear in the Quran, the Sunnah is the secondary, supplementary source; and when the answer to questions needs further clarification the third source for Muslims is reasoning about the intent of the Quran and Sunnah by those men who are recognized as having the training and experience which qualifies them to reason properly.

It is the final revelation, the Word of God given through His Prophet as a guide to all men everywhere, regardless of race, or colour, or nationality. Within two years of the death of the Prophet it was compiled in book form and has been the primary source of Islam for almost fourteen centuries, without question and without variant versions. Since it was revealed in Arabic it has necessitated knowledge of Arabic, and this has been a unifying cultural factor throughout the Muslim world. It was recognized, however, that the people in the various countries often read the Quran in Arabic without understanding its meaning. The uneducated people even thought that it was sufficient to pronounce the words correctly, and that such repetition—even without understanding the meaning—would bring them blessings from God and save their souls. Some even used verses of the Quran as amulets against dangers and diseases! Half a century ago the orthodox Muslims believed that it was forbidden to translate the Quran, fearing that translations would supplant the original Arabic version and that versions in different languages would cause disagreements and misinterpretations of the revelation of God. While it is true that because of its very high literary style it is difficult, if not impossible, to translate the Quran into any other language without losing the beauty and vigour of the original, translations in the languages of the people are necessary in order that they may understand the meaning of this book which is the source of Islam. Today the Quran is available in translation in most of the languages of the world.

Sometimes people ask why the Quran was revealed in Arabic if it is intended to be the Holy Book for all human beings. This question cannot be answered definitely, for if the Quran had been revealed in any other language—for example, in English—the question would still remain as to why that one language was chosen. Thus we have to content ourselves with the fact that, regardless of any possible reasons, the Quran was revealed in Arabic. The second source for Islam is the Sunnah. During Muhammad's lifetime, Muslims could ask him to guide them in solving any problem when they did not find a clear answer in the Quran. For instance, once a man asked him if it would be proper to perform a pilgrimage on behalf of his deceased mother. The Prophet replied that it would be proper since such an act could be compared to a debt which she owed and the son was obligated to pay. When the Prophet was dying, and knew that he would not be present to give such advice, he told the people that they would not go astray so long as they held to the two guides he was leaving for them—the Quran, the Book of God, and the example of his own way of life, the Sunnah. The Quran, in Surah XXXIII, verse 21, establishes the Sunnah as the second source of Islam:

"There is a good example in the Apostle of Allah for those who wish to meet God and the Day of Judgment, and to remember God much."

The Sunnah is made up of the deeds, speech, and approbation of the Prophet. His deeds include the way he prayed, or washed his hands, or took a bath, and the like. His words have been preserved for us, as for example when he said, "I am sent to perfect high morality." By approbation is meant that when Muhammad saw something done, or heard words uttered in his presence and did not object, such actions or words are approved. Approbation was applied chiefly to customs of the Arab society which were not in contradiction to the spirit of Islam. For example, when Muhammad saw a man dancing with a sword he smiled and showed his pleasure, so later jurists concluded that dancing with the sword is permitted. Such approval has been applied to customary practices and laws in all Islamic countries where such customs do not contradict the spirit of Islamic laws—for example, in the marriage ceremonies. The codification of the Sunnah, the Traditions, began a century and a half after the Prophet when Malik Ibn Anas wrote a compilation of the Traditions concerning Islamic laws. The compilation of the Traditions took final form at the hands of Bukhari and Muslim in the third century (ninth century AD), and today most Muslims recognize their work as the two correct books on Traditions. Those two compilers established conditions for determining which Traditions would be accepted as authentic, conditions which related only to the persons who narrated the Traditions. Such persons must be of good moral character, pious, honest, of sound discretion, and blessed with a good memory; and the series of such transmitters must be continuous from generation to generation. The first generation was called the Companions, the second was known as the followers, and the third as the followers of the followers. Thus a tradition narrated by the followers only would not be accepted by Bukhari because there would be a gap of a generation from the time of the Prophet.

It must be explained, however, that those conditions for the correctness of a Tradition did not touch the subject matter, for internal criticism was unknown at the time. Consequently we find in the two compilations some Traditions, such as those about the signs of the approaching of the Day of Judgment, which we do not understand even yet. The lapse of two and a half centuries between the death of the Prophet and the compilation of the Sunnah has resulted in many differences between Muslims which continue in our time. In the civil war and struggle for power in the time of Uthman, the third Caliph, irreligious elements among the Muslim people did not refrain from fabricating traditions concerning the merits of some political figures. Accurate judgments concerning the narrators of Traditions became difficult because the political feuds sometimes made the judgments far from objective. A knowledge of the way in which the Traditions were compiled and transmitted facilitates an understanding of the various attitudes toward the Traditions which are found in Muslim countries today.

The Quran, which was revealed almost fourteen centuries ago, and the Traditions concerning the Prophet who lived that long ago exclusively in a desert society cannot serve as explicit guides for every situation which might arise centuries later, and especially in the complex societies of the present day. This was recognized by the Prophet himself. Once when he was sending one of his Companions to Yemen to serve as governor, he tested the man by asking him what principles he would follow in his new position. He answered that he would hold to the teachings of the Quran. The Prophet asked, "And if you do not find a particular guide in the Quran?" He replied, "I shall look for it in the Sunnah." Then the Prophet asked, "Well, what *if* you do not find it in the Sunnah either?" He replied, "In such a case, I shall make use of my own opinion." The Prophet was very pleased with that answer and said, "Thanks to God who has guided the messenger of the Messenger of Allah."

Thus a third basis for Islam became established, the basis of reasoning. We find in the Quran many verses which mention reasoning, or thinking, or knowing—verses which exhort us to make use of our brains instead of following blindly the traditions which our ancestors followed. Concerning the Unbelievers of old, the Quran says, "Nay, for they say only: Lo we found our fathers following a religion, and we are guided by their footprints" (Surah XLIII, 22). While exhorting us to contemplate nature, the Quran says, "In the creation of skies and the earth, the difference between night and day, the ships which run at sea carrying that which is useful for mankind, the rain water which Allah sends down from the sky to revive the earth after its death, and to spread animals on it, and the arrangement of winds and clouds between sky and earth, in all those things there are evidences (for the existence of

God) for those who make use of their brains" (Surah II, 164). There is even a verse which says that once upon a time the people of Hell said to one another, "If we had made use of our ears or our brains we would not have been the inhabitants of this Hell" (Surah LXVII, 10).

Originally the word used for reasoning, *qiyas,* meant measure, used in the sense of thinking by comparing one thing with another – reasoning by analogy. As the third source of Islamic law it means determining the proper course of action by reasoning from the Quran and the Sunnah. Some men, however, speak of a fourth source of the law of Islam – consensus of opinion, or the agreement of capable men in their judgment on a specific question. This concept was introduced by al Shafii, the founder of one of the schools of law. Some people have misunderstood consensus to mean simply public opinion, and have asserted that if public opinion approves an action it is therefore acceptable to Islam. For Muslim legislators, consensus is the agreement reached among qualified religious leaders in one place at one time. There has never been a means by which such agreement might be found for all Muslims everywhere. True consensus, ijma, was possible only during the time of the first two Caliphs and part of the rule of the third Caliph. Ijma now only means that some agreement has been found in some places concerning the interpretation of certain verses of the Quran. As a basic source for Islam, it is reasoning, not consensus which is the third source. The Quran, the Sunnah, and reasoning are the generally accepted sources of Islam.

There are, as has been seen, some exceptions to the position that these are the three sources of Islam, for some people hold that only the Quran and Sunnah can give us a solid foundation for Islam. Their attitude, however, is easily refuted for it must be admitted that the problems of the world today are very different from those of the time of Muhammad, and their attitude would make Islam a dead religion. Actually, Islam is a dynamic religion, based on the Quran, the Sunnah, and reasoning. Some people confuse ijtihad with reasoning, but if used in the sense of a personal preference it is obviously not the same thing. In the sense of careful reasoning as to the implications of the Quran and the Sunnah, it is the same as reasoning. Unchecked, ijtihad might even lead to disagreement concerning such basic ideas as right and wrong, good and bad! To understand the unity and diversity in

Islam it is necessary to understand these three sources of Islamic law: the Quran, the Sunnah, and the proper use of reason.

THE CREED OF ISLAM

The unity in Islam is shown in the acceptance of the six articles of belief, the fundamentals of Islam—belief in God, Angels, revealed scriptures, prophets, the Day of Judgment, and the destiny of man for good or evil. These beliefs are held by all Muslims.

The proof for the existence of God is found in the Quran through meditation on the beauty and order of nature. The harmony of the natural world shows that there is one benevolent Allah who created the universe and all human beings. The oneness of God is His most distinctive characteristic, as is shown in Surah CXII of the Quran, "He is One. He it is to whom we address our demands. He never gives birth and He was never born, nothing is similar to Him." In addition, all good qualities can be ascribed to God, He is the Merciful, the Generous, the Lover, the Great, the High. Some traditions mention ninety-nine names of God, but it is probable that the number is to be understood, not literally, but only as a very great number. Thus a Muslim may choose among those names of God the one which is psychologically relevant in the circumstances, a practice which is common throughout the Muslim world.

Theological treatises mention that there are twenty attributes of God, usually listed in four divisions. The first division includes only the essential attribute of existence. The second division is made up of the five negative attributes—no beginning, no end (eternity), difference from contingent things, independence of existence, unity (uniqueness). The third division includes the seven abstract attributes of power, will, knowledge, life, and the ability to hear, see, and speak. The fourth division, which is called the correlative of the abstract attributes, is made up of present participles of the abstract attributes of the third division—powerful (overpowering), willing, knowing, living, hearing, seeing, speaking. The theologians stressed that the attributes of God are not separate from the essence of God. This division of attributes is arbitrary and not clear, but most of the people consider it to be an essential element of belief. The series of attributes is clearly an artificial reflection of a reaction to Greek philosophy; it is not found in this form in the Quran or the Hadith, and has made people think in an unhealthy way. It is more appropriate to understand the existence of God through contemplating nature, as is revealed in the Quran. The differences of opinion among Muslims as to whether or not God resembles human beings, and the opinion of some common people that God resembles a medieval absolute king, arise only from different patterns of education; they are not fundamental to Islam.

Angels are creatures who serve as liaison between God the Almighty and His apostles, bringing the Godly messages and revelations to them. Some Traditions speak of Angels who guard Hell, some who guard Paradise, some who ask dead people about their beliefs, and some who record all of a man's actions; there is also an Angel who will blow the trumpet to awaken all human beings on the Day of Judgment. Common people tend to understand such Traditions literally, while educated people prefer to understand them figuratively with an interpretation more or less acceptable to reason. The Quran, the holy revealed Book of Islam, mentions three former revealed books—the Book of Ḍavid, the Book of Moses, and the Book of Jesus. This does not necessarily mean that there were no other revealed books, but only that we do not know whether or not any other books were revealed. Most people believe that there were no other revealed books than those three and the Quran. The names of twenty-five apostles are found in the Quran, beginning with Adam. Muslims depend entirely on the text of the Quran for information concerning those prophets since the Quran is the only source about which there is not the slightest doubt. It is fortunate that the career of Muhammad is well-known, that there is nothing vague in the records of his life. The Traditions picture him in a very human way – dealing in commerce, getting married, having children, losing his wife and his sons, sharing all common experiences—in no sense a supernatural being. The only difference between Muhammad and the rest of mankind is that he received the revelations of God. All Muslims recognize Muhammad as a Prophet, and the last of the prophets. They see that the proof of his revelation lies not in external miracles but in the nature of the revelation itself. When the question is asked as to whether or not the teachers of other religions, such as the Buddha or Confucius, were prophets, no clear answer can be given. The Quran is not explicit on that point, for it says, "I have sent many apostles before you (Muhammad).

I have told you about some of them, and I have not told you about some others" (Surah XL, 78). Some people conclude that the teachers of other religions are included in the "some others" that God has not told about, but other people say that only by studying the spirit and fundamentals of those religions can one determine whether or not they are of the same spirit as Islam, and their founders might be considered to have been prophets.

The Day of Judgment is mentioned in many verses in the Quran. When the sky is split, when the stars collide, when the mountains are like cotton, when the earth quakes—that is the Day of Judgment. On that day all people are awakened and their deeds are weighed; those having a heavy weight of good records will live happily in Paradise and those who have light weights will go to a Hell full of fire. The descriptions of Paradise are in such beautiful language that they make a deep impression on anyone who listens to the recital of the parts of the Quran which refer to it. On the other hand, Hell is described in a horrible way in many passages in the Quran. Although the common people are inclined to understand the descriptive passages in a literal sense, educated people recognize them as figurative. When the passages which describe Paradise and Hell are meditated upon it is easy to understand what great power they have to motivate people toward good actions.

The sixth fundamental belief of Islam is the belief in destiny for good or for evil. There has been much misunderstanding of the meaning of the word destiny. Many people have thought that a belief in destiny implies that everything will happen by itself, whether we wish it or not, and that such a belief will make people apathetic and indifferent toward all progress. The real meaning of belief in destiny, however, is that one believes that God created an orderly world and one should act according to the nature of that world. Thus a man with a sense of destiny will be active in doing anything which he judges to be good, knowing that if anything bad happens in spite of all precautionary measures, then there will be no reason for regret or for blaming oneself. Then he would say that it was the destiny of Allah. This meaning was illustrated by the Caliph Umar Ibn al-Khattab when he decided not to visit Palestine while there was an epidemic there. A companion asked him, "Are you evading the destiny of God?" He answered, "Yes. I run from the destiny of God to another destiny of God." There is no difference among Muslims concerning these six fundamental beliefs of Islam. Every Muslim believes in God, in Angels, in revealed scriptures, in apostles, in the Day of Judgment, and in destiny. The differences are only in the interpretations, as mentioned above, and these differences result primarily from the differences in standards of education.

THE PILLARS OF ISLAM

The fundamental beliefs of Islam have their practical consequences in everyday life. The writers of the other chapters in this book have referred to the practical side of Islam as the consequences of religion, the particular requirements of Islam, or as worship and dealings. Tradition says that the worship obligations, or requirements, of Islam are known as the Pillars of Islam; and the guide for dealings, for the responsibilities of human beings in society, are covered by fiqh, Islamic law.

According to Tradition, Islam is based on five foundations: the confession that there is no God but Allah and that Muhammad is the Apostle of Allah; prayer; almsgiving; fasting during Ramadan; and pilgrimage to Mecca by those who are able to go. Of these five pillars, concerning the first one there is no variation anywhere in the Islamic world. All Muslims know the Word of Witness, the confession of faith in Allah and the recognition of Muhammad as His Messenger, and all Muslims repeat it as their confession of faith.

The prayers are of two kinds, obligatory and optional. The five daily prayers are obligatory, including the obligation to attend the congregational prayer on Friday in the mosque. It is impossible to estimate what proportion of the people perform the five daily prayers regularly, since women usually say their prayers in the home and men may perform the salat at the mosque, at work, or at home.

There is no religious superior who checks on the performance of the prayers. It is possible, however, to observe the attendance at the Friday noon prayers in the mosque. Large number of people will be seen at the mosque on Friday in Indonesia, in Turkey, Egypt, and parts of the Maghrib, and in the Shia mosques of Iran, to mention only the most obvious places. The smallest attendance at the Friday service would be found in China, and in the Soviet Union.

The optional, or facultative, prayers are of many kinds, such as the additional prayers before and after the obligatory prayers, prayers on the holiday after the month of fasting, prayers at the festival which marks the end of the pilgrimage, and prayers in times of need—which are offered by anyone at any time or place when the help of God is sought. Prayer for a person who died is necessary, since the spirit of such a person continues to live. Optional prayers can be performed at any time because a Muslim is in constant relation with God.

There are minor differences from country to country in the manner of praying, differences of no importance which have grown up through varying interpretations in the schools of jurisprudence. Some people emphasize the performance of optional prayers after the Friday prayers, while others do not. There are slight differences in posture; for example, in some countries, while standing, the people put their hands one upon the other in front of the lower part of the chest, while others who follow the school of Malik or of the Shias bend their hands down. Such differences are of no importance, and the unity is shown by the complete harmony among Muslims as to the times of prayer, the ablutions which must be performed before prayer, and the facing toward the Kaaba in Mecca.

The mosques are the centres for prayer, teaching, and service in the Muslim world and are recognized as the distinctive symbol of Islam even though they differ considerably from country to country. Originally the mosque was very simple, for any ground can be made a place for prayer. The first mosque built by Muhammad in Medina was a simple plot of ground with clay walls on all sides and a roof of palm branches. As Islam spread to other countries the mosques adopted the architecture of those countries. In China, for example, we find mosques which resemble pagodas in many ways; in Indonesia most mosques are built near streams which the people can use for ablutions; in Arab countries the big mosques have one section roofed for winter use and an open area for use in summer. In recent years the greatest activity in building new mosques has been in Turkey and Indonesia.

There is great variety in the minarets which are used for the call to prayer. They may be simple square or round towers, as in the Levant; or elaborate architectural designs as in Egypt; or the slender, pencil-shaped minarets of Turkey; in Iraq and Iran the minarets in Shia mosques are often beautifully decorated with colourful ceramic tiles; in Indonesia they stand as separate towers, or in the villages may even be a chair in a high tree; and in China the government did not permit the building of minarets. Indonesia is unique in using drums for the call to prayer.

It is generally agreed that a Muslim should give alms which amount to a tenth of the agricultural yield immediately after harvest, and a fortieth part of his wealth of goods, or of gold after a lapse of one year if it reaches the quantity of thirty.-eight grams – and about the same proportion of wealth in animals. The Quran specifies that such alms are to be given to the poor, the needy, the collectors of zakat, those whose hearts are to be appeased, slaves, travellers, debtors, and those who are on the path of God. While the source and the recipients of zakat are generally agreed upon, there are variations in the practice of distribution, largely because most Islamic countries do not have official collectors or an official organization for administering almsgiving. Turkey has a ministry of waqfs, as a part of the government; some of the Arab countries have governmental departments which are concerned with the administration of religious endowments; but in most countries almsgiving in goods or money is a voluntary gift either to individuals or to pious foundations. In Arabia they still give animals as alms since they have official collectors, but there is no almsgiving of goods or gold. In Indonesia people pay zakat on agricultural products to the religious men in the Islamic country reaches the proportion imposed by religion.

Pilgrimage remains a very important force making for unity in the Muslim world. Each year Muslims from all over the world, Muslims of every colour and race, gather in the Holy Land to fulfill their obligation to make the pilgrimage. After almost fourteen centuries the pilgrimage retains its importance for Islam in spite of the development of new means of communication, for there Muslims from all over the world, religious leaders and common folk, meet and exchange views. Such personal contact is necessary to keep the spirit of universal brotherhood alive. The minor details in practices associated with the pilgrimage are only variations which developed in the different schools of law and are not significant. In modern times the improvement in travel facilities has made it possible for large numbers of people to make the pilgrimage even from distant lands, an important factor in bringing the Muslims of the Far East into closer relations with their brothers of the Turkish and Arab areas of Islam. In recent years the major obstacles to the pilgrimage, other than the ever-present difficulty of being able to afford the expense, have been currency restrictions and the limitations imposed by the governments of the Soviet Union and China. Pilgrimage remains one of the vital pillars of Islam, wisely instituted by the Quran and Sunnah as a form of worship which brings Muslims closer to God and to each other.

ISLAMIC LAW

As we have seen, the practical consequences of the six fundamentals of Islam include both worship, as outlined under the five Pillars of Islam, and dealings, or the responsibilities of Muslims in their everyday life. These practical consequences, the particular requirements of religion, have been codified in the four schools of law which exist amicably side by side in the Muslim world. The Maliki school which was founded during the second century after Muhammad shows preference for the Traditions and practices of Medina where the Prophet lived for thirteen years; it is found today chiefly in North Africa, some parts of Egypt, and in the Sudan. Also in the second century there lived in Baghdad a silk merchant named Abu Hanifah, a rationalist who based his teachings concerning the consequences of religion on the Quran and the Traditions. He wrote no book himself, but his disciples spread his liberal teachings and founded the Hanaifi school of jurisprudence which is found in Turkey, Afghanistan, Central Asia, Pakistan, India, and Egypt. Another of Abu Hanifah's disciples, Muhammad Ibn Idris al-Shafii, founded the Shafii school in the third century; he was a great systematic jurist who took an Intermediate position between extreme legalism and traditionalism. The school of Shafii interpretation is predominant in South Arabia, South India, Thailand, Malaya, Indonesia, and the Philippines. The fourth school of law was also founded in the third century after the Prophet by Ahmad Hanbal, a resident in Baghdad; he stressed the Traditions and distrusted the use of reason. The Hanbalis arc found in Central Arabia, Syria, and some parts of Africa.

These four schools of law – covering the four divisions of rites, contracts, matrimonial law, the penal codes – were worked out so completely by their founders over a thousand years ago that those who came after them found fully adequate systems of law which met all the requirements of their times. A Muslim was free to choose any one of the four systems for his personal guidance, but the prevailing practice was to choose the school of law which was followed in the place of a man's birth. Thus a man born in Indonesia is usually a follower of Shafii law, while a man born in Turkey will be a Hanafite. The influence of birth was so great that many Muslims later became convinced that one did not need to look back to the original sources of the Quran and the Sunnah, for they believed wrongly that no one in these Later days has a capacity for reasoning equal to that of the founders of the schools of law. They became imitators of their predecessors on the basis of a belief that every period since the time of the Prophet has been inferior to the earlier days. While it might be true that those who lived in the time of the Prophet could understand religion better than the people of today who must study Islam by means of documents only, we cannot ignore the considerable change in the social situation and world conditions during the past fourteen centuries. The insistence on imitating the predecessors reflects a loss of self-confidence which was at one time widespread in Islamic communities. The texts of the Quran are still and will always be valid, but we should understand them in the light of present knowledge. One of the great tasks facing religious scholars in our time is the re-examination of the jurisprudence of Islam in the light of reason and modern knowledge. Since Islam does not make a distinction between the secular and the religious, and since a large part of the Muslim world has but recently attained political independence and is now playing a significant role in world affairs, this re-examination of Islamic law is all the more urgently needed.

The relation between Islamic law and the law of the government is a pressing issue in modern times. In Turkey the national law is avowedly secular and even the waqf funds are administered by secular authorities. In Egypt, Pakistan, and India the problem of the relation of Islamic and national law is the subject of frequent public discussion, and in Indonesia several political parties have grown up around this issue. Another problem is the relation between Islamic law and the customary law of a country, as has been noted in China and Indonesia in particular. This will inevitably continue to be a problem as Islam spreads throughout the rest of the world.

Sects in Islam

From the beginning, the basic sources of Islam have been the Quran and the Sunnah. Muslims have always looked to the Quran as their guide and have prayed and fasted and made pilgrimages as the Prophet did. For the details governing their lives, Muslims have relied upon their reason in applying the principles of the Quran and the Sunnah, and this has been the cause of the different schools of law, the various tendencies, and the sects which are found in Islam.

Followers of the Hanafi school of law tend toward rationalism, such as is found among the Mutazilities; the Shafii school follows the moderate theology of the Asharites; the Malikites are predestinationist; and the Hanbalites tend to be literal in their interpretation of theology. These are theological tendencies, but not sectarian differences.

The two major sects in Islam are the Sunnis and the Shias, whose distinctive characteristics have been discussed at length in earlier chapters in this book. Among the Shias the three leading sects are the Ithna Ashariya, the Sabiya, and the Zaidis. The Ithna Ashariya is the major group among the Shias, found primarily in Iraq and Iran; they accept the twelve Imams. The Sabiya, sometimes called the Seveners because they broke away over the claim that Isma'il was the seventh Imam, are also known as the Ismailis. They have divided into several sects, of which the best known is the group which follows the Agha Khan, found in Pakistan, India, Iran, Syria, and East Africa. The Zaidis, now found in Yemen, are a small Shia sect which has drawn closer to the Sunnis over the years.

The Kharijites, who rebelled against Ali, were originally Shia and have been somewhat influenced by Sunni thought. They are found in Oman and Muscat, and in North Africa where they are known as Ibadis.

More than ninety per cent of the Muslims of the world are Sunnis, followers of the Sunnah. The only sects of any importance among the Sunnis are the Wahhabis, the reformist sect of Arabia, and the Qadiani sect of Pakistan which is generally looked upon as somewhat heretical—although its Lahori branch is not always so regarded. The various tendencies among the Sunnis have often led to differences in point of view, but not to the creation of new sects. The most widely accepted theological position is that of the Asharites. The rationalism of the Mu'tazilites at one time almost led to the formation of a recognizable sect, but today the rationalist point of view is only one of several tendencies among the Sunnis. Differences between the firmly orthodox and the modern reformist have not created a sectarian division.

The numerous Sufi orders cannot be classed as separate sects because they are made up of people who consider themselves to be Sunnis or Shias as well as Sufis. Sufi orders have been banned by the government of Turkey, but Sufism continues there as a powerful factor in the Islamic life of the country; both intellectuals and common people study the writings of their famous Sufis and continue their personal Sufi disciplines. The Sufi orders continue to be an important factor in Africa, though their influence in Egypt is declining. There is still, however, a strong interest in Sufi writings among the intellectuals in Egypt. The Shias have pronounced Sufi tendencies which have influenced the devotional life in Iran and Iraq as well as Pakistan and India. The Sufism of Pakistan and India has sometimes been influenced by the mysticism of Hinduism, leading on occasion to pantheistic tendencies there. In Indonesia, as we have seen, Sufism plays a major role in the devotional life of the Muslims, both as organized orders among the common people and as a study and discipline among the intellectuals. Only in China do we find that Sufism has not been an important factor in the Muslim community.

Sufism has been especially susceptible to the influences of Greek, Iranian, and Indian thought which have sometimes led it to excesses and fanaticism which were contrary to the real spirit of Islam. Some Sufis even denounced the Pillars of Islam and taught that union with God is the aim of Islam, a pantheistic doctrine which is heretical. Other Sufis have followed the teachings of Ghazali, combining the rituals of Islam with deep religious feeling. Such Sufis have made, and are making today, a valuable contribution to the religious life of the Muslim world.

CHARACTERISTIC OF ISLAMIC PRACTICES

Muslims are exhorted to follow the straight path of Islam in every detail of their daily lives, guided by the Quran, by the example of the life of the Prophet, and by the Hadith. The life of a Muslim should illustrate the teachings and example of the

Prophet. When a Muslim baby is born, it is recommended that some one should whisper the call to prayer in his ear, "God is Most Great.. there is no God other than Allah.. Muhammad is the Messenger of God... Welcome prayer.. Welcome good fortune... God is Most Great When the baby is one week old it is suggested that the parents sacrifice a sheep—one sheep for a girl and two for a boy—and distribute the meat among the poor. A baby should be given a good name on the seventh day. It is also recommended that boys should be circumcised, and girls also, for the sake of cleanliness. The parents are urged to teach the children how to pray so that by the age of nine they should know everything about the prayers, including the proper ablutions to be done before prayers.

The ablutions before prayer simply require the washing of the hands up to the wrist, washing the face and the head—a part of it is sufficient—and washing the feet up to the ankle. After any pollution or sexual intercourse, a Muslim must take an obligatory bath; in case there is no water, a symbolic action is necessary.

Muslims are required to pray five times a day, with two prostrations in the early morning before sunrise, four a little before midday, four in the afternoon when the shadow of a thing is as tall as the thing itself, three after sunset, and four about one hour later. Each prayer takes not more than five minutes, though it may be lengthened with optional prayers. It is recommended that the prayers be performed collectively, or at least with one companion. In case a person is travelling, two prayers can be performed together and shortened by half. Shias customarily carry a small tablet made of the clay from Karbala which they place on the ground and touch with their forehead as they prostrate themselves in prayer.

All Muslims should attend the Friday midday prayer in the mosque and listen attentively to the address given by an Imam. Women may also go to the mosque, but they must pray behind the men. In practice, women either gather at a separate place in the mosque or do not attend the collective prayers at all.

At the two major festivals, the Id al-Fitr at the end of the Ramadan fast and the Id-ul-Adha—or Id-ul-Qurban—at the end of the pilgrimage, Muslims are urged to perform additional congregational prayers, preferably in the open air, and to listen to the special address by the Imam. Before the prayers at the end of Ramadan they are urged to contribute food to the needy so no one may be hungry that day, and after the pilgrimage prayers they are exhorted to sacrifice a sheep, a cow, or a camel and distribute the meat to the needy. There is no restriction on association between men and women in the Islamic community, the only reservation in the instructions being that there must be no occasion for misconduct. Thus, a woman must not meet a man alone, nor should a woman travel alone. She must protect her body decently but her face need not be covered. The practice of purdah, of veiling the face in public, which is followed in many Islamic countries, is only an exaggeration of the instructions enjoining modesty which has been deeprooted in Islamic communities by long centuries of ignorance.

When a young man wishes to marry he is allowed to see his prospective wife in order to assure the success of the marriage. The girl is protected by her parents, but they must ask her consent before giving her in marriage. If she is a widow, the consent must be explicit, and if she is a virgin tacit consent by silence is suffiecent. The bridegroom must pay a dowry to the bride, which may be only a token. Two male witnesses are necessary for the marriage contract. A celebration after the marriage is recommended, but it should not be extravagant.

The husband must provide maintenance for the wife and children. Divorce is permitted only as a last resort. In case differences arise between a husband and his wife, relatives of both parties should serve as a committee of arbitration. Since divorce is a serious event "by which the throne of God is shaken," in the words of the Prophet, it must be delayed by two stages before it becomes final, and during that time the wife must receive maintenance. A wife can also ask for a divorce on the grounds of cruel treatment, sexual defect, contagious disease, and like conditions which make the marriage intolerable.

Polygamy is neither forbidden nor required. It may be called a necessary evil. If a man needs a son and his wife does not give birth to a male, for example, he might take a second wife. The question is still a subject of controversy among Muslim jurists, but there is general agreement that more than one wife is not permitted for the purpose of satisfying one's lust. Muta, a temporary marriage which may be terminated after even one day upon payment of a gift, is permitted among the Shias. It was originally permitted by the Prophet, but later the permission was abrogated, according to the Sunnis. The Shia still maintain that there was no abrogation, but even those who claim that the permission continues are against the prevalent practice, which does not differ much from prostitution. Adultery is forbidden; if the evidence is sufficient, the prescribed penalty is flogging with eighty lashes or stoning to death if the offender is married.

In case of death a man inherits from his wife or a wife inherits from her husband. The laws of inheritance are given in considerable detail but they follow the general principle that a man inherits twice as much as a woman. This is because the man must bear the responsibility for maintenance of his wife and must provide dowry for the marriage, while a woman who marries will receive both dowry and maintenance.

A dead person must be bathed and given ablution before burial and the community must pray for him. The prayer for a dead person is an obligation of the whole community. If it is neglected, the whole community is sinful, but if one person performs the prayer, the community is considered to have performed its duty. It is recommended that neighbours of the bereaved family should prepare food to be offered to the mourners and their visitors. It is also recommended that relatives should visit the grave from time to time to put flowers on it and to pray for the departed soul. Women, however, are urged not to go to the graveyard to pray for the deceased, since they are too sensitive.

Concerning food, Muslims are permitted to eat anything that is not explicitly forbidden. It is related that the Prophet said, "What God permits in His Book is permitted, and what He forbids is forbidden, and what is not mentioned is in favour, therefore take His favour. God does not forget." According to the Quran, Muslims are forbidden to eat a corpse, blood, pork, a pagan sacrifice, suffocated animals, animals killed other than by slaughtering, animals which died from a fall, animals killed by other animals, remnants of food eaten by a beast, food offered as a sacrifice to idols. All fish which live in the sea may be eaten, according to the ninety-sixth verse of the fifth Surah. All animals which live in the water and on land, such as frogs, crocodiles, turtles, and the like, are forbidden as food. Of land animals, it is permitted to eat camels, cows, sheep, horses, and the like. It is forbidden to eat donkeys; beasts with claws such as lions, tigers, wolves, and bears; birds with talons, such as hawks and falcons; animals which the Prophet ordered killed, such as snakes, mice, crows; creatures which the Prophet forbade killing, such as ants and bees; animals judged to be dirty, and animals which live on dirt. In deciding what food can be eaten and what is forbidden Muslim jurisprudence accepts as guides the Quran, the Hadith, what the Prophet ordered to be killed and what he forbade killing, and the foods which are abhorrent to human feeling.

The verses of the Quran make it clear that all kinds of drinks are permitted except wine. Wine is forbidden because it is intoxicating. On this point the Holy Quran is so clear that no other interpretation is possible. Thus, however small the quantity may be, the drinking of wine is absolutely forbidden. By wine is meant the fermented juice of grapes. As to other fermented drinks, there is a difference of opinion among Muslim jurists. Some maintain that juices extracted from fruits other than grapes, such as apples or dates, are permitted. They base their opinion on some Traditions which say that Muhammad sometimes fermented dates for one or two days.

A Muslim is forbidden to steal, and if he steals a certain amount deliberately the punishment prescribed is the cutting off of the hands. A Muslim must not gamble nor participate in lotteries. He must not deceive concerning measures or weights; he must not break a promise or go back on his word. He is forbidden to pay or receive interest when borrowing or lending money, but a debtor may present a token of gratitude to the creditor.

These requirements and prohibitions, mentioned here only in general outline, are representative of the rules found in the Quran and Traditions which govern the lives of all Muslims.

ISLAMIC SOCIETY

To understand the role of Islam in society one must first realize that Islam is a universal religion in which all Muslims are brothers, regardless of differences in homeland, race, colour, or rank. This brotherhood does not divide the world into Muslims and non-Muslims, for Muslims must be friendly toward non-Muslims so long as they are friendly, so long as they do not attack Islam. Islam has retained its unity and universal characteristics in the midst of such diverse cultures as those of Arabia, Greece,

Rome, and Iran in ancient times, and later in the cultures of Africa, Egypt, Turkey, Central Asia, India, China, and Southeast Asia. Once more the universalism of Islam is being shown as it comes into contact with the new culture of the W/est.

In this interplay between Islam and the various cultures of the world it should be remembered that Islam has no master organization which requires conformity or organizes missionary programmes. The interplay is a spontaneous movement on the part of individual Muslims who seek to follow the straight path of Islam. These Muslims recognize no distinction between the religious and the secular; they try to follow in their social life the rules revealed to them in the Quran and the Sunnah and interpreted in Islamic law. For Islam, the present world is but a transitory existence to be followed by the Eternal World which is better by far, "And verily the latter portion will be better for thee than the former" (Surah XCIII, 4). This does not mean that we must neglect this world; on the contrary, Islam warns us against neglecting it, for the Quran says, "But seek the abode of the Hereafter in that which Allah has given thee and neglect not thy portion of the world, and be thou kind even as Allah has been kind to thee, and seek not corruption in the earth; lo! Allah loves not corrupters" (Surah XXVIII, 77). Islam recognizes the importance of life in the community in this world, but it warns the Muslim against considering this world as the end of existence. Moral and religious values must be seen to be higher than material values.

The importance of social justice is constantly emphasized in Islam through the obligation of zakat and the distribution of gifts at the times of the great festivals. In the older Islamic countries this has been the origin of waqfs for all kinds of service to the community. The teachings concerning zakat stress the principle that the ownership of wealth is a privilege, not a right, and one which imposes obligations to the community. In the Traditions the Prophet exhorts us to give our servants the same food we eat and the same clothes we wear.

In Islam the merit of a person depends upon his deeds, not upon his words, nor his ancestors, nor his rank in the community. The Quran says, "there is nothing for the person but what he has done" (Surah LIII, 39) and again, "The highest among you is the most pious" (Surah XLIX, 13). The only recognized difference in rank in Islam is that which is merited by religious devotion and insight. Such recognition is accorded on the basis of deeds, not on the basis of office. Islam has no ordained clergy, no religious hierarchy with authority over their fellow Muslims. The ulama, the Shaikh, Mullah, Imam, Ahund, Mufti, Mujtahid, Hatib—all are only men like the others in the Muslim community, men who perform special services and are respected and elevated only on the basis of the Quranic principle that the highest is the most pious.

Slavery was customary at the time that Islam was revealed, but Islam prepared the grounds for its elimination. It encourages the emancipation of slaves by giving them the possibility of purchasing their freedom, it urges that part of zakat be given to slaves to help them free themselves, and it offers the possibility of atonement for certain sins, such as having sexual intercourse during fasting days, by releasing slaves.

Women are given equality with men, in principle, for the Quran says, "Whoever, male or female, who is a believer, performs good actions, they will enter into Paradise" (Surah IV, 124), and again, "Men have reward for what they do, and women have reward for what they do" (Surah IV, 32). But we cannot deny that in general men are superior to women and consequently men have authority over women. The Quran says, "Men have authority over women" (Surah IV, 14).

With the rise of nationalism in the modern world, the relation of nationalism to Islam has become a problem which is frequently discussed. Many people think that since Islam is universal it must be against nationalism, but this is not the case. Universalism can begin with national loyalty, for nationalism is simply the result of the organization of a group of people in one political body, regardless of their differences in religion. Islam does not prohibit such political organizations so long as they do not jeopardize the essentials of Islamic teachings. Nationalism can unite or divide, and when it is guided by the universal principles of Islam it can lead men to unity rather than to divisions. In this regard it should be noted that the demand for the Caliphate, in the political sense, has greatly lessened in modern times. Pan-Islamism in our day is not a movement for one super-government over all Muslims, but for cooperation between Islamic nations. Jihad, holy war, has sometimes been misunderstood as meaning that Muslims must declare war on non-Muslims until they accept Islam. This mistake arises from a misreading of the Quran without knowing the context of the verses and the circumstances in which they were revealed.

The verses which call for war against unbelievers were revealed when pagans were still putting obstacles in the way of the activities of Muhammad even after opportunities for reconciliation had been given. War in Islam is only legitimate when it is declared in defense of religion, property, and prestige. The Quran says, 'Fight in the way of God those who wage war on you, and do not commit aggression. God does not like aggressors" (Surah II, 190).

Islam does not approve of hostility toward other religions. Rather, it proclaims freedom of religion and forbids coercion in religion. During his lifetime, Muhammad himself was very kind toward his neighbours and friends of other beliefs, Jews as well as Christians. He even married a Jewish woman, Safijah, and a Christian slave, Marie, who was given him by the ruler of Egypt. When the Emperor of Abyssinia died, Muhammad prayed for him in recognition of his help given to the Muslims who took refuge there in the early days of Islam.

Islamic society has been greatly influenced, and the spread of Islam has been aided, by the educational opportunities offered through the mosques and religious leaders. The Prophet encouraged education by appointing many of his Companions as teachers in Arabia when Islam spread throughout the country. It was ruled that a poor man could marry a woman with a dowry of teaching her a chapter of the Quran. As Islam spread to other lands, centres of study grew up at Baghdad, Kufa, and many other cities of the Muslim world.

The system of education was simple, without organized programme or ceremony. Any pupil could approach a teacher and stay with him as long as he' continued to learn; then he might go on to other teachers, or receive a license to be a teacher himself. In the family the parents educated their children. The teachers did not form a special class but were at the same time landowners, merchants, or government officials. This system continues today in most Muslim countries.

In addition, there have been in most countries the madrassas associated with the mosques, and special schools of higher learning. The oldest Islamic university is the Al Azhar in Cairo, founded in the fourth century (tenth century AD). Other centres for higher

Islamic studies today are found at Fez in Morocco, at Zaitouna University in Tunisia, at Medina, at Istanbul and Ankara in Turkey, at Baghdad and Karbala in Iraq, at Tehran in Iran, at Lahore in Pakistan, at Lucknow and at Alighar and Usmania Universities in India, and at Jogjakarta in Indonesia. In some of these centres the Islamic studies are associated with government-supported universities; there are also government universities in other countries which offer special courses in Islam, as is the case on Taiwan. Instruction in Islam is given in local languages at the lower levels, but for higher studies a good knowledge of Arabic is necessary and mastery of Persian and Turkish is required for any extensive research. Since art and music flourish in times of peace and prospenty, there was little time for them in the early days of the Prophet. Muhammad, however, approved of the music known in his day. He forbade the art which was prevalent in his time, consisting chiefly of human figures, since it was symbolic of idols and would have spread paganism. Because of that, the literal-minded jurists deduced that Islam opposed art and music, which is not correct. The better deduction would have been that we must be careful of the consequences of any kind of art. Art for art's sake is unknown in Islam. As long as art is useful as a means of heightening religion and morality, it is permitted; but if it leads to immorality, it is forbidden.

LATEST DEVELOPMENTS IN ISLAM

When the Mu'tazilite, or rational, movement was suppressed and the political organization of the Muslim world disintegrated, the Muslim people lost their vitality. They neglected the study of the Quran and the Traditions which are the original sources of Islam and instead adopted the teachings of the scholars. They thought that ijtihad was forbidden and that they must only imitate the four schools of law. Instead of making use of reason, they accepted the four schools of law as complete and unchanging and turned to mysticism and belief in the supernatural powers of saints, dead and alive. That gave rise to the worship of the graves of saints which is found today in all Islamic countries from North Africa to Indonesia.

The Wahhabi movement in Arabia was a reaction against the worship of saints, but it made use of force rather than arguments, and failed to establish a general reform. After the French occupied

Egypt many scholars studied in Europe and a renaissance was started which culminated in the work of the great scholar, Muhammad Abduh, who brought new ideas to the people of Egypt. At about the same time the Muslims of India, led by such men as Sir Sayyid Ahmad Khan, who founded Alighar University, became conscious of their cultural importance and their national existence. Within the past half-century the greater ease of communication and travel has brought the peoples of the Muslim world into closer contact with each other and with the cultures of the rest of the world and made them aware of the need for a new evaluation of the ideas of the jurists and thinkers of the middle ages. This is the period in which much of the Muslim world has attained political independence and the people have been preoccupied with political and international problems.

Today the Muslims of Morocco, Tunisia, Egypt, the Levant, Turkey, Iraq, Iran, Pakistan, India, and Indonesia are vitally concerned with problems associated with the establishment of their new, independent governments. At the same time, the Muslims of Algeria and much of Africa, of the Soviet Union and of China, are struggling with political controls which are not encouraging to Islam and are often inimical. These political problems have been faced at the time when the impact of Western culture in the Muslim world has been most pronounced. More than anything else, Islam today needs a period of peace in order that favorable conditions may develop for the growth of Islamic thought. Since the time of Ibn Khaldun, more than five centuries ago, no great thinker has arisen in the Muslim world. Now more than ever there is a need for a time of peace and intellectual freedom in which devout thinkers can interpret the Quran in the light of the progress of human knowledge. The rituals will remain as they are, the fundamentals will remain unchanged, but the understanding of Islam will be illuminated anew for our time.

At the present time, there are four major tendencies in the Islamic world – orthodoxy, reform, Sufism, and Shia. The increase in commumcation and in education is bringing to the followers of each tendency a better understanding of the others. Significant progress is being made in Cairo in encouraging better understanding and reconciliation between Shia and Sunni. Orthodoxy is becoming less reactionary and the reformers less intolerant. The Sufi orders are declining in influence at the same time that the devotional and mystical teachings of the Sufi masters are being studied more sympathetically by intellectuals. In Turkey, Egypt, and Indonesia in particular there are many evidences of a new vitality and interest in Islamic thought. Many books are being published, many students are engaged in Islamic studies, new mosques are being built. Islam spread originally along the trade routes through North Africa, Iran, Central Asia, Indonesia, and China. As Muslim traders settled along those routes they married and established families which often became the nucleus for a new Muslim community. In spite of the diversities of cultures, they maintained the unity of Islam through the centuries. Today, with trade routes easily followed around the world, it is inevitable that the same process will be repeated and Islam will spread to new regions where it has not been known. In this discussion of the unity and variety of Islam we have seen that divergences from the essential unity of Islam have occurred only when there is ignorance among the common people—a low level of education. It is the task of the present generation to provide training in the essentials of Islam, to know Islam deeply, for out of that knowledge of the straight path of Islam will come the unity of belief and practice which has been revealed to mankind in the Quran and the Sunnah.

Origins

Islam means submission to Allah (God). Islam was revealed to the Prophet Muhammad who lived from 570 CE to 632 CE in Mecca in modern-day Saudi Arabia. Muhammad was called to prophethood when God dictated the Quran to him through the archangel Gabriel. Although he gained a small following in his tribe, Muhammad was initially persecuted for his beliefs. In 622 CE he fled to Yathrib, now called Medina, where the first Muslim political community was formed. Enlisting the help of nomadic Arab clans, Muhammad returned to Mecca, stripping the city of all signs of pagan belief. He was generous to those he defeated, however, and many converted to Islam. Two years later, in front of the Kaaba in Mecca, he declared Islam the religion of the people, saying he had fulfilled his mission and that he left behind him the Book of Allah and a set of clear commandments.

History and Spread

By the time of Muhammad's death, many people of the Arabian

Peninsula had begun to follow Islam. A series of caliphs and dynasties led the Muslim community after Muhammad's death, creating an Islamic empire that expanded as far as modern-day Pakistan in the east, Spain in the north, and North Africa to the south. This was a period of great intellectual, cultural and spiritual vitality. In Spain, Islamic civilisation lasted until 1492 when the Christian monarchs regained power. After the collapse of the Empire, Islam remained the dominant religion in most Middle Eastern countries and significant pockets throughout North Africa and Asia.

IN AUSTRALIA

The history of Islam in Australia pre-dates European settlement. From 1650, Muslim fisherman from South East Asia communicated and traded with Aborigines from Australia's north. Some inter-marriage occurred. In the 1860s, some 3000 camel drivers-with camels-came from Afghanistan and the Indian sub-continent. This group contributed to the exploration of the Australian outback, working on both the railway line between Port Augusta and Alice Springs, and the Overland Telegraph Line from Adelaide to Darwin, which connected Australia to London via India. Since the late 1960s there have been a number of significant Muslim migrations into Australia, most notably from Turkey and Lebanon. In the 1990s, refugees and migrants from the Horn of Africa, Afghanistan, Iran, Iraq, Bosnia-Herzegovina, Albania, Indonesia and Malaysia have all made their home in Australia.

Some Islamic societies in Australia are affiliated with AFIC (The Australian Federation of Islamic Councils), which does not control the individual societies but gives a public voice and face to Islam, both in state and federal politics and matters of community representation. Between 1991 and 1996, the Muslim community grew by 36 per cent (approx. 53 000). In 1996, there were over 280,000 Muslims in Australia, belonging to over 70 ethnic groups (ABS).

Key Movements

Islam is divided into two main sects, the Sunni and the Shia. This division arose over the order of caliph succession in the first century of the Islamic calendar. Shiites believe that the true authority and leadership of Muslims after Muhammad's son-in-law, Ali, continued through a line of imams (religious teachers).

Sunnis uphold the supremacy of the caliphs, the line of rulers elected by the people and mandated to guard the prophetic legacy in the administration of community affairs. This gave rise to the development of Sharia law.

Shiites constitute less than 10 per cent of world's Muslims, and possess many internal divisions. The largest contemporary Shia group are the Ithnaasharis, or Travellers. Shiites are a majority in Iran. Sunni Muslims constitute 90% of the world's Muslims and are considered the orthodox face of Islam. There are various mystic strands of Islam, such as Sufism and the Ibadites of Oman, East Africa and Algeria. These are not, strictly speaking, sectarian divisions.

Organisational Structure

Muslims do not require an intermediary between themselves and God. Imams-religious teachers and leaders of prayer in the mosques-do, however, play a significant role. They are often formally educated in matters of religion and jurisprudence, and systems exist for settling questions of law and religious observance. The al-Azahr, a Islamic university in Cairo, is conventionally regarded as the highest authority in Sunni Islam. The Shia developed a hierarchy in line with their beliefs in the succession of rule; in Iran, this finds expression in the system of ayatollahs (senior interpreters and arbiters of religious law). Mosques are not denominational and are run on a number of models depending on the mosque's governing constitution. Some are ethnically-based.

ISLAMISM IN SOUTH ASIAISLAMISM IN SOUTH ASIA

Islamism is a set of ideologies holding that Islam is not only a religion but also a political system; that modern Muslims must return to their roots of their religion, and unite politically.

Islamism is a controversial term and definitions of it sometimes vary. Leading Islamist thinkers emphasized the enforcement of sharia (Islamic law); of pan-Islamic political unity; and of the elimination of non-Muslim, particularly western, military, economic, political, social, or cultural influences in the Muslim world, which they believe to be incompatible with Islam.

Some observers suggest Islamism's tenets are less strict and can be defined as a form of identity politics or "support for [Muslim] identity, authenticity, broader regionalism, revivalism, [and] revitalization of the community". Still others define it as "an Islamic militant, anti-democratic movement, bearing a holistic vision of Islam whose final aim is the restoration of the caliphate". Many of those described as "Islamists" oppose the use of the term, maintaining that they are simply Muslims, and that their political beliefs and goals are an expression of Islamic religious belief. Similarly, some scholars favour the term "activist Islam" instead or "political Islam". Central figures of modern Islamism include Muhammad Iqbal, Jamal al-Din al-Afghani, Abul Ala Maududi, Sayyid Qutb and Ayatollah Ruhollah Khomeini.

Definitions of Islamism

Islamism has been defined as:

- "Islam as a modern ideology and a political program falala",
- "the belief that Islam should guide social and political as well as personal life",
- "the ideology that guides society as a whole and that law must be in conformity with the Islamic sharia",
- "a movement that seeks cultural differentiation from the West and reconnection with the pre-colonial symbolic universe",
- "the organised political trend, owing its modern origin to the founding of the Muslim Brotherhood in Egypt in 1928, that seeks to solve modern political problems by reference to Muslim texts",
- "the whole body of thought which seeks to invest society with Islam which may be integrationist, but may also be traditionalist, reform-minded or even revolutionary", and
- "the active assertion and promotion of beliefs, prescriptions, laws or policies that are held to be Islamic in character."
- a movement of "Muslims who draw upon the belief, symbols, and language of Islam to inspire, shape, and animate political activity." May contain moderate, tolerant, peaceful Islamists or those who "preach intolerance and espouse violence"

Islamism takes several forms and spans a wide range of strategies and tactics, and thus is not a united movement.

Moderate reformists who accept and work within the democratic process include the Justice and Development Party of

Turkey and Tunisian author and reformer Rashid Al-Ghannouchi. The Islamist group Hezbollah in Lebanon participates in both elections and armed attacks, seeking to abolish the state of Israel. Groups such as the Jamaat-e-Islami of Pakistan and the Sudanese Muslim Brotherhood favored a top-down road to power by military coup d'état. The radical Islamists al-Qaeda and Egyptian Islamic Jihad reject democracy and moderate, self-proclaimed Muslims entirely, and preach violent jihad, urging and conducting attacks on a religious basis.

Another major division within Islamism is between the fundamentalist "guardians of the tradition" of the Salafism or Wahhabi movement, and the "vanguard of change" centered on the Muslim Brotherhood. Olivier Roy argues that "Sunni pan-Islamism underwent a remarkable shift in the second half of the 20th century" when the Muslim Brotherhood movement and focus on Islamistation of pan-Arabism was eclipsed by the Salafi movement with its emphasis on "sharia rather than the building of Islamic institutions," and rejection of Shia Islam. Different Islamist groups have come to blows in places such as present day Iraq.

History of Usage

The term *Islamism* was coined in eighteenth-century France as a way of referring to Islam or Mohammedanism, as the faith was often, if inaccurately, labeled as late as the 1970s. Earliest known use of the term identified by the Oxford English Dictionary is 1747. By the turn of the twentieth century it had begun to be displaced by the shorter and purely Arabic term Islam and by 1938, when Orientalist scholars completed *The Encyclopaedia of Islam*, seems to have virtually disappeared from the English language.

The term Islamism is considered to have first begun to acquire its contemporary connotations in French academia between the late 1970s and late 1980s. From French, it began to migrate to the English language in the mid-1980s, and in recent years has largely displaced the term Islamic fundamentalism in academic circles. The use of the term Islamism was at first "a marker for scholars more likely to sympathize" with new Islamic movements; however, as the term gained popularity it became more specifically associated with political groups such as the Taliban or the Algerian Armed Islamic Group, as well as with highly publicized acts of violence.

An article in *Middle East Quarterly* in 2003 states, "In summation, the term Islamism enjoyed its first run, lasting from Voltaire to the First World War, as a synonym for Islam. Enlightened scholars and writers generally preferred it to Mohammedanism. Eventually both terms yielded to Islam, the Arabic name of the faith, and a word free of either pejorative or comparative associations. There was no need for any other term, until the rise of an ideological and political interpretation of Islam challenged scholars and commentators to come up with an alternative, to distinguish Islam as modern ideology from Islam as a faith."

Relation between Islam and Islamism

The concept *Islamism* is controversial, not just because it posits a political role for Islam, but also because Islamists believe their views merely reflect Islam, and the idea that Islam is, or can be, apolitical is an error. Scholars and observers who do not believe that Islam is a political ideology include Fred Halliday and John Esposito. Islamists ask the question, "If Islam is a way of life, how can we say that those who want to live by its principles in legal, social, political, economic, and political spheres of life are not Muslims, but Islamists and believe in Islamism, not [just] Islam?"

On the other hand, Muslim-owned and run media have used the terms "Islamist" and "Islamism"-as distinguished from Muslim and Islam-to distinguish groups such as the Islamic Salvation Front in Algeria or Jamaa Islamiya in Egypt, which actively seeking to implement Islamic law, from other Muslim groups.

Another source distinguishes Islamist from Islamic "by the fact that the latter refers to a religion and culture in existence over a millennium, whereas the first is a political/religious phenomenon linked to the great events of the 20th century". Islamists have, at least at times, defined themselves as "Islamiyyoun/Islamists" to differentiate themselves from "Muslimun/Muslims".

According to Bernard Lewis, Islamists, or as he terms them "activist Muslims", follow the role that the Prophet Muhammad played as a "rebel" during his time in Mecca:

There are in particular two political traditions, one of which might be called quietist, the other activist. The arguments in favor of both are based, as are most early Islamic arguments, on the Holy Book and on the actions and sayings of the Prophet. The quietist tradition obviously rests on the Prophet as sovereign, as judge and statesman. But before the Prophet became a head of state, he was a rebel. Before he traveled from Mecca to Medina, where he became sovereign, he was an opponent of the existing order. He led an opposition against the pagan oligarchy of Mecca and at a certain point went into exile and formed what in modern language might be called a "government in exile," with which finally he was able to return in triumph to his birthplace and establish the Islamic state in Mecca...The Prophet as rebel has provided a sort of paradigm of revolution—opposition and rejection, withdrawal and departure, exile and return. Time and time again movements of opposition in Islamic history tried to repeat this pattern.

The International Crisis Group's (ICG) report makes the point: "...the conception of 'political Islam' inherent in this dichotomy is unhistorical as well as self-serving. The term 'political Islam' is an American coinage which came into circulation in the wake of the Iranian revolution. It implied or presupposed that an 'apolitical Islam' had been the norm until Khomeini turned things upside down. In fact, Islam had been a highly politicised religion for generations before 1979. It only appeared to have become apolitical in the historically specific and shortlived heyday of secular Arab nationalism between 1945 and 1970."

Influence of Islamism

Few observers contest the influence of Islamism. Following the collapse of the Soviet Union, political movements based on the liberal ideology of free expression and democratic rule have led the opposition in other parts of the world such as Latin America, Eastern Europe and many parts of Asia; however "the simple fact is that political Islam currently reigns as the most powerful ideological force across the Muslim world today".

Even those who see Islamism as fraught with contradictions make remarks like "the socioeconomic realities that sustained the Islamist wave are still here and are not going to change: poverty, uprootedness, crises in values and identities, the decay of the educational systems, the North-South opposition, and the problem of immigrant integration into the host societies".

The strength of Islamism draws from the strength of religiosity in general in the Muslim world. Compared to Western, Latin, or Asian cultures, "[w]hat is striking about the Islamic world is that...

it seems to have been the least penetrated by irreligion". Where other peoples may look to the physical or social sciences for answers in areas which their ancestors regarded as best left to scripture, in the Muslim world, religion has become more encompassing, not less, as "in the last few decades, it has been the fundamentalists who have increasingly represented the cutting edge of the culture".

In Egypt and the rest of the Muslim world "the word secular, a label proudly worn 30 years ago, is shunned" and "used to besmirch" political foes. The small secular opposition parties "cannot compare" with Islamists in terms of "doggedness, courage," "risk-taking" or "organizational skills".

In the Middle East and Pakistan, religious discourse dominates societies, the airwaves, and thinking about the world. Radical mosques have proliferated throughout Egypt. Bookstores are dominated by works with religious themes... The demand for sharia, the belief that their governments are unfaithful to Islam and that Islam is the answer to all problems, and the certainty that the West has declared war on Islam; these are the themes that dominate public discussion. Islamists may not control parliaments or government palaces, but they have occupied the popular imagination.

Moderate Islamism has proven successful locally. In Morocco, the Islamist Justice and Development Party (PJD) supported King Muhammad VI's "Mudawana," a startlingly progressive family law which grants women the right to a divorce, raises the minimum age for marriage to 18, and, in the event of separation, stipulates equal distribution of property. Muslim Brothers in Jordan condemned the Iraq War, while their comrades in Iraq sat in the Iraqi government.

As a result of a flexible pragmatism, Islamists are rising to become the only serious opposition. In Egypt, with the Muslim Brotherhood officially banned, it puts forward only independent candidates during election. Pundits have estimated it would receive at least thirty percent of the votes in free elections, and even more with a lower turnout at the polls, because of the ability to mobilize adherents at any time.

Socialists, liberals, and nationalists have long been marginalized in Islamic countries with apparent dictatorship. The fact that many regimes use a threatening theocracy as a pretext to deal with the secular opposition at the same time usually only plays into the hands of Islamists.

As countries like Egypt and Tunisia have demonstrated, the price of suppressing Islamism in the name of freedom is the undermining of democracy. Today Islamists are among the most passionate advocates of freedom of speech, fair elections, and pluralism - genuinely Western values posing a dilemma for the west, much as the Palestinian legislative elections showed.

Sources of Strength

Amongst the various reasons for the global strength of Islamism are:

ALIENATION FROM THE WEST

Muslim alienation from Europe and its ways, including its political ways.

- The memory in Muslim societies of the many centuries of "cultural and institutional success" of Islamic civilization that have created an "intense resistance to an alternative `civilizational order`", such as Western civilization, Outside Islamdom, Christian missionaries from Europe usually succeeded in making converts. Whether for spiritual reasons or for material ones, substantial numbers of American Indians, Africans, Hindus, Buddhists, and Confucians accepted the Gospels. But Muslims did not."
- The proximity of the core of the Muslim world to Europe and Christendom where it first conquered and then was conquered. Iberia in the seventh century, the Crusades which began in the eleventh century, then for centuries the Ottoman Empire, were all fields of war between Europe and Islam.

The Islamic world was aware of European fear and hatred:

For almost a thousand years, from the first Moorish landing in Spain to the second Turkish siege of Vienna, Europe was under constant threat from Islam. In the early centuries it was a double threat - not only of invasion and conquest, but also of conversion and assimilation. All but the easternmost provinces of the Islamic realm had been taken from Christian rulers, and the vast majority of the first Muslims west of Iran and Arabia were converts from Christianity... Their loss was sorely felt and it heightened the fear that a similar fate was in store for Europe. And also felt its own anger and resentment at the much more recent technological superiority of westerners who, are the perpetual teachers; we, the perpetual students. Generation after generation, this asymmetry has generated an inferiority complex, forever exacerbated by the fact that their innovations progress at a faster pace than we can absorb them ... The best tool to reverse the inferiority complex to a superiority complex... Islam would give the whole culture a sense of dignity. For Islamists, the primary threat of the West is cultural rather than political or economic. Cultural dependency robs one of faith and identity and thus destroys Islam and the Islamic community (*ummah*) far more effectively than political rule.

- The end of the Cold War and Soviet occupation of Afghanistan has eliminated the common atheist Communist enemy uniting some religious Muslims and the capitalist west.

Resurgence of Islam

- The resurgence of Islamic devotion and the attraction to things Islamic can be traced to several events. A tenet of the Quran is that Islam will deliver victory and success. For example 23:1: "Successful indeed are the believers"; Sura 9:14 "Fight them and God will punish them at your hands... God will make you victorious over them"; 22:40: "God will certainly aid those who aid His (cause): for verily God is Full of Strength, Exalted in Might."

Yet, by the end of World War I, there was scarcely such a thing left as a Muslim state not dominated by the Christian West. How could this happen? Only two answers were possible. Either the claims of Islam were false and the Christian or post-Christian West had finally come up with another system that was superior, or Islam had failed through not being true to itself. Obviously, a redoubling of faith and devotion by Muslims was called for to reverse this tide.

- The connection between the lack of an Islamic spirit and the lack of victory was underscored by the disastrous defeat of Arab nationalist-led armies fighting under the slogan "Land, Sea and Air" in the 1967 Six Day War, compared to the near-victory of the Yom Kippur War six years later. In that war the military's slogan was "God is Great".

- Along with the Yom Kippur War came the Arab oil embargo where the (Muslim) Gulf oil-producing states' dramatic decision to cut back on production and quadruple the price of oil, made the terms oil, Arabs and Islam synonymous - with power - in the world, and especially in the Muslim world's public imagination. Many Muslims believe as Saudi Prince Saud al Faisal did that the hundreds of billions of dollars in wealth obtained from the Persian Gulf's huge oil deposits were nothing less than a gift from God to the Islamic faithful.
- As the Islamic revival gained momentum, governments such as Egypt's, which had previously repressed (and was still continuing to repress) Islamists, joined the bandwagon. They banned alcohol and flooded the airwaves with religious programming, giving the movement even more exposure.

SAUDI ARABIAN FUNDING

Starting in the mid-1970s the Islamic resurgence was funded by an abundance of money from Saudi Arabian oil exports. The 10s of billions of dollars in "petro-Islam" largess obtained from the recently heightened price of oil funded an estimated "90% of the expenses of the entire faith."

Throughout the Muslim world, religious institutions for people both young and old, from children's maddrassas to high-level scholarships received Saudi funding, "books, scholarships, fellowships, and mosques" (for example, "more than 1500 mosques were built and paid for with money obtained from public Saudi funds over the last 50 years"), along with training in the Kingdom for the preachers and teachers who went on to teach and work at these universities, schools, mosques, etc.

The funding was also used to reward journalists and academics who followed the Saudis' strict interpretation of Islam; and satellite campuses were built around Egypt for Al Azhar, the world's oldest and most influential Islamic university. The interpretation of Islam promoted by this funding was the strict, conservative Saudi-based Wahhabism or Salafism. Some who claim that this movement taught that Muslims should reject absolutely any non-

Muslim ideas and practices, including political ones, offer no evidence to support this view.

In its harshest form it preached that Muslims should not only "always oppose" infidels "in every way," but "hate them for their religion... for Allah's sake," that democracy "is responsible for all the horrible wars of the 20th century," that Shia and other non-Wahhabi Muslims were infidels, etc. While this effort has by no means converted all, or even most, Muslims to the Wahhabist interpretation of Islam, it has done much to overwhelm more moderate local interpretations, and has set the Saudi-interpretation of Islam as the "gold standard" of religion in Muslims' minds.

Grand Mosque Seizure

The strength of the Islamist movement was manifest in an event which might have seemed sure to turn Muslim public opinion against fundamentalism, but did just the opposite. In 1979 the Grand Mosque in Mecca Saudi Arabia was seized by an armed fundamentalist group and held for over a week. Scores were killed, including many pilgrim bystanders in a gross violation of one of the most holy sites in Islam (and one where arms and violence are strictly forbidden). Instead of prompting a backlash against the movement from which the attackers originated, however, Saudi Arabia, already very conservative, responded by shoring up its fundamentalist credentials with even more Islamic restrictions. Crackdowns followed on everything from shopkeepers who did not close for salah and newspapers that showed photos of women, to the selling of dolls, teddy bears (images of animate objects are considered haraam), and dog food (dogs are considered unclean).

In other Muslim countries, blame for and wrath against the seizure was directed not against fundamentalists, but against Islamic fundamentalism's foremost geopolitical enemy – the United States. Ayatollah Khomeini sparked attacks on American embassies when he announced:

It is not beyond guessing that this is the work of criminal American imperialism and international Zionism despite the fact that the object of the fundamentalists' revolt was the Kingdom of Saudi Arabia, America's major ally in the region. Anti-American demonstrations followed in the Philippines, Turkey, Bangladesh, India, the UAE, Pakistan, and Kuwait. The US Embassy in Libya was burned by protestors chanting pro-Khomeini slogans and the embassy in Islamabad, Pakistan was burned to the ground.

Dissatisfaction with the Status Quo

- The original heart of the Muslim world - the Arab world - has been afflicted with economic stagnation. For example it has been estimated that the exports of Finland, a European country of five million, exceeded those of the entire 260 million-strong Arab world, excluding oil revenue. This economic stagnation is argued to have commenced with the demise of the Ottoman Caliphate in 1924, with trade networks being disrupted and societys torn apart with the creation of new nation states-prior to this, the Middle East had a diverse and growing economy and more general prosperity.
- Strong population growth combined with economic stagnation has created urban conglomerations in Cairo, Istanbul, Tehran, Karachi, Dacca, and Jakarta each with well over 12 million citizens, millions of them young and unemployed or underemployed. Such a demographic, alienated from the westernized ways of the urban elite, but uprooted from the comforts and more passive traditions of the villages they came from, is understandably favorably disposed to an Islamic system promising a better world - an ideology providing an "emotionally familiar basis for group identity, solidarity, and exclusion; an acceptable basis for legitimacy and authority; an immediately intelligible formulation of principles for both a critique of the present and a program for the future."

Shelter of the Mosque

While dictatorial regimes can preempt opposition nationalist or socialist campaigns by closing down their networks and headquarters, the center for Islamist political organizing is the mosque. It is exempt from government crackdowns in the Muslim world (and often in the non-Muslim world) by virtue of its sacredness. "It is in the mosque where [Islamists] canvas neighborhoods in the course of providing social services, spread their political messages and campaign for votes where permitted to participate."

Charitable Work

Islamist movements such as the Muslim Brotherhood, "are well known for providing shelters, educational assistance, free or low cost medical clinics, housing assistance to students from out of town, student advisory groups, facilitation of inexpensive mass marriage ceremonies to avoid prohibitively costly dowry demands, legal assistance, sports facilities, and women's groups." All this compares very favorably against incompetent, inefficient, or neglectful governments whose commitment to social justice is limited to rhetoric.

Power of Identity Politics

Islamism can also be described as part of the religiously-oriented nationalism that emerged in the Third World in the 1970s: resurgent Hinduism in India, ultra-Orthodox Judaism in Israel, militant Buddhism in Sri Lanka, resurgent Sikh nationalism in the Punjab, 'Liberation Theology' of Catholicism in Latin America, and of course, Islamism in the Muslim world." (This is distinguished from ethnic or linguistic-based nationalism which Islamism opposes.) These all challenged Westernized ruling elites on behalf of 'authenticity' and tradition.

SPECIFIC EXAMPLES

Earliest History

Some Islamic militant or revivalist movements and leaders pre-dating Islamism include:

- Ibn Taymiyyah, a Syrian Islamic jurist during the 13th and 14th centuries who is often quoted by contemporary Islamists. Ibn Taymiyya argued against the shirking of [Sharia] law, and against practices such as the celebration of the Prophet's birthday or the construction of mosques around the tombs of Sufi sheikhs, believing that these were unacceptable borrowings from Christianity: Many Muslims 'do not even know of the Christian origins of these practices. Accursed be Christianity and its adherents!'
- Shaikh Ahmad Sirhindi (~1564–1624) was part of "a reassertion of orthodoxy within Sufism" and was known to his followers as the `renovator of the second millennium`. It has been said of Sirhindi that he `gave to Indian Islam the rigid and conservative stamp it bears today.`

- Shah Waliullah of India and Muhammad ibn Abd-al-Wahhab of Arabia were contemporaries who met each other while studying in Mecca. Muhammad ibn Abd-al-Wahhab advocated doing away with the later accretions like grave worship and getting back to the letter and the spirit of Islam as preached and practiced by the Prophet Muhammad. He went on to found Wahhabism. Shah Waliullah was a forerunner of reformists like Muhammad Abduh in his belief that there was "a constant need for new ijtihad as the Muslim community progressed and expanded and new generations had to cope with new problems" and in his interest in the social and economic problems of the poor.
- Sayyid Ahmad Barelvi was a disciple and successor of Shah Waliullah's son and emphasized the 'purification' of Islam from un-Islamic beliefs and practices. He anticipated modern Islamists by leading a jihad movement and attempted to create an Islamic state with strict enforcement of Islamic law. While he waged jihad against Sikhs in North-Western India, his followers fought the British after his death and allied itself with the Indian Mutiny.

After the failure of the Indian Mutiny some of Shah Waliullah's followers turned to more peaceful methods of preserving the Islamic heritage and founded the Dar al-Ulum seminary in 1867 in the town of Deoband. From the school developed the Deobandi movement which became the largest philosophical movement of traditional Islamic thought in the subcontinent and led to the establishment of thousands of madrasahs throughout modern-day India, Pakistan and Bangladesh. Today, Deobandism is represented in Pakistan by the Jamiat Ulema-e-Islam organization/ political party and its splinter groups.

The Clash with the West

The end of the 19th century saw the dismemberment of most of the Muslim Ottoman Empire by non-Muslim European colonial powers. The empire spent massive sums on Western civilian and military technology to try to modernize and compete with the encroaching European powers, and in the process went deep into debt to these powers. In this context, the publications of Jamal ad-din al-Afghani (1837–97), Muhammad Abduh (1849–1905) and

Rashid Rida (1865–1935) preached Islamic alternatives to the political, economic, and cultural decline of the empire. Muhammad Abduh and Rashid Rida formed the beginning of the Salafist movement, as well as the Islamic modernist/secularist movement.

Their ideas included the creation of a truly Islamic society under sharia law, and the rejection of taqlid, the blind imitation of earlier authorities, which they believed deviated from the true messages of Islam. Unlike some later Islamists, Salafists strongly emphasized the restoration of the Caliphate.

Sayyid Abul Ala Maududi

Sayyid Abul Ala Maududi was a "Deobandi alumni" and an important early twentieth-century figure in the Islamic revival in India, and then after independence from Britain, in Pakistan. Trained as a lawyer he chose the profession of journalism, and wrote about contemporary issues and most importantly about Islam and Islamic law. In the struggle for the creation of a separate Muslim state in South Asia Maudidi and his party first opposed the establishment of the state of Pakistan but later supported the idea. He was an inspirational figure for modern Islamist groups in South Asia and elsewhere.

Maududi founded the Jamaat-e-Islami party in 1941 and remained its leader until 1972. Although Maududi was educated at Deobandi institution(s) his party is a long-time rival of the Deobandi party/group Jamiat Ulema-e-Islam. Maududi had much more impact through his writing than through his political organizing. His extremely influential book,*Towards Understanding Islam* (*Risalat Diniyat* in Arabic), placed Islam in a modern context and influenced not only conservative ulema but liberal modernizers such as al-Faruqi, whose "Islamization of Knowledge" carried forward some of Maududi's key principles.

Maududi believed that Islam was all emcompassing "Everything in the universe is 'Muslim' for it obeys God by submission to His laws... The man who denies God is called Kafir (concealer) because he conceals by his disbelief what is inherent in his nature and embalmed in his own soul."

Maududi also believed that Muslim society could not be Islamic without Sharia, and Islam required the establishment of an Islamic state. This state should be a "theo-democracy," based on the principles of: *tawhid* (unity of God), *risala* (prophethood) and *khilafa* (caliphate). Because Islam is all-encompassing, Maududi believed that the Islamic state should not be limited to just the "homeland of Islam", it is for all the world: Islam wishes to destroy all States and Governments anywhere on the face of the earth which are opposed to the ideology and programme of Islam regardless of the country or the Nation which rules it. The purpose of Islam is to set up a State on the basis of its own ideology and programme,... the objective of Islamic 'Jihad' is to eliminate the rule of an un-Islamic system"

Although Maududi talked about Islamic revolution, he was both less revolutionary and less politically/economically populist than later Islamists like Qutb.

The Muslim Brotherhood

Roughly contemporaneous with Maududi was the founding of the Muslim Brotherhood in Ismailiyah, Egypt in 1928 by Hassan al Banna. His was arguably the first, largest and most influential modern Islamic political/religious organization. Under the motto "the Qur'an is our constitution," it sought Islamic revival through preaching and also by providing basic community services including schools, mosques, and workshops. Like Maududi, Al Banna believed in the necessity of government rule based on Shariah law implemented gradually and by persuasion, and of eliminating all non-Muslim imperialist influence in the Muslim world. Jihad was declared against European colonial powers.

Some elements of the Brotherhood, though perhaps against orders, did engage in violence against the government, and its founder Al-Banna was assassinated in 1949 in retaliation for the assassination of Egypt's premier Mahmud Fami Naqrashi three months earlier. The Brotherhood has suffered periodic repression in Egypt and has been banned several times, in 1948 and several years later following confrontations with Egyptian president Gamal Abdul Nasser, who jailed thousands of members for several years. In recent years its status has usually been described as "semi-legal." Despite periodic repression, the Brotherhood has become one of the most influential movements in the Islamic world, particularly in the Arab world. Along with being the only opposition group in Egypt able to field candidates during elections, it has fostered several offshoot organizations in many other countries.

Sayyid Qutb

Maududi's political ideas influenced Sayyid Qutb, one of the key philosophers of Islamism, and a leading member of the Muslim Brotherhood movement. Qutb believed things had reached such a state that the Muslim community had literally ceased to exist. It "has been extinct for a few centuries," having reverted to Godless ignorance (Jahiliyya). To eliminate jahiliyya, Qutb argued Sharia, or Islamic law, must be established. Sharia law was not only accessible to humans and essential to the existence of Islam, but also all-encompassing, precluding "evil and corrupt" non-Islamic ideologies like socialism, nationalism, or liberal democracy.

Qutb preached that Muslims must engage in a two-pronged attack of converting individuals while also waging jihad to forcibly eliminate the "structures" of Jahiliyya - not only from the Islamic homeland but from the face of the earth. Qutb was both the most famous member of the brotherhood and enormously influential in the Muslim world at large. Qutb is considered by some to be "the founding father and leading theoretician" of modern jihadis, such as Osama bin Laden. Ironically, the Muslim Brotherhood in Egypt and in Europe has not embraced his vision of armed jihad, something for which they have been denounced by more radical Islamists.

The Six Day War of 1967

The quick and decisive defeat of the Arab troops during the Six-Day War by Israeli troops constituted a pivotal event in the Arab Muslim world. The defeat along with economic stagnation in the defeated countries, was blamed on the Arab nationalism of the ruling regimes. A steep and steady decline in the popularity and credibility of both secular and nationalist politics ensued. Ba'athism, Arab Socialism, and Arab Nationalism suffered, and Islamist movements inspired by Mawlana Maududi, and Sayyid Qutb gained ground.

ISLAMIC REPUBLIC IN IRAN

The first Modern Islamic state (with the possible exception of Zia's Pakistan) was established among the Shia of Iran. In a major shock to the rest of the world, Ayatollah Ruhollah Khomeini led the Iranian Revolution of 1979 to overthrow the oil-rich, well-armed, Westernized and pro-American secular monarchy ruled by Shah Muhammad Reza Pahlavi. Khomeini's beliefs were similar to Sunni Islamic thinkers like Mawdudi and Qutb: He believed that imitation of the early Muslims and the restoration of Sharia law were essential to Islam, that secular, Westernizing Muslims were actually agents of the West serving Western interests, and that the "plundering" of Muslim lands was part of a long-term conspiracy against Islam by the Christian West. But they also differed:

- As a Shia, the early Muslims whom Khomeini looked to were Ali ibn Abî Tâlib and Husayn ibn Ali, not Caliphs Abu Bakr, Omar or Uthman.
- Khomeini talked not about restoring the Caliphate, but about establishing an Islamic state where the leading role was taken by Islamic jurists (*ulama*) as the successors of Shia Imams until the Mahdi returned from occultation. His concept of *velayat-e-faqih* ("guardianship of the [Islamic] jurist"), held that the leading Shia Muslim cleric in society – which Khomeini and his followers believed to be himself – should serve as head of state in order to protect or "guard" Islam and *Sharia* law from "innovation" and "anti-Islamic laws" passed "by sham parliaments."
- The revolution was influenced by Marxism through Islamist thought and also by writings that sought either to counter Marxism (Muhammad Baqir al-Sadr's work) or to integrate socialism and Islamism (Ali Shariati's work). A strong wing of the revolutionary leadership was made up of leftists or "radical populists", such as Ali Akbar Mohtashami-Pur.

While initial enthusiasm for the revolution in the Muslim world was intense, it has waned as "purges, executions, and atrocities tarnished its image". As a model for potential Islamic states, the Islamic Republic has not been notably successful in achieving many of its goals: raising standards of living; ridding Iran of corruption, poverty, political oppression and Westernization, or even protecting Sharia from innovation. Internally, it has been modestly successful in increasing literacy and health care.

It has also maintained its hold on power in Iran in spite of the US economic sanctions, and has created or assisted like-minded

Shia Islamist groups in Iraq (SCIRI) and Lebanon (Hezbollah), (two Muslim countries that also have large Shiite populations). During the 2006 Israel-Lebanon conflict, the Iranian government enjoyed something of a resurgence in popularity amongst the predominantly Sunni "Arab street," due to its support for Hezbollah and to President Mahmoud Ahmadinejad's vehement opposition to the United States and his call for the annihilation of Israel.

Lebanon

The Lebanese Civil War gave radical Shia movements in that country a new power and prominence after 1975. Expatriate Iranian cleric Musa al-Sadr founded the Amal movement well before his native country's own revolution, heading a combination of political party and militia. After his disappearance in 1978 his organization survived, but the opportunity arose for other factions to mobilize potential support from the same social base. The most successful such movement is Hezbollah. Founded in 1985 by Lebanese Shia aided by Iranian Shia Islamists, the movement is dedicated to the expulsion of Western "colonialist entities" from Lebanon and to the destruction of Israel, which it sees as an illegal state that is usurping Islamic territory. Hezbollah was instrumental in driving the Israeli military from Lebanon in 2000, which heightened its popularity in Lebanon even among non-Shia. In 2006, an Israeli attempt to crush Hezbollah by attacking its strongholds in south Lebanon sustained serious casualties and was considered by many observers to be a failure for Israel.

Pakistan's Islamization Campaign

In July 1977 General Zia-ul-Haq overthrew Prime Minister Ali Bhutto's regime in Pakistan. Ali Bhutto, a leftist in political competition with Islamists, had banned alcohol, horse-racing, and nightclubs, and announced that the "sharia would be fully applied" within six months, shortly before he was overthrown. Ul-Haq was much more committed to Islamism, and "Islamization" or implementation of Islamic law (AKA sharia), became a cornerstone of his eleven-year military dictatorship and Islamism became his "official state ideology". An admirer of Mawdudi, Mawdudi's party Jamaat-e-Islami became the "regime's ideological arm", and its members prospered under ul-Haq.

In Pakistan this Islamization from above was "probably" more complete "than under any other regime except those in Iran and

Sudan," but Ul-Haq was also criticized by some Islamists for imposing "symbols" rather than substance, and using Islamization to legitimize his means of seizing power. The program was a dramatic reversal of the traditional secularism of Pakistan's founding Muslim League and its leader Mohammad Ali Jinnah, but unlike neighboring Iran, ul-Haq's policies were intended to "avoid revolutionary excess", and not to strain relations with his American and Persian Gulf state allies. Ul-Haq was killed in 1988 but Islamization is still proceeding in Pakistan.

Afghanistan: Jihad against the Soviets

In 1979 the Soviet Union deployed its 40th Army into Afghanistan, attempting to suppress an Islamic rebellion against an allied Marxist regime in the Afghan Civil War. The conflict, pitting indigenous impoverished Muslims (mujahideen) against an atheist superpower, galvanized thousands of Muslims around the world to send aid and sometimes to go themselves to fight jihad. Leading this pan-Islamic effort was Palestinian sheikh Abdullah Yusuf Azzam. While the military effectiveness of these "Afghan Arabs" was marginal, Azzam's group is said to have organized paramilitary training for more than 20,000 Muslim recruits, from about 20 countries around the world. When the Soviet Union abandoned the Marxist Najibullah regime and withdrew from Afghanistan in 1989 (the regime finally fell in 1992), the victory was seen by many Muslims as the triumph of Islamic faith over superior military power and technology that could be duplicated elsewhere. The jihadists gained legitimacy and prestige from their triumph both within the militant community and among ordinary Muslims, as well as the confidence to carry their jihad to other countries where they believed Muslims required assistance.

The "veterans of the guerrilla campaign" returning home to Algeria, Egypt and other countries "with their experience, ideology, and weapons," were often eager to continue armed jihad. The collapse of the Soviet Union itself in 1991, was seen by many Islamists, including Bin Laden, as the defeat of a superpower at the hands of Islam, the $6 billion in aid given by the US to the mujahideen having nothing to do with the victory. As bin Laden opined: "[T]he US has no mentionable role" in "the collapse of the Soviet Union... rather the credit goes to God and the mujahidin" of Afghanistan.

Persian Gulf War

Another factor in the early 1990s that worked to radicalize the Islamist movement was the Gulf War, which brought several hundred thousand US and allied non-Muslim military personnel to Saudi Arabian soil to put an end to Saddam Hussein's occupation of Kuwait. Prior to 1990 Saudi Arabia played an important role in restraining the many Islamist groups that received its aid. But Saddam embraced Islamic rhetoric and attacked Saudi Arabia, his enemy in the war, for violating Islamic unity and its role as custodian of the two holy cities by allowing non-Muslims on its soil (traditional Muslim belief holds that non-Muslims must not be allowed on the Arabian peninsula), and he also accused the Kingdom of being a puppet of the west. These attacks resonated with conservative Muslims and the problem did not go away with Saddam's defeat either, since American troops remained stationed in the kingdom, and a defacto cooperation with the Palestinian-Israeli peace process developed. Saudi Arabia attempted to compensate for its loss of prestige among these groups by repressing those domestic Islamists who attacked it (bin Laden being a prime example), and increasing aid to Islamic groups (Islamist madrassas around the world and even aiding some violent Islamist groups) that did not, but its pre-war influence on behalf of moderation was greatly reduced. One result of this was a campaign of attacks on government officials and tourists in Egypt, a bloody civil war in Algeria and Osama bin Laden's terror attacks climaxing in 9/11 attack.

Jihad Movements of Egypt

While Qutb's ideas became increasingly radical during his imprisonment prior to his execution in 1966, the leadership of the Brotherhood, led by Hasan al-Hudaybi, remained moderate and interested in political negotiation and activism. Fringe or splinter movements inspired by the final writings of Qutb in the mid-1960s (particularly the manifesto "Milestones," aka Ma'alim fi-l-Tariq) did, however, develop and they pursued a more radical direction. By the 1970s, the Brotherhood had renounced violence as a means of achieving its goals.

The path of violence and military struggle was then taken up by the Egyptian Islamic Jihad organization responsible for the assassination of Anwar Sadat in 1981. Unlike earlier anti-colonial movements, Islamic Jihad directed its attacks against what it believed were "apostate" leaders of Muslim states-leaders who held secular leanings or who had introduced or promoted Western/ foreign ideas and practices into Islamic societies. Its views were outlined in a pamphlet written by Muhammad Abd al-Salaam Farag, in which he states:...there is no doubt that the first battlefield for jihad is the extermination of these infidel leaders and to replace them by a complete Islamic Order... Another of the Egyptian groups which employed violence in their struggle for Islamic order was al-Gama'a al-Islamiyya (Islamic Group).

Victims of their campaign against the Egyptian state in the 1990s included the head of the counter-terrorism police (Major General Raouf Khayrat), a parliamentary speaker (Rifaat al-Mahgoub), dozens of European tourists and Egyptian bystanders, and over 100 Egyptian police. Ultimately the campaign to overthrow the government was unsuccessful, and the major jihadi group, Jamaa Islamiya (or al-Gama'a al-Islamiyya), renounced violence in 2003. Other lesser known groups include the Islamic Liberation Party, Al-Najun min al-nar and Al-Takfir wa al-Hijra and these groups have variously been involved in activities such as attempted assassinations of political figures, arson of video shops and attempted takeovers of government buildings.

Sudan

For many years Sudan had an Islamist regime under the leadership of Hassan al-Turabi. His National Islamic Front first gained influence when strongman General Gaafar al-Nimeiry invited members to serve in his government in 1979. Turabi built a powerful economic base with money from foreign Islamist banking systems, especially those linked with Saudi Arabia. He also recruited and built a cadre of influential loyalists by placing sympathetic students in the university and military academy while serving as minister of education.

After al-Nimeiry was overthrown in 1985 the party did poorly in national elections but in 1989 it was able to overthrow the elected post-al-Nimeiry government with the help of the military. Turabi was noted for his commitment to the democratic process and a liberal government before coming to power, but strict application of sharia law, and an intensification of the long-running war in southern Sudan, human rights abuses, once in power. The

NIF regime also harbored Osama bin Laden for a time (before 9/11), and worked to unify Islamist opposition to the American attack on Iraq in the 1991 Gulf War.

After Sudanese intelligence services were implicated in an assassination attempt on the President of Egypt, UN economic sanctions were imposed on Sudan, a very poor country, and Turabi fell from favor. He was imprisoned for a time in 2004-5. Some of the NIF policies, such as the war with the non-Muslim south, have been reversed, though the National Islamic Front (now named the National Congress Party) still holds considerable power in the Sudanese government.

Algeria

An Islamist movement influenced by Salafism and the jihad in Afghanistan, as well as the Muslim Brotherhood, was the FIS or Front Islamique de Salut (the Islamic Salvation Front) in Algeria. Founded as a broad Islamist coalition in 1989 it was led by Abbassi Madani, and a charismatic radical young preacher, Ali Belhadj. Taking advantage of liberalization by the unpopular ruling leftist/nationalist FLN regime, it used its preaching to advocate the establishment of a legal system following Sharia law, education in Arabic rather than French, and gender segregation, with women staying home to alleviate the high rate of unemployment among young Algerian men. The FIS won sweeping victories in local elections and it was going to win national elections in 1991 when voting was canceled by a military coup d'état. As Islamists took up arms to overthrow the regime, the FIS's leaders were arrested and it became overshadowed by Islamist guerilla groups particularly the Islamic Salvation Army, MIA and Armed Islamic Group (or GIA). A bloody and devastating civil war ensued in which between 150,000 and 200,000 people were killed over the next decade. Civilians – including foreigners, University academics, intellectuals, writers, journalists, and medical doctors – were targeted by Islamist extremists. although government forces were also accused of killing civilians and of manipulating the brutal takfiri GIA The civil war was not a victory for Islamism. By 2002 the main guerrilla groups had either been destroyed or had surrendered. The popularity of Islamist parties has declined to the point that "the Islamist candidate, Abdallah Jaballah, came a distant third with 5% of the vote" in the 2004 presidential election.

Afghanistan Taliban

In Afghanistan the mujahideen's victory did not lead to justice and prosperity but to a vicious and destructive civil war between warlords, making Afghanistan one of the poorest countries on earth. In 1996, a new movement known as the Taliban, rose to power, defeated most of the warlords and took over roughly 80% of Afghanistan. The Taliban were spawned by the thousands of madrasahs the Deobandi movement established for impoverished Afghan refugees and supported by governmental and religious groups in neighboring Pakistan.

The Taliban differed from other Islamist movements to the point where they might be more properly described as Islamic fundamentalist or neofundamentalist, interested in spreading "an idealized and systematized version of village customs to an entire country." Despite Afghanistan's great poverty, they had little interest in social, economic and technological development - at one time explaining that "we Muslims believe God the Almighty will feed everybody one way or another." Their ideology was also described as being influenced by Pashtunwali tribal law, Wahhabism, and the jihadism pan-Islamism of their guest Osama bin Laden.

The Taliban considered "politics" to be against Sharia and thus did not hold elections. They were led by Mullah Mohammed Omar who was given the title "Amir al-Mu'minin" or Commander of the Faithful, and a pledge of loyalty by several hundred Taliban-selected Pashtun clergy in April 1996. Like most Islamists, the Taliban enforced strict prohibitions on women, but these were so severe - for example effectively forbidding most employment and schooling - that they created an international outcry.

The Taliban were also famous for other activities they banned - music, TV, videos, photographs, pigeons, kite-flying, beard-trimming, etc. - and for the energy and the resources which they used to enforce the bans, including hundreds perhaps thousands of religious police officers armed with "whips, long sticks and Kalashnikovs." The Taliban also opposed Shi'ism and have been accused by human rights groups of indiscriminately killing thousands of Shia. They were also overwhelmingly Pashtun and were accused of not sharing power with the approximately 60% of Afghanis who belonged to other ethnic groups.

The Taliban's hosting of Osama bin Laden, despite the attacks he organized against the United States, led to an American-organized attack against which drove them from power following the 9/11 attacks. Taliban are still very much alive and fighting a vigorous insurgency from bases in the frontier regions of Pakistan with suicide bombings and armed attacks being launched against NATO, Afghan government targets and civilians.

Attacks on Civilians

Some Islamist groups call for and/or engage in attacks on not only police/military enemies, but non-combatants as well. These groups include several mentioned above: al-Gama'a al-Islamiyya (Islamic Group) of Egypt, Islamist groups in Algeria, Hamas and Islamic Jihad in Gaza and the West Bank, and perhaps most famously Osama bin Laden and his al-Qaeda group.

Both Muslims and non-Muslims have been among the targets and victims. Some of the groups have proudly proclaimed the attacks, others have been silent or denied involvement.

Justification for attacks on Muslims often comes as takfir, an implicit death threat since under traditional Sharia law the punishment for apostasy in Islam is death. Justification for attacks on non-Muslims is often the allegation that the targets had "waged war against God," are occupiers of Musilm land, or tourists unwelcome on Muslim land. Suicide or "martyrdom operations" are a lethal technique among radical Islamists, sometimes motivated by the much disputed explanation that "God will give" those who kill themselves in the path of jihad 70 or 72 female "virgins" and "everlasting happiness."

Religious or sectarian attacks in situations where Islamists are active have been particularly serious following 2004. In Iraq, 8,262 people were killed in terror attacks in 2005 and 13,340 in 2006, although not all of theses casualties came from attacks by Islamist groups. Islamist or fundamentalist attacks are also on the increase in Afghanistan and in Pakistan, where hundreds have been killed in 2006 and 2007, although in both countries not all of the attacks have been on civilians.

Hizb ut-Tahrir

An influential international Islamist movement is the 'party' Hizb ut-Tahrir, founded in 1953 by a Sufi and Islamic Qadi *(judge)*

Taqiuddin al-Nabhani. HT is unique from most other Islamist movements in that the party focuses not on local issues or on providing social services, but on unifying the Muslim world under its vision of a new Islamic caliphate spanning from North Africa and the Middle East to much of central and South Asia. To this end it has drawn up and published a constitution for its proposed caliphate state. The constitution's 187 articles specify specific policies such as sharia law, a "unitary ruling system" headed by a caliph elected by Muslims, an economy based on the gold standard, public ownership of utilities, public transport, and energy resources, and Arabic as the "sole language of the State."

In its focus on the Caliphate, HT takes a different view of Muslim history than some other Islamists such as Muhammad Qutb. HT sees Islam's pivotal turning point as occurring not with the death of Ali, or one of the other four rightly guided Caliphs in the 7th century, but with the 1918 or 1922 abolition of the Ottoman Caliphate. This is believed to have ended the true Islamic system, something for which it blames "the disbelieving (Kafir) colonial powers" working through Turkish modernist Mustafa Kamal.

HT does not engage in armed jihad or vote-getting, but works to take power through "ideological struggle" to change Muslim public opinion, and in particular through elites who will "facilitate" a "change of the government," i.e. launch a bloodless coup. It allegedly attempted and failed such coups in 1968 and 1969 in Jordan, and in 1974 in Egypt, and is now banned in both countries.

The party is sometimes described as "Leninist" and "rigidly controlled by its central leadership," with its estimated one million members required to spend "at least two years studying party literature under the guidance of mentors *(Murshid)*" before taking "the party oath." HT is particularly active in the ex-soviet republics of Central Asia and in Europe. In the UK its rallies have drawn thousands of Muslims, and the party is said to have outpaced the Muslim Brotherhood in both membership and radicalism.

Turkey

In Turkey, something of an anomaly among Islamist movements and parties is the Justice and Development Party (Turkey) (*Adalet ve Kalkinma Partisi*) (AKP) of Turkey headed by Recep Tayyip Erdogan. The successor to earlier Islamist parties of Necmettin Erbakan – National Order Party (*Milli Nizam Partisi*), National Salvation Party (*Milli Selamet Partisi*), Welfare Party (*Refah Partisi*) – AKP was the first Islamist party in history to win a free national election and form a government. In July 2007 it won 46% of the vote, (a landslide in Turkey's multiparty political landscape).

Since its victory in 2002 elections, the tensions between the AKP and those claiming secularism-the bureacracy (particularly the judiciary), the Armed Forces, and an important fraction of society, including the heterodox Alevi sect-have been on the boil. In 2008, Turkey's chief prosecutor filed a case asking that the AKP be banned for "anti-secular activities". The Constitutional Court accepted the case but decided against a ban. Instead the court ruled that the party's public financing be cut in half, as well as issue a "serious warning" that it was steering the country in too Islamic a direction. Despite the aggressive opposition in Turkey, the AKP has been praised in the west for policies supporting "integration into the global economy, and membership in the EU," rather than aligning with Islamic countries. On the other hand, the AKP has also been criticised in the west for its alleged hidden agenda of transforming Turkey into an Islamic state and its procrastination in improving human rights, democracy, and freedom of speech in Turkey.

Criticism

Islamism has been criticised for: repression of free expression, rigidity, hypocrisy, lack of true understanding of Islam, misinterpreting the Quran and Sunna, and for innovations to Islam (bid'ah), notwithstanding Islamists' proclaimed opposition to any such innovation. Despite this, Islamism remains very popular among many Muslims.

Action Against

Several governments, including the U.S. government have engaged in efforts to counter Islamism, or violent Islamism, since 2001. These efforts were centered in the U.S. around public diplomacy programs conducted by the State Department. There have been calls to create an independent agency in the U.S. with a specific mission of undermining Islamism and jihadism. Christian Whiton, an official in the George W. Bush administration, called for a new agency focused on the nonviolent practice of "political warfare" aimed at undermining the ideology. U.S. Defense

Secretary Robert Gates called for establishing something similar to the defunct U.S. Information Agency, which was changed with undermining the communist ideology during the Cold War.

Post 9/11 Issues

It is important to distinguish between Islamists and Islamist terrorists: "While ignoring the overwhelming majority of Islamists who have nothing to do with terror and making them virtually irrelevant and stigmatized in Western political discourse... To ignore the complexity of political Islam and tar all Islamists with the same brush of terrorism guarantees Bin Laden's success." International Crisis Group warns that the tendency of "policy-makers... to lump all forms of Islamism together, brand them as radical and treat them as hostile... is fundamentally misconceived." Furthermore, it states:

"...the issues and grievances which have been grist to the mill of Sunni jihadism across the Muslim world have not been resolved or even appreciably attenuated since 2001, but, on the contrary, aggravated and intensified. The failure to address the Palestinian question and, above all, the decision to make war on Iraq and the even more extraordinary mishandling of the post-war situation there have unquestionably motivated and encouraged jihadi activism across the Muslim world. Unsophisticated Western understanding and rhetoric that tends to discredit all forms of political Islamism, coupled with the lumping together of the internal, irredentist and global jihadis..."

OTHER COUNTRIES

In the 1990s, Islamist conflicts erupted around the world. In 1995 a series of terrorist attacks were launched against France. Malaysia is described as a "soft" Islamist state, whereas Iran is considered a "hard" Islamist state. A considerable effort has been made to fight against Western targets, especially the United States. The United States, in particular, was made a target of Islamist fire because of its support for Israel, its presence on Saudi Arabian soil, what Islamists regard as its aggression against Muslims in Iraq and Afghanistan, and because of its support of the regimes that Islamists oppose.

In addition, some Islamists have concentrated their activity against Israel, and nearly all Islamists view Israel with hostility.

Osama bin Laden, at least, believes that this is of necessity due to the historical conflict between Muslims and Jews, and believes that there is a Jewish/American alliance against Islam. On the other extreme (i.e. the moderate end) of the Islamist movement, the Muhammadiyah movement in Indonesia has stated that it is concerned with "far more important issues than the application of Sharia," namely strengthening the education, health, economy and society of that Muslim nation, a task they maintain represents "the greater Shari'a" or path of God.

Other moderate Islamist groups include the Islamist Justice and Development Party (PJD) in Morocco which supports King Muhammad VI's "Mudawana," a progressive family law which grants women the right to a divorce, raises the minimum age for marriage to 18, and, in the event of separation, stipulates equal distribution of property. Muslim Brothers in Jordan condemned the Iraq War, while their comrades in Iraq sat in the Iraqi government. There is some debate as to how influential Islamist movements remain. Some scholars assert that Islamism is a fringe movement which is dying, following the clear failures of Islamist regimes like the regime in Sudan, the Habitué's Saudi regime and the Deobandi Taliban to improve the lot of Muslims.

However, others (such as Ahmed Rashid and Graham E. Fuller) feel that the Islamists still command considerable support and cite the fact that Islamists in Pakistan and Egypt regularly win 10 to 30 percent in electoral polls, despite the fact that they are prosecuted and that many believe the polls are rigged against them.

10

Present Status of Islam

The last two hundred years have seen enormous challenges to all religions. Intellectually, Darwin, Freud, Marx, Nietzsche and the development of modern scientific ways of thinking have transformed the way we see the world and man and woman's place in it. Critical study of religious texts has implied that these are human creations rather than divine revelations. Politically, two of the major ideologies which dominated the twentieth century, Fascism and Communism, were anti-religious. Technologically, patterns of life have changed dramatically in the more affluent parts of the world. Religion, as we have suggested, has to some extent, especially in the West, been pushed to the margins of life, although the secular society of which many people spoke so confidently in the sixties and seventies is now more questionable. Secularism is a word used to cover several phenomena. It implies the autonomy of daily life. It excludes the interference of religious authorities in government and in political and economic life.

Thus in the USA, there is a clear separation of church and state. Likewise, India, constitutionally – if not in practice – is a secular state in the sense that no religion is meant to be given favored treatment. A secular society may also mean one in which individual citizens do not have any moral pattern of behavior imposed upon them by the state. For example in many Western countries homosexual acts, which were until quite recently illegal and punishable by law, are now considered a private matter for consenting individuals. In the same way, in many countries, abortion, with certain restrictions, is no longer illegal. Secularism may also describe a change of mood by which people no longer seek to explain life by reference to religious beliefs. They will look for a natural rather than a divine cause of illness or disaster. Some sociologists of religion suggest that in the West religion should be regarded as a private or even a 'leisure time' activity. This, of course, is not a view that a committed Christian would accept and is even more alien to the devout Muslim, who, if he or she has been brought up to think of Britain or America as 'Christian' countries, is puzzled by what seems to him or her their moral decadence, especially in terms of permissive sexuality and drug-taking.

In addition to these challenges, which all religions have had to face, much of the Islamic world has had to cope with Western imperialism and the political, economic and military dominance of the super-powers, and now particularly of the USA. Many of the challenges to religion mentioned above were cradled in Western society, so they can seem to Muslims a Western threat. It is hard to generalize about two centuries and large areas of the world. Individual Muslim countries are each different. The responses of religious people to change can, however, usually be classified in terms of those who seek to maintain the tradition, those who claim to be returning to the pure faith, reformers who allow for alterations to practice, but no substantive change and those, often labeled modernists by their critics, who draw on outside sources in their reinterpretation of a faith. Different writers use rather varying labels for these four categories.

The Cambridge scholar Akbar Ahmed includes amongst those who maintain the tradition, scholars such as Ali Shariati and Ali Ashraf, as well as Ismail Faruqi and Hossein Nasr, both of whom I had the privilege of getting to know through the World Congress of Faiths. These writers concentrate on the larger message of Islam and avoid narrower sectarian quarrels. Often, their scholarship has been inaccessible to and rather remote from ordinary Muslims. The term modernist is used by Akbar Ahmed of creative thinkers in the nineteenth and twentieth centuries, such as Sir Sayyed Ahmed Khan, who established the Muhammadan Anglo-Oriental College at Aligarh, which was consciously modeled on Oxbridge, and which I once briefly visited. Another modernist, who I take him as an example, was Sir Muhammad Iqbal (1876-1938). One of the best known Muslim exponents of Renewal, he wished to create a synthesis of Muslim and Western thought. Iqbal tried to reinterpret Islam in the light of the Sufi heritage and Western philosophy, especially the creative evolution of Bergson.

The key feature of Iqbal's thought was the notion of reality as pure duration, with God and human beings interrelating dynamically in the universe. He believed that the marriage of intellect and love could transform human beings into a higher level of being. Iqbal's constant theme was 'Arise, and create a new world'. His poetry in Urdu and Persian inspired Indian Muslims in the first half of the twentieth century to shape and improve their condition of life and was a factor behind the creation of Pakistan. In his *Reconstruction of Religious Thought in Islam* (1928), Iqbal gave a more systematic elaboration of his Islamic vision, arguing for a return to independent judgement, *ijtihad,* and the establishment of a legislative institution for the reformation of Islamic law.

One Indian Muslim professor of philosophy drawing attention to the word 'reconstruction' rather than 're-interpretation' said that Iqbal 'while he seems to be elaborating the meaning of a verse of the Qur'an, is really using it as a peg to hang his own ideas on.' Wilfred Cantwell Smith, who taught in Pakistan and later became Professor of the History of Comparative Religion at Harvard, wrote, in a book published in the middle of the last century, 'Today if Islam would function in this radically new world in which we find ourselves, it must be refashioned to give dynamic initiative and vision to man facing a life of opportunity and to give him creative love towards the community of his fellow men. Such a refashioning was a service rendered to Islam chiefly by the outstanding Muslim poet and thinker of the century, Muhammad Iqbal.'

Cantwell Smith's comment, which he might well have revised later in his life, is interesting for the assumption, common at the time that he wrote it, that liberal re-interpretation must be the way forward for religion in the modern world. As a long standing member of the Modern Church People's Union, I sympathize with this, but it is not the dominant mood in Islam today, although Iqbal's influence is not forgotten. The term modernist is also used by Akbar Ahmed of some contemporary writers, but in a different sense to that in which we have been using it. The common feature, he says, 'is the general belief that religion as a force or guide is no longer valid in our age.' He mentions writers such as Tariq Ali, Salman Rushdie, who have been influenced by Marxism and, on the right, Shahid Burki and Rana Kabbani, although the latter has moved closer to the traditionalists. Writers on both flanks, he says, echo ideas and concepts from outside the Islamic tradition. Far more common than modernists are those who are concerned to reform abuse or corruption, but who in no way wish to question the message of Islam. Reform, of course, can be quite superficial but it can be far reaching. I take too examples: Maulana Wahiduddin Kahn, who is a member of the Indian Muslim minority, and Farid Esack, who is a from South Africa, where again Muslims are in a minority. Maulana Wahiduddin Kahn 'stands out as a voice in the wilderness', said Dr Yoginder Sikand, in a paper I heard recently at a conference at the Punjabi University in Patiala. Kahn called for an understanding of Islam that is both rooted in the original sources of Islam, while at the same time willing wholeheartedly, although critically, to engage with modernity, responding positively to serious concerns such as questions of peace, inter-religious dialogue and political activism.'

Maulana Wahiduddin Kahn was born in what is now Uttar Pradesh in 1925. At first he joined the Jama'at-i-Islami Hind, which was founded by Abul 'Ala Maududi. Kahn was searching for a socially engaged spirituality, but he came to see that the agenda of the Jama'at, which was working for the establishment of an Islamic state in India was impractical. He moved for a time to the Tablighi Jama'at, but by 1975 he had cut his links with it because of its hostility to the creative application of Islamic law to the challenges of changing social conditions. In 1976 Khan set up his own research center in New Delhi. He believed that a new understanding of Islam was necessary to appeal to modern educated Indians. Khan accepts that Muslims in India are and are likely to remain a minority. They need to seek a solution to their problems by internal reform rather than by conflict with the state or the dominant Hindu majority. He takes seriously the issue of pluralism and inter-community relations and stresses the need to build bridges with people of other faiths. He quotes from the Qur'an the saying 'Unto you your religion and unto me mine.' (109, 6). Islam enjoins Muslims to live with others as brothers in spirit. Khan argues that the Muslims of India today find themselves in a position similar to that of the Prophet and his followers in Mecca, when the nascent community was small and relatively powerless. Just as the Prophet at that time concentrated on peaceful preaching so Muslims in India today should do the same. They should also concern themselves with the problems and issues of the whole country instead of just thinking about their own communal interests.

Khan suggests that the traditional distinction between the 'house of Islam' or lands ruled by Muslims, *dar-ul islam,* and lands ruled by non-Muslims, traditionally known as *dar-ul harb* or 'the house of war' needs to be rethought. The term 'house of war' only applied to those lands where Muslims were persecuted for their faith and had to resort to violence in self-defense. There should be a third category, which he calls the 'house of invitation' or *dar-ul da'wah,* to refer to lands under non-Muslim control but where Muslims are welcome and have full civil rights. Here the Muslim responsibility is to address non-Muslims with the message of Islam but not to seek confrontation. A similar view was expressed when a delegation from the World Muslim League visited Oxford in March 2002. In answer to a question Dr Abdullah of the League said that the distinction between the 'house of war' and the 'house of Islam' was a historical concept which does not apply today. He stressed that Muslims in Britain should see themselves as good British citizens.

Maulana Wahiduddin Khan also insists that non-Muslims should not be spoken of a *kafirs.* To do so is 'to violate God's injunctions.' The term *kafir* should only be applied to someone who knowingly rejects or conceals the truth. Khan has not created a 'movement' and he has been attacked for collusion with the 'enemies of Islam.'

Reference has already been made to Dr Farid Esack's book *On being A Muslim.* This and another book, *Qur'an, Liberation and Pluralism.*, are both written in the context of the struggle in South Africa against apartheid – a struggle with which many Muslims, including Esack, identified. This struggle led Farid Esack to reflect on key Qur'anic passages used in the context of oppression to rethink the role of Islam in a plural society. He shows how traditional interpretations of the Qur'an were used to legitimize an unjust order, but that these same texts, if interpreted within a contemporary socio-historical context, support active solidarity with people of other religions in the struggle for change. In describing the objectives of his book, Esack puts first the wish 'to show that it is possible to live in faithfulness to both the Qur'an and to one's present context alongside people of other faiths, working with them to establish a more humane society.' Towards the end of the book, he refers to a Call of Islam publication *Women Arise! The Qur'an Liberates You,* which says that 'we must unleash a debate on the question of women so that equality and freedom become achievable.' But the document hastens to add that 'this debate need not depart from the pages of the Qur'an at all for within these pages there is sufficient evidence to suggest that Muslim women can and must play a full role in our society.'

The key difference, which is not always easy to make in practice, between those I label Reformers and those who seek Renewal is that those who are Reformers do not question Islam's authoritative sources, but are willing to debate how these have been interpreted. Those who speak of Renewal seek to marry the teachings of Islam with philosophical ideas drawn from external sources. There are other examples of reformers who could be mentioned, such as Chandra Muzaffar, from Malaysia, who is President of the International Movement for a Just World and whose spiritual commitment has led him to participate actively in politics. Most reformers are also involved in inter-faith activity. Where, the application of faith to the search for peace and social justice is a high priority, it is natural to look for allies among people of other faiths who share this passion.

Others who share this social passion blame the West for many of the ills and are less interested in interfaith dialogue. Akbar Ahmed uses the term radical to group together thinkers, such as Shabbir Akhtar, Parvez Manzoor, Ziauddin Sardar and Kalim Siddiqui, known for his leadership of the British Muslim Parliament, who all reject the possibility of a *modus vivendi* with the West. In this they are similar to those who seek a return to the pure faith, who are sometimes called reactionaries and sometimes labeled radicals, although I am by no means suggesting that they would support violent opposition. Reactionaries are those who recognize the challenges of the modern world to Islam and seek to resist them. They may welcome technological advance and scientific discovery, but reject many of the assumptions of secular society. I think it is necessary to repeat the distinction I made in the chapter on the Qur'an between reactionaries and traditionalists – using the word in a very different sense than when I referred above to Seyyed Hossein Nasr and other scholars. Traditionalists live much as their parents did and continue to practice the religion in which they were brought up without much awareness of the challenges to it posed by modern society. Reactionaries consciously reject and resist those challenges. For a very small minority, that resistance may be expressed by violence.

As an example, I take the Wahhabiya movement, partly because of its influence. Muhammad ibn Abd al-Wahhab (1703-87) initiated an ultra-conservative puritanical movement, which adhered to Hanbalite law in the Arabian peninsula during the eighteenth century. The movement rejected centuries of legal interpretation as well as the mysticism of the Sufis. Al-Wahhab found a champion in the tribal leader Muhammad ibn Sa'ud and the Saudis became the main supporters of the movement. In 1801, the Wahhabis slaughtered two thousand ordinary citizens in the streets of Qarbala, so violence is nothing new to this movement.

Another influential figure was al-Afghani (1838-97), who was born in Iran but who spent his formative years in Afghanistan. He aimed to rally the Muslim world to realize its power as an international community and by raising its political and intellectual standards to combat Western colonialism. Freedom from foreign rule was he hoped to be followed by the establishment of a pan-Islamic state and the union of all Muslims under a caliph. He regarded the Arabic language as of primary importance in promoting Muslim unity. His programme, he believed, would lead to improvements in the living standards of all Muslims. He affirmed the transcendental truth of Islam in his *The Refutation of the Materialists*. Towards the end of his life, he was hunted down by the Iranian authorities, but although three of his colleagues were hanged, he himself died of cancer. In the early part of the twentieth century, the Muslim struggle against the West turned into a mass movement. In 1928 an Egyptian called al-Banna (1906-49) founded the Muslim Brotherhood, al-Ikhwan al-Muslimun, which rapidly gained support across the Middle East. Banna, who like many other radicals was a middle class intellectual, was in sympathy with the ideas of Afghani and deplored the disunity and moral laxity of Egyptian society, which he blamed on British occupation. One day, he wrote, six laborers from a British camp came to see him and said:

'We are weary of this life of humiliation and restriction. Lo, we see that Arabs and the Muslims have no status and no dignity. They are not more than mere hirelings belonging to the foreigners. We possess nothing but this blood... and these souls... and these few coins... We are unable to perceive the road to action as you perceive it, or to know the path to the service of the fatherland, the religion and the nation as you know it. All that we desire now is to present you with all we possess, to be acquitted by God of the responsibility, and for you to be responsible before Him for us and for what we must do.'

So the Muslim Brotherhood was born. By 1949, it had 2,000 branches and some half million members. Banna told his followers in 1943, 'You are not a benevolent society, nor a political party, nor a local organization having limited purposes. Rather, you are a new soul in the heart of the nation to give it life by means of the Qur'an.' Banna's aim was to free Egypt from British control and to establish an Islamic state, eliminating such Western influences as night-clubs, casinos and pornography. After the Second World War, al-Banna took up the cause of the Palestinians, but his activities were restricted by the Egyptian government. At the end of 1948, many members of the Muslim Brotherhood were arrested. Soon afterwards a young member of the movement shot and killed the prime minister of Egypt, Nuqrashi Pasha and seven weeks later Hasan al-Banna was himself assassinated by secret servant agents.

The Brotherhood never fully recovered from the death of its founder, although the writings of Sayyid Qutb, who was executed in 1966, had considerable influence. His widely read *Malim fi al-Tariq* argued that social systems were of two types. Either there was a Nizam Islami – a true Islamic order – or a Nizam Jahli, that is the rule of pre-Islamic ignorance. As Egypt did not belong to the first category, it belonged to the second and therefore it was the duty of true Muslims to wage jihad against ignorant and despotic governments. In passing it is worth emphasizing that radical Muslims are often as critical of many Muslim governments, which they consider in the pay of the West, as they are of Western powers themselves. Members of the Muslim described Egypt's defeat in the Six-Day War 'as a sign of God's punishment for leaving the path of Islam.' They too were responsible for the assassination of President Sadat, whom they accused of treachery against Islam and the Palestinian people by his agreement to the Camp David Accord.

The most spectacular victories for militant Islam have been the Iranian revolution in 1979 and the capture of Kabul by the

Taliban in 1979. The Shah of Iran and his father had tried to westernize their country. Traditional Muslim style of dress were banned and western education promoted. Opponents ran foul of the much feared secret police. When Muslim clergy protested, the Shah dismissed them as 'black reactionaries'. He expelled the most vociferous protester, Ayatollah Khomeini (1902-89), a leader of the Twelve Shi'ite Muslims, who in exile became more dangerous and eventually succeeded in overthrowing the Shah in 1979. As leader of the revolution, he purged Iran of Western influences. His *fatwa* or ban against Salman Rushdie's *The Satanic Verses* was widely accepted in the Muslim world. The Taliban was originally a military group, formed in response to the invasion of Afghanistan by the Soviet Union. As part of the Cold War against the Soviet Union both America and Britain trained Taliban fighters in guerrilla warfare and supplied arms and money. When they gained power, the Taliban showed themselves even more rigorous than Ayatollah Khomeini in imposing a version of Islamic law, which most Muslims regard as crude and distorted.

Recent years have also seen a revival of the original militant movement founded by al-Wahhab with a network of organizations, under various names. These groups have been involved in prolonged struggles in Algeria, where the Islamic party won a general election but were denied power and where there have been atrocities on both sides Militants are said to be responsible for the deaths of seventy tourists at Luxor in 1997 and to be linked with armed groups in Kashmir. The most notorious group is, of course, al-Qaida, led by Osama bin-Laden, which the USA accuses of responsibility for the twin tower tragedy on September 11th, 2001. It must be emphasized that the great majority of Muslims want nothing to do with violence and most have condemned the terrorist attacks on America. Even so, it is important to hear what some of these militants are saying so as to see how the world is seen through the eyes of the most alienated Muslims. Terror draws its sustenance from disaffection which is caused by the hopelessness of those who feel victimized by poverty and injustice.

Ayatollah Khomaini was a long standing critic of the Shah of Persia's regime, but during his exile, he broadened his opposition to attack the institution of monarchy itself and to call not just for adherence to Islamic law, but for the establishment of an Islamic state. In about 1969 he gave a series of lectures to his students, which were published as a book entitled *Velayat-e Faqih.* It is a blueprint for the reorganization of society. It is a handbook for revolution. There are four main themes. First the book condemns the institution of monarchy as alien to Islam, abhorrent to the Prophet and the source of all Iran's misfortunes over 2,500 years. Secondly, it presents the Islamic state, which is based on the Qur'an and modeled after the Islamic community governed by the Prophet in the seventh century, as a practical form of government realizable in the lifetime of the present generation and not as some distant ideal. Thirdly, and this is particular to the Shi'ite tradition, the claim of the clerical class, as heirs of the Prophet, to the leadership of the community is forcefully asserted. Justice and an expertise in Islamic law are essential for those who rule. 'The real governors', he says, 'are the Islamic jurists themselves.' Although leadership is vested collectively in the religious leadership (*ulama*), it can be vested in a single leader. Fourthly, *Velayat-e Faqih* calls on all believers to work actively for the overthrow of the non-Islamic state. 'We have no choice', Khomaini wrote, 'but to shun wickedness, and to overthrow governors who are traitorous, wicked, cruel and tyrannical.' He urged revolution, but not violence.

The statements of Osama bin-Laden are more directly political in tone. In a 'World Islamic Front Statement' entitled 'Jihad Against Jews and Crusaders', he argues that the United States of America has created a state of war against the Muslim world and in particular the people of the Arabian Peninsula. He speaks of the occupation of the Arabian Peninsula, which contains Islam's most holy places, arguing that it is being used by the Americans as a staging post for continuing aggression against the Iraqi people, of whom he claims more than one million have been killed. Further he complains of the 'occupation of Jerusalem and the murder of Muslims there' – Israel, being seen as an American puppet state. These American actions, in his view, amount to a 'clear declaration of war on God, his messenger, and Muslims.' Further because 'the *ulema* have throughout Islamic history unanimously agreed that the *jihad* is an individual duty if the enemy destroys Muslim countries', Osama bin-Laden, therefore, declared that it is a duty for every Muslim who can to kill Americans and their allies and he quotes from the Qur'an (2, 193 and 4,75) to justify this call.

This is an extreme position, which I in no way seek to justify, but if there is to be an alternative to violent reaction to violence, then at least we need to hear the complaint of those who sympathize with Osama bin-Laden's attack on America and the West. Two years ago, not for the first time, I visited a Palestinian Refugee camp. In the bitterness and despair of those we talked to I felt more than ever their deep sense of injustice and of a wasted life. The causes of the situation are complex and neighboring Arab nations have been almost as much responsible as Israeli governments. The human tragedy is overwhelming as also is the suffering of many families in Iraq, because of sanctions imposed by the USA and Britain (although nominally by the UN). One could add to the political complaints, the failure of Western powers to protect the Bosnian Muslims or to curb the ruthless Russian suppression of Chechnyan rebels. Terrorism is not to be condoned and I deplore all violence, but in every age victims of ruthless regimes have been driven to armed resistance. One person's terrorist is another person's freedom-fighter.

There is also a sense amongst some Muslims that Western concern for human rights is selective and that the world economic system operates largely to the benefit of the West and certain Arab rulers who are in league with them. To some eyes globalization is seen as bed-fellow of modernism. I do not want to pursue the political analysis, but it is impossible to separate political and religious issues in the present situation. What is felt by many Muslims as injustice, contributes to oppositional attitudes and the rejection of all that the West stands for. Raficq Abdullah, a Muslim lawyer who lives in London, writes that for millions of Muslims who live in poverty and who feel profoundly marginalized, modernity has nothing to offer them. It embodies 'the virulent return of *jahilliyah* or ungodliness which now infests the whole world including Muslim societies... It is justified by man-made laws which transgress God's legislative authority as enshrined in the religious law or *Shariah.* This comprehensive failure to abide by the only sovereign law which is God's exclusive attribute and prerogative is the cause of moral decay and spiritual bankruptcy. A true Muslim's only shield against this seemingly intractable threat to his or her identity is a reversion to the authentic experience of Islam as it was practiced during the lives of the Prophet and the rightly-guided Caliphs.' Raficq Abdullah is at pains to make clear that Islam is not a monolithic entity, but adds that the rejection of modernity and the 'West' is shared by both Sunni and Shi'a

Islamists. As Raficq Abdullah makes clear, he does not share these views, and accuses those who take this position of committing 'epistemological legerdemain by projecting their deeply nostalgic version of events of the founding moment of Islam as ahistorical categories, as givens which it would be sacrilegious, indeed blasphemous, to place under critical scrutiny'.

Raficq uses the term Islamists. I have tried to avoid the term 'fundamentalist', which as I have already explained is misleading and 'extremist', which may be an excuse for not listening to the call for justice of those who feel marginalized. As Raficq Abdullah points out the way in which some in the West speak of all Muslims as if they were terrorists is as bad as the way some Muslims see all Westerners as enemies of the true faith. As Edward Said has observed, 'the real battle is not a clash of civilizations, but a clash of definitions.'

The struggle should not be the West against the world of Islam, rather a struggle is going on for the soul of Islam. Professor Khalid Duran, of the Foreign Policy Research Institute in Philadelphia, writing well before the tragic events of September 11th, made a distinction between *Muslims* and *Islamists.'* He compares the distinction to that in Germany between *evangelisch* and *evangelikal* (Protestant and Protestant fundamentalist). Similarly before the fall of the Berlin Wall both regimes in Germany claimed they were democratic. Two titles which sound almost the same may have sharply different meanings. One Muslim explained the difference by saying that 'Muslims say "God is most great", whereas Islamists say "Islam is most great", although that is rather too simple.

Most of the Muslims I know and the ones whom we are likely to meet in dialogue are Muslims – in the sense I am using it. They are also usually heirs to the Enlightenment so share many of the assumptions of the modern paradigm. Even so, we need to try to understand something of the appeal of the Islamists. As we have seen, the origins of the Islamic Movement lie with the Wahhabi movement that emerged in Central Arabia in the eighteenth and nineteenth century. Its aim was to revive the Muslim society of seventh century Medina in its 'pristine purity'. A similar vision inspired Hasan al-Banna who founded the Muslim Brotherhood Party. He wanted to return to original Islam 'cleansed of all later accretions such as theology, philosophy and mysticism. Compare this to the motto of Z. A. Bhutto's Pakistan People's Party 'Our religion is Islam, our political system is democracy, our economic orientation is socialism' – a slogan that was anathema to Islamists. There is a real ideological struggle in many Muslim countries reflecting radically different understandings of the Muslim religion.

In part, the Islamists, as we have seen, reject centuries of legal scholarship and the mystical tradition. They are fundamentalist in the sense that scriptural statements are not seen in their historical context and are treated as absolute-whereas any revealed statement ought to be open to interpretation. This points to the very different assumptions of those who are and are not heirs to the Enlightenment. In his book on Judaism, Hans Küng speaks of paradigm shifts and suggests that you can have periods when people of the same faith are living in different paradigm times, which means that they have few shared assumptions about life and the world. Islamists reject 'modernism', partly because their view of life starts from different basic assumptions. The struggle within Islam is primarily a matter for Muslims, but sympathetic friends need to be aware of the struggle that is taking place, and to be supportive of those Muslims who are willing to take the risk of dialogue. They can help to make known the views of the latter group, thereby resisting the stereotyping of Muslims which will make prophecies of a clash of civilizations self-fulfilling. This is also a time when more than ever Christians need to seek dialogue with those Muslims who are willing to take part in it.

It is also vital to help Muslims in Europe and America feel that they are accepted as full citizens and that they have a stake and share in our society. One of the dangers in some urban areas of Britain is that young Muslims not only feel alienated from 'white English society' but are also increasingly alienated from the mosques and the leaders of the Muslim community. In 2001, I was invited to the Awards for Excellence ceremony organized by the *Muslim News* and also to the opening of a new Muslim center near Paddington Station by Prince Charles. It made me more aware how many Muslims are making a rich contribution to British life at all levels of our society. But many others, like a young Muslim woman at a check-out in Cowley or a Rhodes scholar at one of the colleges in Oxford have told me that they feel marginalized and have experienced discrimination and racial abuse. The search for a genuinely multi-cultural and multi-religious society is more important than ever and the work of the various interfaith organization needs to be strongly supported.

On the international scene, governments, *all* governments have to address the root causes of poverty and injustice – and this includes tackling trade discrimination, the arms trade as well as seeking solutions for long-standing areas of tension in the Middle East and in Kashmir and Sudan. People of faith have constantly to call upon the leaders of the nations to live up to their responsibilities. The tragic events of September 11th could be a wake-up call to seek for the new world order that some of us talked about and hoped for with the start of a new millennium.

MODERN AGE OF ISLAM

Every religion prescribes its own prayer system, Islam also does. Every religion has its own unique system and it is this uniqueness which is precious. Islam prescribes its prayer system without challenging prayer systems of other religions as it recognises the uniqueness of prayer systems of other religions. It puts it succinctly as under: "And everyone has direction to which he turns (himself), so vie with one another in good works." (2:148). Thus it is clear that everyone has ones own way of worshipping and one should not denounce each others way of worship. According to Imam Raghib the word 'wijhat' is more comprehensive. It means not only direction but also entire 'shari`ah'. Thus according to Raghib what Qur'an states in the above verse is that each religion has its own 'shari`ah' which has its own uniqueness.

There are different words used by the Qur'an for worship, the most frequent being 'ibadah'. The word 'ibadah' is also used in senses more than one. It is derived from the word 'ubudiyyah' which means to express ones humility and humbleness. But the word ' ibadah' carries in it even greater sense of humility; it, in fact, carries the utter sense of humility. Thus the first requirement of worship in Islam is to feel utterly humble before the Greatest Being and Most Powerful Allah.

Human beings are created by All Mighty Allah and to worship Him they must develop within themselves the utter sense of humility. Thus the Islamic concept of worship implies humility. Thus by implication it also becomes an essential part of Islamic ethic. Thus arrogance is unethical. No wonder than that Qur'an repeatedly denounces arrogance and calls it 'istikbar'. Its opposite is both ' istid`af' (to be weak) and ' ubudiyyat'.

Pharaoh (Fir'aun) has been described in the Qur'an as 'mustakbir' (having arrogance of power) as also the Satan. The direct implication is that those who are arrogant are like Pharaoh or Satan. The true servant of Allah has a sense of utter humility and believes that only Allah is the Greatest-'Allahu Akbar.'

This is very basic formula of Islamic worship. Anyone who is arrogant and has a feeling of powerful cannot be true worshipper of Allah. A true worshipper of Allah is one who has no trace of arrogance, of 'ananiyyah' or egotism. This has another important implication. It negates the very concept of one being ruler over the other and thus creates democratic ethos and human dignity.

Elsewhere also the Qur'an lays emphasis on dignity of entire humanity-children of Adam when it says: " And surely, We have honoured the children of Adam, and We carry them in the land and the sea, and We provide them with good things, and We have made them to excel highly most of those whom We have created." (17:70)

Thus once we accept Allah as the Greatest by implication all human beings are His humble servant without any distinction of caste, colour, creed or race and all are equal before Him and no one is superior to the other. The Qur'an clearly sates that " O mankind, surely We have created you from a male and a female, and made your tribes and families that you may know each other. Surely the noblest of you with Allah is the most pious (God-conscious) of you." (49:13).

It will be seen that it is very important statement of the Qur'an and is quite fundamental to the concept of worship in Islam. All human beings are equal in the sight of Allah and distinction of tribes, families etc. are only to know each other and not to take pride-leading to arrogance in ones belonging to one nation or the other, or one tribe or family or other. The real distinction could be only of piety, honesty and integrity of character and most honoured in the eyes of Allah is one who is most pious. Any Muslim who feels superior to the other on the basis of tribe or family or nation or colour cannot be true worshipper of Allah as this air of superiority leads to arrogance which is quite contrary to the very concept of ' ibadah' and ' ubudiyyah'. One who worships

Allah must intrinsically subscribe to the concept of equality of all human beings. There is no place in Islam of low or high status at all.

This is further symbolised by the congregational prayer in Islam. All have to stand in one line in Islamic congregational prayer. A true worshipper of Allah would show equal respect to all human beings irrespective of their origin, their identity and their status. Any worshiper who apparently stands in one line but carries the feeling of superiority over others in his heart, cannot be construed as true and free worshipper. Such a person is not bondsman of Allah but of his vain desire. He who is bondsman of his ow n desire cannot be a free person and can never claim to enjoy the pleasure of a free man's worship. Thus a false sense of superiority is the very negation of true worship. A free man's worship is based on passionate belief in freedom and dignity of all human beings as Allah alone is creator of all and He alone is real object of worship. Thus a passionate belief in one God also assumes great significance in Islamic tradition. Because only such belief in oneness of God leads to the negation of worshipping lesser beings. It can lead to worship of human being by another human being and thus deifying some among us or deifying some other objects. This would also lead to superiority of some over others negating the concept of equal dignity for all children of Ada m as stated in the Qur'an.

The Sufis, the mystics of Islam, base their concept of 'wahdat al-wujud' (unity of Being) on this concept of 'tawhid' (unity of Godhood) and it is this concept of unity of Being which demolishes all distinctions. The concept of Absolute Being is possible only if we believe in the concept of absolute unity of humankind. And sufis made no such distinctions. Distinctions invariably lead to a sense of superiority and hence go against the concept of worship of a True Being. In Islam an act of worship is a means, not a goal. The goal is a true moral and ethical conduct. The Qur'an says "Surely prayer keeps (one) away from indecency and evil; and certainly the remembrance of Allah is the greatest (act)." (29:45) Many treat prayer 'salah' as a goal, not a means as stated in the above Qur'anic verse. A real worshipper would never indulge in any indecent act ('fahsha)' or would never go near an evil. The important question is what is evil? The word used for evil here is 'munkar' i.e. anything which is rejected by the society as harmful.

Anything which is harmful to human society must be rejected and must be desisted from. There are some evils which are absolute in nature and must be avoided irrespective of time and place. Injustice and falsehood are such evils. The greatest evil thus is being untruthful.

One of the names of Allah is 'Haq' i.e.truth. Thus truthfulness becomes the important element of Allah\rquote s worship. Anyone who deviates from the path of truth cannot claim to be worshipper of Allah. A true worshipper of Allah will never compromise on the question of truth. He will gladly sacrifice his own interests to uphold the cause of truth. Those who sacrifice everything including their own lives deserve to be true worshiper of Allah. A true worshiper would not entertain falsehood in any form. A true worshiper's tongue will speak nothing but truth. He will never utter anything which is not truth. One has to be fearless to be truthful. Only one who fears Allah and no one else can speak truth and avoid falsehood.

Also, Allah is Just and one who worships Allah cannot be but just. Justice is part of worship and one who works tirelessly for establishing justice in the society is real worshiper of Allah. The path of truth and justice is paved with difficulties and sacrifices and a true worshiper does not mind in the least to face these difficulties and make sacrifices for the cause of justice and truth. To court martyrdom for the cause of truth and justice is the highest form of worship one can think of. Thus the Qur'an describes true worshiper as follows: "The patient and the truthful, and the obedient, and those who spend and those who ask Divine protection in the morning times." (3:16). Truth requires inexhaustible degree of patience and hence the above verse refers to the quality of patience along with truthfulness. Allah has been described as 'Rabb al-`Alamin' in the Qur'an i.e. Sustainer of the universe. 'Rabb', according to Imam Raghib, is one who takes a thing from one stage of perfection to another stage until it reaches the final stage of perfection. Allah is 'Rabb' in this sense and any of His worshiper has to work tirelessly for achieving this objective. He or she will do nothing which will obstruct this path of perfection. This also includes the protection of environment and ecological balance. For the perfection of our world its ecological balance is very vital. The greed for consumption leads to destruction of ecological balance. Thus a worshiper can not be insensitive to the destruction of environment. The quality of 'rububiyyat' (sustaining) will be incomplete without mercy and compassion. Thus in the very first chapter of the Qur'an Allah is described as 'Rabb, Merciful and Compassionate'. Only one who is merciful and compassionate can take this universe from one stage of perfection to another stage until it reaches the ultimate stage of perfection. And one who engages oneself in this work on human plane has to have qualities of mercy and compassion for all i.e. for entire humanity on one hand, and, for all the creation of Allah, on the other. A person who is compassionate will not wantonly destroy anything and would show feeling of loving care for all creatures. Thus a worshiper has to be compassionate and merciful towards all.

The Qur'an also makes it clear that the act of prayer is not merely a ritual to be performed. It is an act which transforms ones inner being and makes him or her a perfect person. Perfection of inner being is very important aspect of act of worship. Thus Qur'an describes the act of worship as under: " It is not righteousness that you turn your faces towards the East and West, but righteous is one who believes in Allah, and the Last Day, and the angels and the Book and the prophets, and gives away wealth out of love for Him to the near of kin and the orphans and the needy and the wayfarer and to those who ask and to set slaves free and keeps up prayer and pays the poor rate; and the performers of their promise when they make a promi se, and the patient in distress and affliction and in the time of conflict; and these are they who keep their duty.\rdblquote (2:177)

This is very seminal verse which describes the basic features of worship. Thus worship is not a mere physical act of bowing and prostrating; it is much more than that. The Islamic concept of ' ibadah' is as much social as spiritual. Thus among ' ibadat' are included 'fasting, zakat' and 'Hajj'. These have their own significance. Fasting ('saum') again is not mere an act of going hungry from sunrise to sun set. It is to learn to control ones desires and make ones soul pure by removing all impurities. Controlling ones desires (what the Qur'an calls 'nafs ammarah') is very important element of fasting.

It amounts in fact to developing a spirit of renunciation in the midst of having and developing sensitivity towards others suffering. To be sensitive is very important element of ' ibadah'. And fasting is meant to sensitize the people. Only a sensitive soul can stand up and fight against untruth and injustice. Thus the real significance of fasting is to develop sensitivity towards misery and suffering and devote oneself to eradication of all forms of suffering and misery. Thus in the above verse (2:177) describing the act of true worship emphasis is laid on spending ones wealth out of love for Him for the near of kin and the orphans and the needy and the wayfarer and to those who ask and to set slaves free. In those days of slavery Islam talked of dignity of all human beings and repeatedly laid emphasis on setting the slaves free. Here in the above verse setting slaves free has been described as an act of worship.

Slaves suffer intensely and slavery deprives human beings of their human dignity and hence setting slaves free is an important ingredient of act of worship. A believer or a worshiper would not tolerate any act of indignity to any human being. Thus he has to be passionately committed to human freedom and dignity and has to work to abolish all forms of human unfreedom, slavery being the most abominable for of human indignity. The above verse also emphasises the need for spending for the poor, the orphans, the widows and the wayfarers. This is precisely what the payment of zakat (poor rate) is meant for. Thus the Qur'an says: " Zakat (charity) is only for the poor and the needy, and those employed to administer it, and those whose hearts are made to incline (to truth), and (to free) the captives, and those in debt, and in the way of Allah and for the wayfarer-an ordinance from Allah." (9:60).

Thus it will be seen that zakat is basically meant for the weaker sections of society so that their sufferings could be minimised. Zakat is also required to be spent on paying off the debts of indebted. It is poor who are indebted. The poor are generally indebted and they must be freed of it if their sufferings are to be eliminated. Again, it is for this reason that the Qur'an prohibits interest. It is the poor who have to pay high rates of interest for fulfilling their basic needs. Those who charge high rates of interest on consumption loans are real blood suckers and they can never qualify for worship. On the other hand, Qur'an warns them to be prepared for war with Allah if they do not waive off interest on such loans. In fact war against interest is war against poverty and suffering. Thus it will be seen that establishing social justice is as important part of act of worship as an act of praying. It also has a macro dimension. Entire third world is poor and indebted today. It is the rich countries of the West who exploit the people of the third world and put burden of indebtedness on them. There is need for setting up funds on the line of zakat to waive off debts of third world countries and interest thereon. This would greatly relieve the third world of its suffering and for the West it will be an act of worship. But all of us know that Western countries are not going to oblige the third world. This socio-economic dimension should not be lost sight of. The Qur'an is so sensitive to various dimensions of suffering that it specially mentions the problem of wayfarers also. In those days the wayfarers had to face number of difficult problems while traveling. No basic facilities were available on the long and arduous course of journey. The Qur'an thus required a part of the zakat fund be spent on alleviating the sufferings of these wayfarers. It indicates the degree of sensitivity Qur'an desires to create in us. It is, therefore, highly necessary that a worshiper be hyper sensitive to others sufferings in every form. He should work tirelessly for the welfare of an entire humanity. Hajj is also included in the act of Islamic worship. It is desirable that Muslims should go, if he has means, for 'Hajj' once in life time. What is its significance as an act of worship? What is its social dimension? As pointed out earlier Islam teaches equality of all human beings irrespective of tribe, nation or family. When one meets other human being one should meet him/her on plane of equality. Hajj provides this opportunity to a Muslim. Muslims from all over the world congregate for Hajj in Mecca. They belong to different nations, different tribes, different races and colours. Also they are made to wear a simple 'un-sewn' white cloth to further emphasise their equality before God. This huge congregation of human beings from all over globe without any distinction of nation or tribe, caste or colour is recognition of equality of all human beings and it is a practical lesson in ordering a world free of ethnic, national or racial distinctions.

This is a great act of worship and the greatest service of humanity, provided it is taken in that spirit. Ka'ba is a house of Allah and all those who come there are equal before Him in every respect. If the hajj is taken in its real spirit it can lead to creating of a world free of all ethnic and racial tensions.

Thus it will be seen that an act of worship is not merely a ritual as it has come to be widely practiced. A real act of worship is much more than mere physical act of bowing and prostrating, or fasting mechanically as a ritual or performing hajj by merely going to Mecca. These acts of worship have other dimensions, which are very important in reordering and refashioning our world, a world without suffering, a world without discrimination, a world without inequalities and without bondage. Such a world can be created only with a passionate commitment to dignity and freedom of humanity. It is this passionate commitment with humility before Allah which can constitute a real act of a free man's worship which has spiritual as well as social dimension.

The great philosophers of Islam like al-Farabi, Averros and Avicina rose to the height of their fame after the Abbasid power began to decline. Of course, the encyclopedic work like Ikhwanus Safa (The Brethren of Purity) was written and compiled during the heydays of the Abbasids. There is a great deal of controversy as to who compiled the work which could be described as most modern of its time for its liberalism, openness and sweep. The Isma'ilis claim that the work was compiled by their Imam Husain al-Mastur to effectively reply to the Abbasids through their own weapon. However, others feel that there was a society in Basra which met secretly and discussed the most burning religious and philosophical questions of the time and written records of these were maintained and these records were later on compiled under the title Ikhwanus Safa. Whatever the truth, the fact is that this encyclopedic work was very comprehensive and it runs into 52 volumes, each volume devoted to some subject or the other. It adopted the then most modern approach to the problems and discussed everything in the light of reason and proved their contentions, even of faith, by use of intellect and not blind belief.

It will be interesting to quote here from some philosophical and theological works to show how philosophical and theological controversies were debated in the light of reason. Even most orthodox theological propositions were examined in the light of reason. I quote passages from Al-Ghazali's Al-Munqidh min al-Dalal (i.e. That Which Delivers from Error) to show the nature of debates. It should be borne in mind that al-Ghazali was an orthodox theologian and opposed to philosophical reasoning. He wrote a book Tahafut al-Falasifa (i.e. Bewilderment of Philosophers). Ibn Rushd, a great philosopher and the contemporary of Ghazali replied by writing Tahafut, Tahafut al-Falasifa (i.e. Stupefication of the Bewilderment of Philosophers). Thus al-Ghazali says in one of his passages in his Munqidh min al-Dalal: "In this and similar cases of sense-perception the sense as judge forms his judgments, but another judge, the intellect, shows him repeatedly to be wrong; and charge of falsity cannot be rebutted. "To this I said: 'My reliance on sense-perception also has been destroyed. Perhaps only those intellectual truths which are first principles (or derived from first principles) are to be relied upon, such as the assertion that ten are more than three, that the same thing cannot be both affirmed and denied at one time, that one thing is not both generated in time and eternal, nor both existent and non-existent, nor both necessary and impossible.';"

Further Ghazali continues: "Sense-perception replied: 'Do you not expect that your reliance on intellectual truth will fare like your reliance on sense-perception? You used to trust in me, then along came the intellect-judge and proved me wrong; if it were not for the intellect-judge you would have continued to regard me as true. Perhaps behind intellectual apprehension there is another judge who, if he manifests himself, will show the falsity of intellect in its judging, just as, when intellect manifested itself, it showed the falsity of sense in its judging. The fact that such a supra-intellectual apprehension has not manifested itself is no proof that it is impossible.' "

QUALITY OF ARGUMENTS

Ghazali then gives the example of dream: "My ego hesitated a little about the reply to that, and sense-perception heightened the difficulty by referring to dreams. 'Do you not see', it said, 'how when you are asleep, you believe things and imagine circumstances, holding them to be stable and enduring, and, so long as you are in that dream-condition, have no doubts about them? And is it not the case that when you awake you know that all you have imagined and believed is unfounded and ineffectual? Why then are you confident that all your waking beliefs, whether from sense or intellect, are genuine? They are true in respect of your present state; but it is possible that a state will come upon you whose relation to your waking consciousness is analogous to the relation of the latter to dreaming.' " The argument goes on. The question is not which point of view was right or wrong; the more important question is the quality of arguments, their objectivity and methodology which was quite modern. So the theological and philosophical debates were intellectually rich and based on certain agreed methodology which could be construed as quite modern from the norms of those days. Another parameter of modernity, though not insisted upon by Bernard Lewis, but by some other Western scholars, is gender justice and human rights. If we go by the Islamic ideals and not the practice in Muslim societies, Islam stood for gender justice. The Qur'anic pronouncements in this respect were quite revolutionary from the standards of those days. What is most important is that Islam accepted the woman as a legal entity with definite rights in terms of marriage, divorce, inheritance, maintenance, property and so on. But the conservative 'Ulama, under the influence of their own societies, interpreted, in many cases through inventions of a Hadith (Prophet's sayings), the Qur'anic verses in such a manner as to rob her of the very rights granted to her, in many cases in the most unambiguous terms, by the Divine Book. No other legal system by then had granted her legal individuality, not even the Roman law, which was the most advanced law in the pre-Islamic world.

However, the time was not ripe to practice gender justice as we understand today, much less gender equality. Whatever was given to women was taken away by the Muslim society through the backdoor. In that sense too, Islam was a modern religion which, at least theoretically, brought about radical change in the status of women. There is, therefore, an urgent need to rethink women's rights related issues in the Muslim world. It is ironical that the Muslim world is charged today with oppressing their women and denying them justice.

As for democracy, the Qur'an requires the Holy Prophet to consult people in secular matters, or matters relating to the community (see verses 3:159 and 42:38). This approach could have produced a democratic culture and the early companions of the Prophet did practice it for a limited period of time. However, soon such efforts were sabotaged by some power-hungry people who converted Islamic democracy into dynastic rule. And the tryst with democracy ended there and Muslim society has not known democracy and democratic values ever since.

Feudalism and authoritarianism which were totally alien to the Islamic spirit came to be legitimised and most oppressive and exploitative regimes came into existence in the Islamic history. The early democratic spirit was never re-discovered. it is only in our time that some Islamic countries have ushered in democracies to varying degrees. But, it must be admitted that most of the Muslim countries are ruled by monarchs or military dictators. Thus we have to face the odium that Islam is against modernity.

MODERNITY OF ISLAMIC WORLD

The response of Islamic countries to the concept of modernity as it obtains today varies from country to country. One thing in common, again with one or two honourable exceptions, is that all of these countries have accepted domination of the West, particularly the USA. Some of them even consider this domination as the ultimate in modernity although their societies continue to be utterly feudalistic in values. Neither do they have democracy nor any trace of gender justice. However, most of these countries vie one with the other in buying latest weaponry from the West. This also is considered by them as a symbol of modernity.

In Saudi Arabia, Saudis are governed by a highly authoritarian monarchy with no trace of democracy or gender justice. In this so-called Islamic regime women enjoy no independence worth the name. Though they are allowed to work in establishments run only by women, they are not free to work anywhere else. They are not allowed to go out alone without being accompanied by a mehram i.e. a man within the prohibited degree of marriage. No independent thinking in the fields of religion, philosophy and other social sciences is permitted. In every field there are pre-established official dogmas to which all Saudi citizens have to conform. There is no respect for human rights as there is no democracy. So all parameters of modernity are absent.

Yet one finds a superficial aura of modernity. The Saudi cities are concrete jungles including the holy cities of Mecca and Madina. There is so much blind imitation of the West in designing buildings that no trace of Islamic heritage has been left. There is no Islamic ambiance even outside the holiest mosque of the Islamic world to which millions of pilgrims flock every year i.e. K'aba. Just outside the holiest mosque of the Islamic world there are huge concrete buildings. Mecca appears to be like any other Western city. No attempt has been made to preserve its Islamic heritage, not even in architecture. Could this be construed modernity? If it is, it is very superficial. There is no re-thinking of Islamic issues, no freedom of thought, no critical evaluation of Saudi practices but only blind imitation of the West in its worst aspects mindless urbanisation and disruption of old patterns of living. Also, the Saudi rulers buy huge stockpiles of Western arms which only increases their servility to the West. More arms they purchase from the West, more dependent they become on it.

EQUAL MODERNITY OF HUMAN RIGHTS

Earlier the Shah of Iran had also followed similar policies. He tried to impose forcibly the western modernism on a highly traditional society. The Shah also wanted to become regional satrap by stockpiling Western arms. There was no trace of democracy in Iran during his regime and no respect for human rights which are important parameters of modernism. Also, if women were allowed to wear mini skirts, could it be taken as sign of gender justice? In fact women were far from enjoying higher status in the Shah's Iran. After the revolution Ayatollah Khomeini also tried to impose many restrictions on women. Chador was made compulsory. Also, the traditional laws as regards women were not changed. However, women in post-revolutionary Iran are becoming quite conscious of their rights. Iran is one of the few Islamic countries which allows women to contest elections and now a woman has also become Vice-President of Iran. In Kuwait it is still being debated whether women could be given right to vote. In appearance Kuwait is one of the most modern cities of the world but its society still continues to be medieval. In all these countries except Iran there is total dependence on the West for arms as well as for economic development. They have no ability for developing modern science and technology or independent thinking in social or religious matters. Egypt produced many modern thinkers but it is also regressing now and fundamentalism has raised its head. In Egypt also there is a lack of democracy and human rights. In relation to women too, the 'Ulama of al-Azhar are resisting change. So the record of gender justice is not very bright in Egypt too. However, compared to other Islamic countries, Egypt is relatively more advanced.

11

Chronology of Islamic History

ISLAMIC HISTORY (CHRONOLOGY) 6TH CENTURY (500-599) C.E.

545: Birth of Abdullah, the Holy Prophet's father.

569-571: Year of the Elephant. Invasion of Makkah by Abraha the Viceroy of Yemen, his retreat.

577: The Holy Prophet visits Madina with his mother. Death of his mother.

580: Death of Abdul Muttalib, the grandfather of the Holy Prophet.

583: The Holy Prophet's journey to Syria in the company of his uncle Abu Talib. His meeting with the monk Bahira at Bisra who foretells of his prophethood.

586: The Holy Prophet participates in the war of Fijar.

591: The Holy Prophet becomes an active member of "Hilful Fudul", a league for the relief of the distressed.

594: The Holy Prophet becomes the Manager of the business of Lady Khadija, and leads her trade caravan to Syria and back.

595: The Holy Prophet marries Hadrat Khadija. Seventh century Islamic History (Chronology)

7th Century (600-699) C.E.

605: The Holy Prophet arbitrates in a dispute among the Quraish about the placing of the Black Stone in the Kaaba.

610: The first revelation in the cave at Mt. Hira. The Holy Prophet is commissioned as the Messenger of God.

613: Declaration at Mt. Sara inviting the general public to Islam.

614: Invitation to the Hashimites to accept Islam.

615: Persecution of the Muslims by the Quraish. A party of Muslims leaves for Abyssinia.

616: Second Hijrah to Abysinnia.

617: Social boycott of the Hashimites and the Holy Prophet by the Quraish. The Hashimites are shut up in a glen outside Makkah.

619: Lifting of the boycott. Deaths of Abu Talib and Hadrat Khadija. Year of sorrow.

620: Journey to Taif. Ascension to the heavens.

621: First pledge at Aqaba.

622: Second pledge at Aqaba. The Holy Prophet and the Muslims migrate to Yathrib. 623: Nakhla expedition.

624: Battle of Badr. Expulsion of the Bani Qainuqa Jews from Madina.

625: Battle of Uhud. Massacre of 70 Muslims at Bir Mauna. Expulsion of Banu Nadir Jews from Madina. Second expedition of Badr.

626: Expedition of Banu Mustaliq.

627: Battle of the Trench. Expulsion of Banu Quraiza Jews.

628: Truce of Hudaibiya. Expedition to Khyber. The Holy Prophet addresses letters to various heads of states.

629: The Holy Prophet performs the pilgrimage at Makkah. Expedition to Muta (Romans).

630: Conquest of Makkah. Battles of Hunsin, Auras, and Taif.

631: Expedition to Tabuk. Year of Deputations.

632: Farewell pilgrimage at Makkah.

632: Death of the Holy Prophet. Election of Hadrat Abu Bakr as the Caliph. Usamah leads expedition to Syria. Battles of Zu Qissa and Abraq. Battles of Buzakha, Zafar and Naqra. Campaigns against Bani Tamim and Musailima, the Liar.

633: Campaigns in Bahrain, Oman, Mahrah Yemen, and Hadramaut. Raids in Iraq. Battles of Kazima, Mazar, Walaja, Ulleis, Hirah, Anbar, Ein at tamr, Daumatul Jandal and Firaz.

634: Battles of Basra, Damascus and Ajnadin. Death of Hadrat

Abu Bakr. Hadrat Umar Farooq becomes the Caliph. Battles of Namaraq and Saqatia.

635: Battle of Bridge. Battle of Buwaib. Conquest of Damascus. Battle of Fahl.

636: Battle of Yermuk. Battle of Qadsiyia. Conquest of Madain.

637: Conquest of Syria. Fall of Jerusalem. Battle of Jalula.

638: Conquest of Jazirah.

639: Conquest of Khuizistan. Advance into Egypt.

640: Capture of the post of Caesaria in Syria. Conquest of Shustar and Jande Sabur in Persia. Battle of Babylon in Egypt.

641: Battle of Nihawand. Conquest Of Alexandria in Egypt.

642: Battle of Rayy in Persia. Conquest of Egypt. Foundation of Fustat.

643: Conquest of Azarbaijan and Tabaristan (Russia).

644: Conquest of Fars, Kerman, Sistan, Mekran and Kharan.Martyrdom of Hadrat Umar. Hadrat Othman becomes the Caliph.

645: Campaigns in Fats.

646: Campaigns in Khurasan, Armeain and Asia Minor.

647: Campaigns in North Africa. Conquest of the island of Cypress.

648: Campaigns against the Byzantines.

651: Naval battle of the Masts against the Byzantines.

652: Discontentment and disaffection against the rule of Hadrat Othman.

656: Martyrdom of Hadrat Othman. Hadrat Ali becomes the Caliph. Battle of the Camel.

657: Hadrat Ali shifts the capital from Madina to Kufa. Battle of Siffin. Arbitration proceedings at Daumaut ul Jandal.

658: Battle of Nahrawan.

659: Conquest of Egypt by Mu'awiyah.

660: Hadrat Ali recaptures Hijaz and Yemen from Mu'awiyah. Mu'awiyah declares himself as the Caliph at Damascus.

661: Martyrdom of Hadrat Ali. Accession of Hadrat Hasan and his abdication. Mu'awiyah becomes the sole Caliph.

662: Khawarij revolts.

666: Raid of Sicily.

670: Advance in North Africa. Uqba b Nafe founds the town of Qairowan in Tunisia. Conquest of Kabul.

672: Capture of the island of Rhodes. Campaigns in Khurasan.

674: The Muslims cross the Oxus. Bukhara becomes a vassal state.

677: Occupation of Sarnarkand and Tirmiz. Siege of Constantinople.

680: Death of Muawiyah. Accession of Yazid. Tragedy of Kerbala and martyrdom of Hadrat Hussain.

682: In North Africa Uqba b Nafe marches to the Atlantic, is ambushed and killed at Biskra. The Muslims evacuate Qairowan and withdraw to Burqa.

683: Death of Yazid. Accession of Mu'awiyah II.

684: Abdullah b Zubair declares himself aS the Caliph at'Makkah. Marwan I becomes the Caliph' at Damascus. Battle of Marj Rahat.

685: Death of Marwan I. Abdul Malik becomes the Caliph at Damascus. Battle of Ain ul Wada.

686: Mukhtar declares himself as the Caliph at Kufa.

687: Battle of Kufa between the forces of Mukhtar and Abdullah b Zubair. Mukhtar killed.

691: Battle of Deir ul Jaliq. Kufa falls to Abdul Malik.

692: The fall of Makkah. Death of Abdullah b Zubair. Abdul Malik becomes the sole Caliph.

695: Khawarij revolts in Jazira and Ahwaz. Battle of the Karun. Campaigns against Kahina in North Africa. The' Muslims once again withdraw to Barqa. The Muslims advance in Transoxiana and occupy Kish.

ISLAMIC HISTORY (CHRONOLOGY) 8TH CENTURY (700-799) C.E.

700: Campaigns against the Berbers in North Africa.

702: Ashath's rebellion in Iraq, battle of Deir ul Jamira.

705: Death of Abdul Malik. Accession of Walid I as Caliph.

711: Conquest of Spain, Sind and Transoxiana.

712: The Muslims advance in Spain, Sind and Transoxiana.

713: Conquest of Multan.

715: Death of Walid I. Accession of Sulaiman.

716: Invasion of Constantinople.

717: Death of Sulaiman. Accession of Umar b Abdul Aziz.

720: Death of Umar b Abdul Aziz. Accession of Yazid II.

724: Death of Yazid II. Accession of Hisham.

725: The Muslims occupy Nimes in France.

732: The battle of Tours in France.

737: The Muslims meet reverse at Avignon in France.

740: Shia revolt under Zaid b Ali. Berber revolt in North Africa. Battle of the Nobles.

741: Battle of Bagdoura in North Africa.

742: The Muslim rule restored in Qiarowan.

743: Death of Hisham. Accession of Walid II. Shia revolt in Khurasan under Yahya b Zaid.

744: Deposition of Walid I1. Accession of Yazid II1 and his death. Accession of Ibrahim and his overthrow. Battle of Ain al Jurr. Accession of Marwan II.

745: Kufa and Mosul occupied by the Khawarjites.

746: Battle of Rupar Thutha, Kufa and Mosul occupied by Marwan II.

747: Revolt of Abu Muslim in Khurasan.

748: Battle of Rayy.

749: Battles of lsfahan and Nihawand. Capture of Kufa by the Abbasids. As Saffah becomes the Abbasid Caliph at Kufa.

750: Battle of Zab. Fall of Damascus. End of the Umayyads.

751: Conquest of Wasit by the Abbasid. Murder of the Minister Abu Salama.

754: Death of As Saffah. Accession of Mansur as the Caliph.

755: Revolt of Abdullah b Ali. MUrder of Abu Muslim. Sunbadh revolt in Khurasan.

756: Abdul Rahman founds the Umayyad state in Spain.

762: Shia revolt under Muhammad (Nafs uz Zakia) and Ibrahim.

763: Foundation of Baghdad. Defeat of the Abbasids in Spain.

767: Khariji state set up by Ibn Madrar at Sijilmasa. Ustad Sees revolt in Khurasan.

772: Battle of Janbi in North Africa. Rustamid. state set up in Morocco.

775: Death or the Abbasid Caliph Mansur, Accession of Mahdi,

777: Battle of Saragossa in Spain.

785: Death of the Caliph Mahdi. Accession of Hadi.

786: Death of Hadi. Accession of Harun ur Rashid.

788: Idrisid state set up in the Maghrib. Death of Abdul Rahman of Spain, and accession of Hisham.

792: Invasion of South France.

796: Death of Hisham in Spain; accession of al Hakam.

799: Suppression of the revolt of the Khazars. Ninth century.

ISLAMIC HISTORY (CHRONOLOGY) 9TH CENTURY (800-899) C.E.

800: The Aghlabid rule is established in North Africa.

803: Downfall of the Barmakids. Execution of Jafar Barmki.

805: Campaigns against the Byzantines. Capture of the islands of Rhodes and Cypress.

809: Death of Harun ur Rashid. Accession of Amin.

814: Civil war between Amin and Mamun. Amin killed and Mamun becomes the Caliph.

815: Shia revolt under Ibn Tuba Tabs.

816: Shia revolt in Makkah; Harsama quells the revolt. In Spain the Umayyads capture the island of Corsica.

817: Harsama killed.

818: The Umayyads of Spain capture the islands of Izira, Majorica, and Sardinia.

819: Mamun comes to Baghdad.

820: Tahir establishes the rule of the Tahirids in Khurasan.

822: Death of AI Hakam in Spain; accession of Abdul Rahman. II.

823: Death of Tahir in Khurasan. Accession of Talha and his deposition. Accession of Abdullah b Tahir.

827: Mamun declares the Mutazila creed as the state religion.

833: Death of Mamun. Accession of Mutasim.

836: Mutasim shifts the capital to Samarra. 837 Revolt of the Jats.

838: Revolt of Babek in Azarbaijan suppressed.

839: Revolt of Maziar in Tabaristan. The Muslims occupy South Italy. Capture of the city of Messina in Sicily.

842: Death of Mutasim, accession of Wasiq.

843: Revolts of the Arabs.

847: Death of Wasiq, accession of Mutawakkil.

850: Mutawakkil restores orthodoxy.

849: Death of the Tahirid ruler Abdullah b Tahir; accession of Tahir II.

852: Death of Abdur Rahman II of Spain;. accession of Muhammad I.

856: Umar b Abdul Aziz founds the Habbarid rule in Sind.

858: Mutawakkil founds the town of Jafariya.

860: Ahmad founds the Samanid rule in Transoxiana.

861: Murder of the Abbasid Caliph Mutawakkil; accession of Muntasir.

862: Muntasir poisoned to death; accession of Mutasin.

864: Zaidi state established in Tabaristan by Hasan b Zaid.

866: Mutasim flies from Samarra, his depostion and accession of Mutaaz.

867: Yaqub b Layth founds the Saffarid rule in Sistan.

868: Ahmad b Tulun founds the Tulunid rule in Egypt.

869: The Abbasid Caliph Mutaaz forced to abdicate, his death and accession of Muhtadi.

870: Turks revolt against Muhtadi, his death and accession of Mutamid.

873: Tahirid rule extinguished.

874: Zanj revolt in South Iraq. Death of the Samanid ruler Ahmad, accession of Nasr.

877: Death of Yaqubb Layth in Sistan, accession of Amr b Layth.

885: Death of Ahmad b Tulun in Egypt, accession of Khamarwiyiah.

866: Death of Muhammad I the Umayyad ruler of Spain, accession of Munzir. Death of Abdullah b Umar the Habbari ruler of Sind.

888: Death of Munzir the Umayyad ruler of Spain, accession of Abbullah.

891: The Qarmatian state established at Bahrain.

892: Death of the Samanid ruler Nasr, accession of Ismail.

894: The Rustamids become the vassals of Spain.

896: Death of the Tulunid ruler Khamarwiyiah; accession of Abul Asakir Jaish.

897: Assassination of Abul Asakir Jaish; accession of Abu Musa Harun. 898: Qarmatians sack Basra,

Islamic History (Chronology) 10th Century (900-999) C.E.

902: Death of the Abbasid Caliph Muktafi; death of the Saffarid ruler Amr.

903: Assassination of the Qarmatian ruler Abu Said; accession of Abu Tahir.

905: Abdullah b Hamdan founds the Hamdanid rule in Mosul and Jazira. End of the Tulunid rule in Egypt.

907: Death of the Abbasid Caliph Muktafi; accession of Muqtadir,

908: End of the Saffarid rule, annexation of their territories by the Samanids.

909: Ubaidullah overthrows the Aghlablds and founds the Fatimid rule in North Africa.

912: Death of the Umayyad Amir Abdullah in Spain, accession of Abdur Rahman III.

913: Assassination of the Samanid ruler Ahmad II, accession of Nasr II.

928: Mardawij b Ziyar founds the Ziyarid rule in Tabaristan.

929: Qarmatians sack Makkah and carry away the Black Stone from the Holy Kaaba. In Spain, Abdur Rahman III declares himself as the Caliph.

931: Deposition and restoration of the Abbasid Caliph Muqtadir. Death of the Qarmatian ruler Abu Tahir; accession of Abu Mansur.

932: Death of the Abbasid Caliph Muqtadir; accession of Al Qahir.

934: Deposition of the Abbasid Caliph Al Qahir; accession of Ar Radi. Death of the Fatimid Caliph Ubaidullah; accession of Al Qaim.

935: Assassination of the Ziyarid ruler Mardawij; accession of Washimgir. Death of Hamdanid ruler Abdullah b Hamdan accession of Nasir ud Daula.

936: By coup Ibn Raiq becomes the Amir ul Umara.

938: By another coup power at Baghdad is captured by Bajkam.

940: Death of the Abbasid Caliph Ar Radi, accession of Muttaqi.

941: Assassination of Bajkam, capture of power by Kurtakin.

942: Ibn Raiq recaptures power.

943: Al Baeidi captures power. The Abbasid Caliph Muttaqi is forced to seek refuge with the Hamdanids. Sail ud Daula captures power at Baghdad and the Caliph returns to' Baghdad. Power is captured by Tuzun and Sail ud Daula retires' to Mosul. Death of the Samanid ruler Nasr II, accession of Nuh.

944: Muttaqi is blinded and deposed, accession of Mustakafi.

945: Death of Tuzun. Shirzad becomes Amir ul Umra. The Buwayhids capture power. Deposition of the Abbasid Caliph Mustakafi.

946: Death of the Fatimid Caliph A1 Qaim. accession of Mansur. Death of the Ikhshid ruler Muhammad b Tughj, accession of Abul' Qasim Ungur.

951: The Qarnaatiana restore the Black Stone to the Holy Kaaba.

954: Death of the Sasanid ruler Nuh, accession of Abdul Malik.

961: Death of the Samanid ruler Abdul Malik, accession of Manauf. Alptgin founds the rule of the Ghazanavids. Death of the Umayyad Caliph Abdul Rahman III in Spain; accession of Hakam. Death of the Ikhshid ruler Ungur accession of Abul Hasan Ali.

965: Death of the Qarmatian ruler Abu Mansur; accession of

Hasan Azam. Assassination of the Ikhshid ruler Abul Hasan Ali; power captured by Malik Kafur.

967: Death of the Buwayhid Sultan Muiz ud Daula, accession of Bakhtiar. Death of the Hamdanid ruler Sail ud Daula.

968: Byzantines occupy Aleppo. Death of the Ikhshid ruler Malik Kafur; accession of Abul Fawaris.

969: The Fatimids conquer Egypt.

972: Buluggin b Ziri founds the rule of the Zirids Algeria.

973: Shia Sunni disturbances in Baghdad; power captured in Baghdad by the Turkish General Subuktgin.

974: Abdication of the Abbasid Caliph AI Muttih; accession of At Taii.

975: Death of the Turk General Subuktgin. Death of the Fatimid Caliph Al Muizz.

976: The Buwayhid Sultan Izz ud Daula recaptures power with the help of his cousin Azud ud Daula. Death of the Samanid ruler Mansur, accession of Nuh II. In Spain death of the Umayyad Caliph Hakam, accession of Hisham II.

978: Death of the Buwayhid Sultan Izz ud Daula, power captured by Azud ud Daula. The Hamdanids overthrown by the Buwayhids.

979: Subkutgin becomes the Amir of Ghazni.

981: End of the Qarmatian rule at Bahrain.

982: Death of the-Buwayhid Sultan Azud ud Daula; accession of Samsara ud Daula.

984: Death of the Zirid ruler Buluggin, accession of Mansur.

986: The Buwyhid Sultan Samsara ud Daula overthrown by Sharaf ud Daula.

989: Death of the Buwayhid Sultan Sharaf ud Daula, accession of Baha ud Daula.

991: Deposition of the Abbasid Caliph At Taii, accession of AI Qadir.

996: Death of the Zirid ruler Mansur, accession of Nasir ud Daula Badis.

997: Death of the Samanid ruler Nuh II, accession of Mansur II.

998: Death of the Samanid ruler Mansur II, accession of Abdul Malik II.

Mahmud becomes the Amir of Ghazni. 999 End of the Samanids.

Islamic History (Chronology) 11th Century (1000-1099) C.E.

1001: Mahmud Ghazanavi defeats the Hindu Shahis.

1004: Mahmud captures Bhatiya.

1005: Mahmud captures Multan and Ghur.

1008: Mahmud defeats the Rajput confederacy.

1010: Abdication of Hisham II in Spain. accession of Muhammad.

1011: In Spain Muhammad is overthrown by Sulaiman.

1012: In Spain power is captured by Bani Hamud. Death of the Buwayhid Baha ud Daula, accession of Sultan ud Daula.

1016: Death of the Zirrid ruler Nasir ud Daula Badis; accession of AI Muizz.

1018: In Spain power is captured by Abdul Rahman IV.

1019: Conquest of the Punjab by Mahmud Ghazanavi.

1020: The Buwayhid Sultan ud Daula is Overthrown by Musharaf ud Daula, Death of the Fatimid Caliph AI Hakim, accession of Al Zahir.

1024: In Spain assassination of Abdul Rahman IV, accession of Mustafi.

1025: Death of the Buwayhid Mushgraf ud Daula, accession of Jalal ud Daula.

1029: In Spain death of Mustaft, accession of Hisham III.

1030: Death of Mahmud Ghazanavi.

1031: In Spain deposition of Hisharn III, and end of the Umayyad rule. Death of the Abbasid Caliph Al Qadir, accession of Al Qaim.

1036: Death of the Fatimid Caliph AI Zahir, accession of Mustansir. Tughril Beg is crowned as the king of the Seljuks.

1040: Battle of Dandanqan, the Seljuks defeat the Ghazanavids. Deposition of Masud the Ghazanavid Sultan, accession of Muhammad. AI Moravids come to power in North Africa.

1041: The Ghazanavid Sultan Muhammad is overthrown by Maudud.

1044: Death of the Buwayhid Jalal ud Daula, accession of Abu Kalijar.

1046: Basasiri captures power in Baghdad.

1047: The Zirids in North Africa repudiate allegiance to the Fatimid and transfer allegiance to-the Abbasids.

1048: Death of the Buwayhid Abu Kalijar, accession of Malik ur Rahim.

1050: Yusuf b Tashfin comes to power.in the Maghrib.

1055: Tughril Beg overthrows the Buwayhids.

1057: Basasiri recaptures power in Baghdad, deposes Al Qaim and offers allegiance to the Fatimid Caliph.

1059: Tughril Beg recaptures power in Baghdad, al Qaim is restored as the Caliph.

1060: Ibrahim becomes the Sultan of Ghazni. Yusuf b Tashfin founds the city of Marrakesh. The Zirids abandon their capital Ashir and establish their capital at Bougie.

1062: Death of the Zirid ruler AI Muizz, accession of Tamin.

1063: Death of the Seljuk Sultan Tughril Beg; accession of Alp Arsalan.

1071: Battle of Manzikert, the Byzantine emperor taken captive by the Seljuks.

1073: Death of Alp Arsalan, accession of Malik Shah.

1077: Death of the Abbasid Caliph AI Qaim, accession of AI Muqtadi.

1082: The A1 Moravids conquer Algeria.

1086: Battle of Zallakha. The AI Moravids defeat the Christians in Spain. Death of the Rum Sejuk Sultan Sulaiman, accession of Kilij Arsalan.

1091: The Normans conquer the island of Sicily; end of the Muslim rule.

1092: Death of the Seljuk Sultan Malik Shah, accession of Mahmud.

1094: Death of Mahmud; accession of Barkiaruk. Death of the Abbasid Caliph AI Muqtadi, accession of Mustahzir.

1095: The first crusade.

1099: The crusaders capture Jerusalem.

ISLAMIC HISTORY (CHRONOLOGY) 12TH CENTURY (1100-1199) C.E.

1101: Death or the Fatimid Caliph Al Mustaali, accession of Al Aamir.

1105: Death of the Seljuk Sultan Barkiaruk, accession Of Muhammad.

1106: Death of the AI Motavid Yusuf b Tashfin.

1107: Death of the Rum Seljuk Sultan Kilij Arsalan, succession of Malik Shah.

1108: Death of the Zirid ruler Tamin, accession of Yahya.

1116: Death of the Rum Seljuk Sultan Malik Shah. accession of Rukn ud Din Masud.

1118: Death of the Seljuk Sultan Muhammad; accession of Mahmud II. Death of the Abbasid Caliph Mustahzir, accession of Mustarshid. In Spain the Christians capture Saragossa.

1121: Death of the Fatimid Caliph AI Aamir, accession of AI Hafiz.

1127: Imad ud Din Zangi establishes the Zangi rule In Mosul.

1128: Death of the Khawarzam Shah Qutb ud Din Muhammad; accession of Atsiz.

1130: Death of the Seljuk Sultan Mahmud II; accession of Tughril Beg II.

1134: Assassination of the Abbasid Caliph Mustarshid; accession of Al Rashid. Death of the Seljuk Sultan Tughril Beg II, accession of Masud.

1135: Deposition of the Abbasid Caliph AI Rashid, accession of AI Muktafi.

1144: Imad ud Din Zangi captures Edessa from the Christians, second crusade.

1146: Death of Imad ud Din Zangi, accession of Nur ud Din Zangi.

1147: In the Maghrib AI Moravids overthrown by the Al Mohads under Abul Mumin.

1148: End of the Zirid rule' in North Africa.

1149: Death of the Fatimid Caliph AI Hafiz, accession of AI Zafar.

1152: Death of the Seljuk Sultan Masud, accession of Malik Shah II. Hamadid rule extinguished in North Africa.

1153: Death of the Seljuk Sultan Malik Shah I1, accession of Muhammad II.

1154: Death of the Fatimid Caliph AI Zafar, accession of AI Faiz.

1156: Death of the Rum Seljuk Sultan Rukn ud Din Masid, accession of Arsalan II.

1159: Death of the Seljuk Sultan Muhammad II, accession of Gulaiman.

1160: Death of the Abbasid Caliph AI Mukta, accession of Al Mustanjid. Death of the Fatimid Caliph Al Faiz, accession of Al Azzid.

1161: Death of the Seljuk Sulaiman, accession of Arsalan Shah.

1163: Death of the AI Mohad ruler Abul Mumin, accession of Abu Yaqub Yusuf.

1170: Death of the Abbasid Caliph Mustanjid, accession of Al Mustazii.

1171: Death of the Fatimid Caliph AI Azzid. End of the Fatimids. Salah ud Din founds the Ayyubid dynasty in Egypt.

1172: Death of the Khawarzam Shah Arsalan, accession of Sultan Shah.

1173: The Khawarzam Shah Sultan Shah is overthrown by Tukush Shah.

1174: Salah ud Din annexes Syria.

1175: The Ghurids defeat the Guzz Turks and occupy Ghazni.

1176: Death of the Seljuk Sultan Arsalan Shah, accession of Tughril Beg III.

1179: Death of the Abbasid Caliph AI Mustazaii, accession of AI Nasir. Shahab ud Din Ghuri captures Peshawar.

1185: Death of the AI Mohad ruler Abu Yaqub Yusuf, accession of Abu Yusuf Yaqub.

1186: The Ghurids overthrow the Ghaznvaids in the Punjab.

1187: Salah ud Din wrests Jerusalem from the Christians, third crusade.

1191: Battle of Tarain between the Rajputs and the Ghurids.

1193: Death of Salah ud Din; accession of Al Aziz. Second battleof Tarain.

1194: Occupation of Delhi by the Muslims. End of the Seljuk rule.

1199: Death of the Khawarzam Shah Tukush Shah; accession of Ala ud Din. Death of the AI Mohad ruler Abu Yusuf Yaqub; accession of Muhammad Nasir. Conquest of Northern India and Bengal by the Ghurids.

Islamic History (Chronology) 13th Century (1200-1299) C.E.

1202: Death of the Ghurid Sultan Ghias ud Din; accession of Mahmud.

1204: Shahab ud Din Ghuri defeated by the Ghuzz Turks.

1206: Death of Shahab ud Din Ghuri. Qutb ud Din Aibik crowned king in Lahore.

1210: Assassination of the Ghurid Sultan MahmUd, accession of Sam. Death of Qutb ud Din Aibak, accession of Aram Shah in India.

1211: End of the Ghurid rule, their territories annexed by the Khawarzam Shahs. In India Aram Shah overthrown by Iltutmish.

1212: Battle of AI Uqab in Spain, end of the AI Mohad rule in Spain. The AI Mohads suffer defeat by the Christians in Spain at the Al-Uqba. The AI Mohad Sultan An Nasir escapes to Morocco where he dies soon after. Accession of his son Yusuf who takes over title of AI Mustansir.

1214: In North Africa death of the AI Mohad ruler Al Nasir, accession of Al Mustansir. The Banu Marin under their leader Abdul Haq occupy the north eastern part of Morocco.

1216: The Banu Marin under their leader Abdul Haq occupy north eastern part of Morocco. The AI Mohads suffer defeat by the Marinids at the battle of Nakur. The Banu Marin defeat the AI Mobads at the battle of Nakur.

1217: The Marinids suffer defeat in the battle fought on the banks of the Sibu river. Abdul Haq is killed and the Marinids evacuate Morocco. In the battle of Sibu the Marinids suffer defeat; their leader Abdul Haq is killed and they evacuate Morocco.

1218: Death of the Ayyubid ruler AI Adil, accession of AI Kamil. The Marinids return to Morocco under their leader Othman and occupy Fez.

1220: Death of the Khawarzam Shah Ala ud Din, accession of Jalal ud Din Mangbarni.

1222: Death of the Zangi ruler Nasir ud Din Mahmud, power captured by Badr ud Din Lulu.

1223: Death of the Al Mohad ruler Muntasir, accession of Abdul Wahid. Death of Yusuf AI Mustansir, accession of Abdul Wahid in Morocco.. In Spain a brother of Yusuf declares his independence and assumes the title of AI Adil. In Spain Abu Muhammad overthrows AI Adil. AI Adil escapes to Morocco and overthrows Abdul Wahid.

1224: Death of the AI Mohad ruler Abdul Wahid, accession of Abdullah Adil.

1225: Death of the Abbasid Caliph AI Nasir, accession of AI Mustansir.

1227: Death of the AI Mohad ruler Abdullah Adil, accession of Mustasim. Assassination of Al Adil, accession of his son Yahya who assumes the throne under the name of Al Mustasim.

1229: Death of the AI Mohad ruler Mustasim, accession of Idris. The Ayyubid AI Kamil restores Jerusalem to the Christians. Abu Muhammad dies in Spain and is succeeded by Al Mamun. AI Mamun invades Morocco with Christian help. Yahya is defeated and power is captured by Al Mamun. He denies the Mahdiship of Ibn Tumarat.

1230: End of the Khawarzam Shah rule.

1232: Death of the AI Mohad ruler Idris, accession, of Abdul Wahid II. Assassination of Al Mamun; accession of his son Ar-Rashid.

1234: Death of the Ayyubid ruler AI Kamil, accession of AI Adil.

1236: Death of Delhi Sultan Iltutmish. Accession of Rukn ud Din Feroz Shah.

1237: Accession of Razia Sultana as Delhi Sultan.

1240: Death of Ar-Rashid; accession of his son Abu Said.

1241: Death of Razia Sultana, accession of Bahram Shah.

1242: Death of Bahram Shah, accession of Ala ud Din Masud Shah as Delhi Sultan. Death of the AI Mohad rules Abdul Wahid, accession of Abu Hasan. Death of the Abbasid Caliph Mustansir, accession of Mustasim.

1243: Death of the AI Mohad ruler Abdul Walid II, accession of.

1244: The Al Mohads defeat the Marinids at the battle of Abu Bayash. The Marinids evacuate Morocco.

1245: The Muslims reconquer Jerusalem.

1246: Death of the Delhi Sultan Ala ud Din Masud Shah, accession of Nasir ud Din Mahmud Shah.

1248: Death of the AI Mohad ruler Abul Hasan, accession of Omar Murtaza. Abu Said attacks Tlemsen, but is ambushed and killed; accession of his son Murtada.

1250: The Marinids return to Morocco, and occupy a greatar part thereof.

1258: The Mongols sack Baghdad. Death of the Abbasid Caliph Mustasim. End of the Abbasid rule. Fall of Baghdad, end of the Abbasid caliphate. The Mongol Il-Khans under Halaku establish their rule in Iran and Iraq with the capital at Maragah. Berek Khan the Muslim chief of the Golden Horde protests against the treatment meted out to the Abbasid Caliph and withdraw his Contingent from Baghdad.

1259: Abu Abdullah the Hafsid ruler declares himself as the Caliph and assumes the name of AI Mustamir.

1260: Battle of Ayn Jalut in Syria. The Mongols are defeated by the Mamluks of Egypt, and the spell of the invincibility of the Mongols is broken. Baybars becomes the Mamluk Sultan.

1262: Death of Bahauddin Zikriya in Multan who is credited with the introduction of the Suhrawardi Sufi order in the IndoPakistan sub-continent.

1265: Death of Halaku. Death of Fariduddin Ganj Shakkar the Chishti saint of the Indo-Pakistan sub-continent.

1266: Death of Berek Khan the first ruler of the Golden Horde to be converted to Islam. The eighth crusade. The crusaders invade Tunisia. Failure of the crusade.

1267: Malik ul Salih establishes the first Muslim state of Samudra Pasai in Indonesia. Murtada seeks the help of the Christians, and the Spaniards invade Morocco. The Marinids drive away the Spaniards from Morocco. Assassination of Murtada; accession of Abu Dabbas.

1269: Abu Dabbas is overthrown by the Marinida, End of the Al Mohads. End of the rule of the AI Mohads in Morocco, the Marinids come to power in Morocco under Abu Yaqub.

1270: Death of Mansa Wali the founder of the Muslim rule in Mali.

1272: Death of Muhammad I the founder of the state of Granada. Yaghmurason invades Morocco but meets a reverse at the battle

1273: Death of Jalaluddin Rumi.

1274: Death of Nasiruddin Tusi. The Marinids wrest Sijilmasa from the Zayenids. Ninth crusade under Edward I of England. The crusade ends in fiasco and Edward returns to England.

1277: Death of Baybars.

1280: Battle of Hims.

1283: Death of Yaghmurasan. Accession of his son Othman.

1285: Tunisis splits in Tunis and Bougie.

1286: Death of Ghiasuddin Balban. Death of Abu Yusuf Yaqub. Bughra Khan declares his independence in Bengal under the name of Nasiruddin.

1290: End of the slave dynasty Jalaluddin Khilji comes into power. Othman embarks on a career of conquest and by 1290 C.E. most of the Central Maghreb is conquered by the Zayanids.

1291: Saadi.

1296: Alauddin Ghazan converted to Islam.

1299: Mongols invade Syria. The Marinids besiege Tlemsen the capital of the Zayanids.

14th Century (1300-1399) C.E.

1301: In Bengal, Death of Ruknuddin the king of Bengal, succeeded by brother Shamsuddin Firuz.

1302: In Granada, Death of Muhammad II; succession of Muhammad III.

1304: In the Mongols Il Khans empire, Death of Ghazan, succession of his brother Khudabanda Ul Jaytu. In Algeria, Death of Othman, succession of his son Abu Zayan Muhammad.

1305: In the Khiljis empire, Alauddin Khilji conquers Rajputana.

1306: In the Chughills empire, Death of Dava, succession of his son Kunjuk.

1307: In the Marinids empire, Assassination of the Marinid Sultan Abu Yaqub Yusuf; accession of Abu Thabit

1308: In the Chughills empire, Deposition of Kunjuk, power captured by Taliku. In Algeria, Death of Abu Zayan Muhammad, succession of his brother Abu Hamuw Musa. In the Marinids empire, Abu Thabit overthrown by Abu Rabeah Sulaiman.

1309: In the Chughills empire, Assassination of Taliku, accession of Kubak. In Granada, Muhammad III overthrown by his uncle Abul Juyush Nasr.

1310: In the Chughills empire, Kubak overthrown by his brother Isan Buga. In the Marinids empire, Abu Rabeah Sulaiman overthrown by Abu Said Othman. In the Khiljis empire, Alauddin conquers Deccan.

1312: In Tunisia, In Tunis Abul Baqa is overthrown by Al Lihiani.

1313: In the Mongols Il Khans empire, Invasion of Syria, the Mongols repulsed. In the Golden Horde empire, Death of Toktu, accession of his nephew Uzbeg.

1314: In Kashmir, Rainchan an adventurer from Baltistan overthrows Sinha Deva the Raja of Kashmir. Rainchan is converted to Islam and adopts the name of Sadrud Din. In Granada, Abul Juyush overthrown by his nephew Abul Wahid Ismail.

1315: In Tunisia, War between Bougie and Tunis, Lihani defeated and killed. Abu Bakr becomes the ruler of Bougie and Tunis.

1316: In the Mongols Il Khans empire, Death of Khudabanda Ul Jaytu, succession of Abu Said. In the Khiljis empire, Death of Alauddin, accession of Shahabuddin Umar, usurpation of power by Malik Kafur, a Hindu convert.

1318: In the Khiljis empire, Assassination of Malik Kafur, deposition of Shahabuddin Umar, accession of Qutbuddin Mubarak. In the Chughills empire, Isan Buga overthrown by Kubak.

1320: In the Khiljis empire, Assassination of Qutbuddin Mubarak, usurpation of power by Khusro Khan a Hindu convert. Khusro Khan overthrown by Ghazi Malik. End of the rule of Khiljis. In Tunisia, Abu Bakr expelled from Tunis by Abu Imran. In the Tughluqs empire, Ghazi Malik founds the rule of the Tughluq dynasty.

1321: In the Chughills empire, Death of Kubak, succession of Hebbishsi who is overthrown by Dava Temur.

1322: In the Chughills empire, Dava Temur overthrown by Tarmashirin, who is converted to Islam. In Bengal, Death of Shamsuddin Firuz. The kingdom divided into two parts. Ghiasuddin Bahadur became the ruler of East Bengal with the capital at Sonargaon, Shahabuddin became the ruler of West Bengal with the capital at Lakhnauti.

1324: In Bengal, Shahabuddin dies and is succeeded by his brother Nasiruddin.

1325: In the Tughluqs empire, Death of Ghazi Malik (Ghiasuddin Tughluq); accession of his son Muhammad Tughluq. In Granada, Assassination of Abul Wahid Ismail, succession of his son Muhammad IV. Assassination of Muhammad IV. Accession of his brother Abul Hallaj Yusuf. In the Samudra Pasai empire, Death of Malik al Tahir I, accession of Malik al Tahir II. In Bengal, With the help of Ghiasuddin Tughluq, Nasiruddin over-throws. Ghiasuddin Bahadur and himself become's the ruler of United Bengal.

1326: In the Ottoman Turks empire, Death of Othman, succession of Orkhan. Orkhan conquers Bursa and makes it his capital.

1327: In the Ottoman Turks empire, The Turks capture the city of Nicaea.

1329: In the Tughluqs empire, Muhammad Tughluq shifts the capital from Delhi to Daulatabad in Deccan.

1330: In the Chughills empire, Death of Tramashirin, succession of Changshahi. Amir Hussain establishes the rule of the Jalayar dynasty at Baghdad. In Tunisia, Abu Bakr overthrows Abu Imran and the state is again united, under him. In Bengal, Muhammad b Tughluq reverses the policy of his father and restores Ghiasuddin Bahadur to the throne of Sonargeon.

1331: In the Marinids empire, Death of Abu Said Othman, sucession of Abul Hasan. In Bengal, Annexation of Bengal by the Tughluqs.

1335: In the Mongols II Khans empire, Death of Abu Said, power captured by Arpa Koun. In the Chughills empire, Assassination of Changshahi, accession of Burun.

1336: In the Mongols II Khans empire, Arpa defeated and killed, succeeded by Musa. Birth of Amir Temur. In the Jalayar empire, Death of Amir Hussain, succession of Hasan Buzurg. In the Ottoman Turks empire, The Turks annex the state of Karasi. In Bengal, The Tughluq Governor at Sonargeon assassinated by armour bearer who captured power and declared his independence assuming the name of Fakhruddin Mubarak Shah.

1337: In the Mongols II Khans empire, The rule of Musa overthrown, Muhammad becomes the Sultan. In the Sarbadaran empire, On the disintegration of the Il-Khan rule, Abdur Razaq a military adventurer establishes an independent principality in Khurasan with the capital at Sabzwar. In the Muzaffarids empire, On the disintegration of the II Khan rule Mubarazud Din Muhammad established the rule of the Muzaffarid dynasty. In the Ottoman Turks empire, The Turks capture the city of Nicomedia. In Algeria, Algeria is occupied by Marinids.

1338: In the Mongols II Khans empire, Muhammad overthrown, succession of Sati Beg. Sati Beg marries Sulaiman who becomes the co-ruler.

1339: In Kashmir, Death of Sadrud Din, throne captured by a Hindu Udyana Deva. In the Chughills empire, Deposition of Burun, accession of Isun Temur. In Bengal, The Tughluq Governor at Lakhnauti-Qadr Khan assassinated and power is captured by the army commander-in-chief who declares his independence and assumes the title of Alauddin Ali Shah.

1340: In the Muzaffarids empire, The Muzaffarids conquer Kirman. In the Chughills empire, Deposition of Isun Temur, accession of Muhammad.

1341: In the Golden Horde empire, Death of Uzbeg, succession of his son Tini Beg.

1342: In the Golden Horde empire, Tini Beg overthrown by his brother Jani Beg.

1343: In the Chughills empire, Muhammad overthrown, power captured by Kazan. In Bengal, Ilyas an officer of Alauddin murders his patron and captures the throne of West Bengal.

1344: In the Mongols II Khans empire, Deposition of Sulaiman, succession of Anusherwan.

1345: In the Samudra Pasai empire, Death of Malik al Tahir II, accession of Tahir III. His rule lasted throughout the fourteenth century. In Bengal, llyas captures East Bengal and under him Bengal is again united. He establishes his capital at Gaur.

1346: In the Chughills empire, Deposition of Kazan, accession of Hayan Kuli. In Tunisia, Death of Abu Bakr, succession of his son Fadal. In Kashmir, Death of Udyana Deva, throne captured by Shah Mirza who assumed the name of Shah Mir, and rounded the rule of Shah Mir dynasty.

1347: The Marinids capture Tunisia. In the Bahmanids empire, Hasan Gangu declares his independence and establishes a state in Deccan with the capital at Gulbarga.

1349: In Kashmir, Death of Shah Mir, accession of his son Jamsbed. In Algeria, The Zayanids under Abu Said Othman recapture Algeria.

1350: In the Sarbadaran empire, Revolt against Abdur Razaq. Power captured by Amir Masud. In Tunisia, Deposition of Fadal, succession of his brother Abu Ishaq. In Kashmir, Jamshed overthrown by his step brother Alauddin Ali Sher.

1351: In the Marinids empire, Death of Abul Hasan, succession of Abu Inan. In the Tughluqs empire, Death of Muhammad Tughluq accession of Firuz Shah Tughluq.

1352: In Algeria, The Marinids again capture Algeria. Abu Said Othman is taken captive and killed.

1353: End of the Mongol II Khan rule. In the Ottoman Turks empire, The Turks acquire the fortress of Tympa on the European side of the Hollespoint. In the Muzaffarids empire, The Muzaffarids conquer Shiraz and establish their capital there.

1354: In the Muzaffarids empire, The Muzaffarids annex Isfahan. In Granada, Assassination of Abu Hallaj Yusuf, succession of his son Muhammad V.

1356: In the Jalayar empire, Death of Hasan Buzurg, succession of his son Owaia.

1357: In the Golden Horde empire, Death of Jani Beg, succession of Kulpa.

1358: In the Bahmanids empire, Death of Hasan Gangu, accession of his son Muhammad Shah. In the Muzaffarids empire, Death of Mubarazuddin Muhammad; accession of Shah Shuja. In the Marinids empire, Assassination of Abu Inan, succession of Abu Bakr Said. In Bengal, Death of Ilyas, succession of his son Sikandar Shah.

1359: In the Ottoman Turks empire, Death of Orkhan, succession of Murad. In the Muzaffarids empire, Shah Shuja deposed by his brother Shah Mahmud. In Tunisia, Abul Abbas a nephew of Abu Ishaq revolts and establishes his rule in Bougie. In Algeria, The Zayanids under Abu Hamuw II recapture Algeria. In the Marinids empire, Abu Bakr Said overthrown by Abu Salim Ibrahim. In Granada, Muhammad V loses the throne in palace revolution, succeeded by Ismail.

1360: In the Muzaffarids empire, Death of Shah Mahmud. Shah Shuja recaptures power. In the Chughills empire, Power captured by Tughluq Temur. In Granada, Ismail overthrown by his brother-in-law Abu Said.

1361: In the Ottoman Turks empire, Murad conquers a part of Thrace and establishes his capital at Demolika in Thrace. In the Golden Horde empire, Kulpa overthrown by his brother Nauroz. In the Marinids empire, Abu Salim Ibrahim overthrown by Abu Umar. Abu Umar overthrown by Abu Zayyan.

1362: In the Golden Horde empire, State of anarchy. During 20 years as many as 14 rulers came to the throne and made their exit. In Granada, Abu Said overthrown by Muhammad V who comes to rule for the second time. In Kashmir, Death of Alauddin Ali Sher, succeeded by his brother Shahabuddin.

1365: In the Ottoman Turks empire, The Turks defeat the Christians at the battle of Matiza, the Byzantine ruler becomes a vassal of the Turks.

1366: In the Marinids empire, Assassination of Abu Zayyan, succession of Abu Faris Abdul Aziz.

1369: Power captured by Amir Temur. End of the rule of the Chughills. Amir Temur captures power in Transoxiana. In Tunisia, Death of Abu Ishaq. Succession of his son Abu Baqa Khalid.

1370: In Tunisia, Abu Baqa overthrown by Abul Abbas under whom the state is reunited. In the Sarbadaran empire, Death of Amir Masud, succession of Muhammad Temur.

1371: In the Ottoman Turks empire, Invasion of Bulgaria, Bulgarian territory upto the Balkans annexed by the Turks.

1372: In the Marinids empire, Death of Abu Faris, succession of Abu Muhammad.

1374: In the Marinids empire, Abu Muhammad overthrown by Abul Abbas.

1375: In the Sarbadaran empire, Deposition of Muhammad Temur, power captured by Shamsuddin. In the Jalayar empire, Death of Owais, succession by his son Hussain.

1376: In Kashmir, Death of Shahabuddin, succeeded by his brother Qutbuddin.

1377: In the Bahmanids empire, Death of Muhammad Shah, succeeded by his son Mujahid.

1378: In the Bahmanids empire, Mujahid assassinated, throne captured by his uncle Daud.

1379: Turkomans of the Black Sheep empire, Bairam Khawaja found the independent principality of the Turkomans of the Black Sheep and established his capital at Van in Armenia. In the Bahmanids empire, Assassination of Daud; accession of Muhammad Khan.

1380: In the Golden Horde empire, Power is captured by Toktamish, a prince of the White Horde of Siberia. In Amir Temur's empire, Amir Temur crosses the Oxus and conquers Khurasan and Herat. Amir Temur invades Persia and subjugates the Muzaffarids and Mazandaran.

1381: In Amir Temur's empire, Annexation of Seestan, capture of Qandhar.

1384: In Amir Temur's empire, Conquest of Astrabad, Mazandaran, Rayy and Sultaniyah. In the Muzaffarids empire, Death of Shah Shuja, accession of his son Zainul Abdin. In the Marinids empire, Abul Abbas overthrown by Mustansir. Turkomans of the Black Sheep empire, Death of Bairam Khawaja, succession of Qara Muhammad.

1386: In Amir Temur's empire, Annexation of Azarbaijan, Georgea overrun. Subjugation of Gilan and Shirvan. Turkomans of the Black Sheep defeated. In the Marinids empire, Death of Mustansir, succession of Muhammad.

1387: In the Marinids empire, Muhammad overthrown by Abul Abbas who comes to power for the second time.

1388: In Algeria, Death of Abu Hamuw II, succession of Abu Tashfin. In the Tughluqs empire, Death of Firuz Shah Tughluq, succeeded by his grandson Ghiasuddin Tughluq II.

1389: In the Muzaffarids empire, Death of the poet Hafiz Shirazi. In the Tughluqs empire, Death of Ghiasuddin Tughluq II, accession: of Abu Bakr Tughluq Shah. Turkomans of the Black Sheep empire, Death of Qara Muhammad. succession of Qara Yusuf.

1390: In the Tughluqs empire, Abu Bakr overthrow by Nasiruddin Tughluq. In Bengal, Death of Sikandar Shah, accession of his son Ghiasud. In the Burji Mamluks empire, The rule of the Burji Mamluks rounded by Saifuddin Barquq.

1391: In Amir Temur's empire, Annexation of Fars. In the Muzaffarids empire, Annexation of the Muzaffarids by Amir Temur. In Granada, Death of Muhammad V, succession of his son Abu Hallaj Yusuf II.

1392: In the Jalayar empire, Death of Hussain, succession of his son Ahmad. In Granada, Death of Abu Hallaj; succession of Muhammad VI.

1393: Amir Temur defeats Tiktomish, the ruler of the Golden Horde. Capture of the Jalayar dominions by Amir Temur. In the Marinids empire, Death of Abul Abbas; succession of Abu Faris II.

1394: Amir Temur defeats the Duke of Moscow. In the Tughluqs empire, Death of Nasiruddin Tugluq, accession of Alauddin Sikandar Shah. In Kashmir, Death of Qutbuddin. Turkomans of the White Sheep empire, Qara Othman established the rule of the White Sheep Turkomans in Diyarbekr.

1395: In the Golden Horde empire, Amir Temur defeated Toktamish and razes Serai to the ground. End of the rule of the Golden Horde. Annexation of Iraq by Amir Temur. In the Tughluqs empire, Death of Sikandar Shah. Accession of Muhammad Shah.

1396: In the Amir Temur's empire, Destruction of Sarai, and of the rule of the Golden Horde. In the Sarbadaran empire, Principality annexed by Amir Temur.

1397: In the Bahmanids empire, Death of Muhammad Khan.

1398: In the Amir Temur's empire, Campaign in India. In the Marinids empire, Death of Abu Faris II. In the Tughluqs empire, Invasion of Amir Timur, Mahmud Shah escapes from the capital. In Morocco, Death of the Marinid Sultan Abu Faris II; succession of his son Abu Said Othman.

1399: In the Amir Temur's empire, Campaign in Iraq and Syria. In the Burji Mamluks empire, Death of Saifuddin Barquq, succession of his son Nasiruddin in Faraj.

ISLAMIC HISTORY (CHRONOLOGY) 15TH CENTURY (1400-1499) C.E.

1400: In the Burji Mamluks empire, The Mamluks lost Syria which was occupied by Amir Timur.

1401: In the Golden Horde empire, Death of Timur Qutluq, the ruler, installed by Amir Timur. accession of Shadi Beg.

1402: In the Ottoman Turks empire, Defeat of Bayazid at the battle of Ankara, taken captive Amir Timur.

1403: In the Ottoman Turks empire, Muhammad I, the son of Bayazid ascended the throne.

1405: In the Timurids empire, Death of Amir Timur, succession of his son Shah Rukh.

1407: In the Golden Horde empire, Deposition of Shadi Beg, installation of Faulad Khan by the king maker Edigu.

1410: In the Golden Horde empire, Deposition of Faulad Khan, installation of Timur.

1412: In the Golden Horde empire, Deposition of Timur, installation of Jalaluddin. In the Burji Mamluks empire, Death of Nasiruddin Faraj, succession of Al Muayyad.

1413: In the Golden Horde empire, Deposition of Jalaluddin, installation of Karim Bardo.

1414: In the Golden Horde empire, Deposition of Karim Bardo, installation of Kubak Khan.

1416: In the Golden Horde empire, Deposition of Kubak Khan, installation of Jahar Balrawi. Deposition of Jahar Balrawi, installation of Chaighray.

1419: In the Golden Horde empire, Death of Edigu, overthrow of Chaighray, power captured by Ulugh Muhammad.

1420: In the Golden Horde empire, Ulugh Muhammad overthrown by Daulat Bairawi. 1420: Turkomans of the Black Sheep empire, Death of Qara Yusuf; succession of his son Qara Iskandar. In Morocco, Assassination of Abu Said Othman; succession of his infant son Abdul Haq.

1421: In the Ottoman Turks empire, Death of Muhammad I; accession of his son Murad II. In the Burji Mamluks empire, Death of Al Muayyad, succession of Muzaffar Ahmad. Muzaffar Ahmad overthrown by Amir Saifuddin Tata, Death of Saifuddin Tata, succession of his son Muhammad. Muhammad overthrown by Amir Barsbay.

1424: In the Golden Horde empire, Death of Daulat Bairawi, succession of Berk. In Algeria, The Halsida of Tunisia occupy Algeria. This state of affairs continued throughout the fifteenth century.

1425: In the Uzbegs empire, Abul Khayr, a prince of the house of Uzbeg declare his independence in the western part of Siberia,

1427: In the Golden Horde empire, Berk overthrown by Ulugh Muhammad who captured power for the second time.

1430: In the Uzbegs empire, Abul Khayr occupies Khawarazm.

1434: Turkomans of the Black Sheep empire, Deposition of Qara Iskandar; installation of his brother Jahan Shah. Turkomans of the White Sheep empire, Death of Qara Othman, succession of his son Ali Beg. In Tunisia, Death of Abul Faris after a rule of forty years, succession of his son Abu Abdullah Muhammad.

1435: In Tunisia, Deposition of Abu Abdullah Muhammad, power captured by Abu Umar Othman.

1438: In the Burji Mamluks empire, Death of Barsbay, accession of his minor son Jamaluddin Yusuf; Yusuf overthrown and power captured by the Chief Minister Saifuddin Gakmuk. Turkomans of the White Sheep empire, Ali Beg overthrown by his brother Hamza.

1439: In the Golden Horde empire, Ulugh Muhammad withdrew from Sarai and found the principality of Qazan. Said Ahmad came to power in Sarai.

1440: Turkomans of the White Sheep empire, Hamza overthrown by Jahangir a son of Ali Beg.

1441: In the Golden Horde empire, Crimea seceded from Sarai.

1446: In the Timurids empire, Death of Shah Rukh, succession of Ulugh Beg. In the Ottoman Turks empire, Second battle of Kossova resulting in the victory of the Turks. Serbia annexed to Turkey and Bosnia became its vassal.

1447: In the Golden Horde empire, Astra Khan seceded from Sarai.

1449: In the Uzbegs empire, Abul Khayr captures Farghana. In the Timurids empire, Death of Ulugh Beg, succession of Abdul Latif.

1450: In the Timurids empire, Assassination of Abdul Latif, accession of Abu Said.

1451: In the Ottoman Turks empire, Death of Murad II; accession of his son Muhammad II.

1453: In the Ottoman Turks empire, Capture of Constantinople by the Turks. Turkomans of the White Sheep empire, Death of Jahangir; accession of his son Uzun Hasan. In the Burji Mamluks empire, Death of Gakmuk. succession of his son Fakhruddin Othman. Othman overthrown by the Mamluk General Saifuddin Inal.

1454: In the Ottoman Turks empire, Attack against Wallachia, Wallachia became a vassal state of Turkey.

1456: In the Ottoman Turks empire, Annexation of Serbia.

1461: In the Ottoman Turks empire, Annexation of Bosnia and Herzogovina. In the Burji Mamluks empire, Death of Saifuddin Inal, succession of his son Shahabuddin Ahmad. Shahabuddin Ahmad overthrown by the Mamluk General Saifuddin Khushqadam.

1462: In the Ottoman Turks empire, Annexation of Albania.

1465: In the Golden Horde empire, Death of Said Ahmad, succession of his son Khan Ahmad. In Morocco, Assassination of Abdul Haq. End of the Marinid rule. Power snatched by Sharif Muhammad al Jati.

1467: Turkomans of the Black Sheep empire, Death of Jahan Shah, end of the rule of the Black Sheep Turkoman rule. Turkomans of the White Sheep empire, Jahan Shah of the Black Sheep attacked the White Sheep. Jahan Shah was defeated and the Black Sheep territories annexed by the White Sheep. In the Burji Mamluks empire, Death of Khushqadam, accession of his son Saifuddin Yel

Bey. Deposition of Yel Bey, power captured by the Mamluk General Temur Bugha.

1468: In the Uzbegs empire, Death of Abul Khayr, succession of his son Haidar Sultan. Turkomans of the White Sheep empire, Uzun Hasan defeated the Timurids at the battle of Qarabagh whereby the White Sheep became the masters of Persia and Khurasan. In the Burji Mamluks empire, Deposition of Femur Bugha, power captured by the Mamluk General Qait Bay.

1469: In the Timurids empire, Death of Abu Said, disintegration of the Timurid state. In Khurasan Hussain Baygara came to power and he ruled during the remaining years of the fifteenth century.

1472: In Morocco, Sharif Muhammad al Jati overthrown by the Wattisid chief Muhammad al Shaikh who establishes the rule of the Wattisid dynasty.

1473: In the Ottoman Turks empire, War against Persia; Persians defeated.

1475: In the Ottoman Turks empire, Annexation of Crimea. War against Venice. Tukey became the master of the Aegean Sea.

1478: Turkomans of the White Sheep empire, Death of Uzun Hasan, succession of his son Khalil.

1479: Turkomans of the White Sheep empire, Khalil overthrown by his uncle Yaqub.

1480: In the Golden Horde empire, Assassination of Khan Ahmad, succession of his son Said Ahmad II.

1481: In the Golden Horde empire, Said Ahmad I1 overthrown by his brother Murtada. In the Ottoman Turks empire, Death of Muhammad II, accession of Bayazid II.

1488: In the Uzbegs empire, Death of Haider Sultan, succession of his nephew Shaybani Khan. In Tunisia, Death of Abu Umar Othman after a rule of 52 years, succession of Abu Zikriya Yahya.

1489: In Tunisia, Abu Zikriya Yahya overthrown by Abul Mumin.

1490: In Tunisia, Abul Mumin overthrown, power recaptured by Abu Yahya.

1493: Turkomans of the White Sheep empire, Death of Yaqub, accession of his son Bayangir.

1495: Turkomans of the White Sheep empire, Bayangir overthown by his cousin Rustam.

1496: In the Burji Mamluks empire, Abdication of Qait Bay, succession of his son Nasir Muhammad.

1497: Turkomans of the White Sheep empire, Rustam overthrown by Ahmad Anarchy and fragmentation.

1498: In the Burji Mamluks empire, Deposition of Nasir Muhammad, power captured by Zahir Kanauh.

1499: In the Uzbegs empire, Shayhani Khan conquered Transoxiana. In the Golden Horde empire, Death of Murtada, succession of Said Ahmad III." In the Ottoman Turks empire, The Turks defeated the Venetian fleet in the battle of Lepanto.

ISLAMIC HISTORY (CHRONOLOGY) 16TH CENTURY (1500-1599) C.E.

1500: In the Burji Mamluks empire, Zahir Kanauh overthrown by Ashraf Gan Balat.

1501: Isamil I establishes the Safavid dynasty in Persia, and the Twelve-Imam Shi'ism becomes the state religion.

1507: The Portuguese under d'Albuquerque establish strongholds in the Persian Gulf.

1508: Turkomans of the White Sheep empire, End of the White Sheep dynasty and the annexation of their territories by the Safawids.

1511: D'Albuquerque conquers Malacca from the Muslims.

1517: The Ottoman Sultan Selim Yavuz ("the Grim") defeats the Mamluks and conquers Egypt.

1520: The reign of Sulayman the Magnificent begins.

1526: Louis of Hungary dies at the Battle of Mohacs.

1526: The Battle of Panipat in India, and the Moghul conquest; Babur makes his capital at Delhi and Agra.

1528: The Ottomans take Buda in Hungary.

1529: Unsuccessful Ottoman siege of Vienna.

1550: The architect Sinan builds the Suleymaniye mosque in Istanbul.

1550: The rise of the Muslim kingdom of Atjeh in Sumatra.

1550: Islam spreads to Java, the Moluccas, and Borneo.

1556: The death of Sulayman the Magnificent.

1568: Alpujarra uprising of the Moriscos (Muslims forcibly converted to Catholicism) in Spain.

1571: The Ottomans are defeated at the naval Battle of Lepanto, and their dominance in the Mediterranean is brought to a close.

1578: The Battle of the Three Kings at Qasr al-Kabir in Morocco. King Sebastian of Portugal is killed.

1588: Reign of Safavid Sultan Shah Abbas I begins.

1591: Mustaili Ismailis split into Sulaymanis and Daudis.

ISLAMIC HISTORY (CHRONOLOGY) 17TH CENTURY (1600-1699) C.E.

1600: Sind annexed by the Mughals. End of the Arghun rule in Sind.

1601: Khandesh annexed by the Mughals.

1603: Battle of Urmiyah. Turks suffer defeat. Persia occupies Tabriz, Mesopotamia. Mosul and Diyarbekr. Death of Muhammad III, Sultan of Turkey, accession of Ahmad I. In Morocco al Shaikh died.

1604: In Indonesia death of Alauddin Rayat Shah, Sultan of Acheh, accession of Ali Rayat Shah III.

1605: Death of the Mughal emperor Akbar; accession of Jahangir.

1607: Annexation of Ahmadnagar by the Mughals.

1609: Annexation of Bidar by the Mughals

1611: Kuch Behar subjugated by the Mughals.

1612: Kamrup annexed by the Mughals.

1617: Death of Ahmad I, Sultan of Turkey, accession of Mustafa; Deposition of Mustafa: accession of Othman II.

1618: Tipperah annexed by the Mughals.

1620: In Turkey deposition of Mustafa, accession of Othman II.

1623: In Turkey Mustafa recaptured power.

1625: In Turkey deposition of Mustafa, accession of Murad IV.

1627: Death of the Mughal emperor Jahangir, accession of Shah Jahan.

1628: Reign of Safavid Sultan Shah Abbas I comes to an end.

1629: In Persia death of Shah Abbas; accession of grandson Safi.

1631: Death of Mumtaz Mahal, wife of Mughal Emperor Shah Jahan and the lady of Taj Mahal, Agra.

1637: Death of Iskandar Muda in Indonesia; accession of Iskandar II.

1640: Death of Otthman Sultan Murad IV. Accession of his brother Ibrahim.

1641: Turks capture Azov. In Indonesia death of Iskandar II; accession of the Queen Tajul Alam.

1642: In Persia death of Shah Safi, accession of Shah Abbas II.

1648: In Turkey Ibrahim deposed; accession of Muhammad IV.

1656: Muhammad Kuiprilli becomes the Grand Minister in Turkey.

1658: Deposition of the Mughal emperor Shah Jahan, accession of Aurangzeb.

1661: Death of Muhammad Kuiprilli, accession of his son Ahmad Kuiprilli.

1667: Death of Shah Abbas II; accession of Shah Sulaiman.

1675: Execution of the Sikh Guru Tegh Bahadur. In Indonesia death of the queen Tajul Alam, accession of the queen Nur ul Alam.

1676: Death of the Grand Wazir of Turkey Ahmad Kuiprilli, succession by Kara Mustafa.

1678: In Indonesia death of the queen Nur ul Alam, accession of the queen Inayat Zakia.

1680: Death of Marhatta chieftain Shivaji.

1682: Assam annexed by the Mughals. Aurangzeb shifts the capital to Aurangabad in the Deccan.

1683: The Turks lift the siege of Vienna and retreat. Kara Mustafa the Grand Wazir executed for the failure of the expedition.

1686: Annexation of Bijapur by the Mughals.

1687: Golkunda annexed by the Mughals. Second battle of Mohads. Defeat of the Turks by Austria. Deposition of Muhammad IV. Accession of Sulaiman II.

1688: In Indonesia death of queen Inayat Zakia, accession of the queen Kamalah.

1690: Death of the Ottoman Sultan Sulaiman II, accession of Ahmad II.

1692: Death of the Turk Sultan Ahmad II, accession of Mustafa II.

1694: In Persia death of Shah Safi, accession of Shah Hussain.

1699: In Indonesia death of Queen Kamalah.

ISLAMIC HISTORY (CHRONOLOGY) 18TH CENTURY (1700-1799) C.E.

1700: Murshid Quli Khan declares the independence of Bengal and establishes his capital at Murshidabad.

1703: Ahmad 11I becomes the Ottoman Sultan. Birth of Shah Wali Ullah. Birth of the religious reformer Muhammad b Abdul Wahab.

1707: Death of the Mughal emperor Aurangzeb, accession of his son Bahadur Shah.

1711: War between Turkey and Russia. Russia defeated at the battle of Pruth.

1712: Death of the Mughal emperor Bahadur Shah, accession of Jahandar Shah.

1713: Jahandar Shah overthrown by his nephew Farrukh Siyar.

1718: In the war against Austria, Turkey suffers defeat. By the treaty of Passarowich Turkey loses Hungary.

1719: Deposition of the Mughal emperor Farrukh Siyar Muhammad Shah ascends the throne. In Sind the Kalhoras came to power under Nur Muhammad Kalhora.

1722: Saadat Khan found the independent state of Oudh. Battle of Gulnabad between the Afghans and the Persians. The Persians were defeated and the Afghans under Shah Mahmud became the masters of a greater part of Persia. Shah Hussain taken captive, accession of Shah Tahmasp II.

1730: Zanzibar freed from Portugese rule and occupied by Oreart.

1747: Ahmad Shah Durrani established Afghan rule in Afghanistan.

1752: Death of Shah Abdul Latif Bhitai, writer of Sassi Pannu, Sohni Mahinwal and Umer Marvo.

1752: Ahmed Shah Durrani captured Punjab, Kashmir and Sind.

1761: Death of Shah Waliullah Dehlavi.

1761: Battle of Panipat. Ahmad Shah Durrani came to India at the invitation of Shah Waliullah Dehlavi and smashed rising Maratha power in the battle of Panipat.

1764: Conversion to Islam of Areadi Gaya. ruler of Futa Bandu State in West Sudan.

1773: Death of Ahmad Shah Durrani.

1783: End of Kalhora rule in Sind.

1797: Death of Muhammad Khan Qachar, king of Persia.

1797: Russia occupied Daghestan.

1799: Ranjit Singh declared himself Maharajah of Punjab defeating Afghans.

1799: Khoqand declared independent Islamic State.

ISLAMIC HISTORY (CHRONOLOGY) 19TH CENTURY (1800-1899) C.E.

1803: Shah Abdul Aziz ibn Saud assassinated by a Shia fanatic. Shah Shuja proclaimed as King of Afghanistan.

1805: Ibn Saud captured Madinah defeating the Turk garrison. 1804: Othman Dan Fodio established Islamic State of Sokoto in Central Sudan.

1805: Faraizi movement launched in Bengal. Muhammad Ali appointed Pasha of Egypt by the Turks.

1806: Khanate of Khiva came into limelight under the rule of Muhammad Rahim Khan.

1807: Darqawi sect revolted against Turkish domination. Tunisia repudiated suzerainty of Algeria.

1811: Birth of Ali Muhammad Bab founder of Bab movement. 1811: British occupied Indonesia. 1812: Madina fell to Egyptians.

1813: Makkah and Taif captured by Egyptian forces and Saudis expelled from Hijaz.

1814: Iran executed treaty of alliance with the British known as Definitive Treaty.

1814: Death of Ibn Saud II.

1814: King Othman of Tunisia assassinated by his cousin Mahmud. 1816: British withdrew from Indonesia restoring it to the Dutch. 1822: Death of Maulay Ismail in Morocco.

1827: Malaya became a preserve of the British according to Anglo-Netherland treaty in 1824. 1828: Russia declared war against Turkey. 1829: Treaty of Adrianople. 1830: French forces landed near Algiers and occupied Algeria ending 313 years rule of Turks.

1831: Syed Ahmad Barelvi and Shah Ismail leaders of Jihad movement in India fell fighting the Sikhs in Balakot.

1832: Turks defeated in the battle of Konia by Egyptian forces.

1832: Sayyid Said, King of Oman, shifted his capital to Zanzibar.

1834: Abdul Qadir recognised as ruler of the area under his control by the French.

1839: Defeat of Turkey by the Egyptians in the battle of Nisibin.

1840: Quadruple Alliance by the European powers to force Egypt to relinquish Syria.

1840: British frees occupied Aden.

1841: State of Adamawa established by Adams adjacent to Nigeria.

1842: Amir Abdul Qadir, ousted from Algeria by the French. Crossed over to Morocco.

1842: Shah Shuja assassinated ending the Durrani rule in Afghanistan.

1847: Amir Abdul Qadir surrendred to France under the condition of safe conduct to a Muslim country of his choice but France violated its pledge and sent him as a captive to France.

1849: Death of Muhammad Ali pasha.

1850: Ali Muhammad Bab arrested and executed by Iranian government.

Qurratul Ain Tabira, a renowned poetess and staunch advocate of Babism also shot dead.

1852: Release of Amir Abdul Qadir by Napolean III. He settled in Turkey.

1855: Khiva annexed by Russia.

1857: British captured Delhi and eliminated Mughal rule in India after 332 years. Last Mughal Emperor Bahadur Shah Zafar was exiled to Rangoon in Burma. This was also the end of 1000 years of Muslim rule over India.

1859: Imam Shamil laid down arms before Russian forces and the Islamic State of Daghestan became a Russian province.

1860: Maulay Muhammad defeated by Spain.

1861: Death of Sultan Abdul-Majid of Turkey.

1862: Faraizi movement fizzled out after the death of Dadu Miyan..

1865: Khoqand State liquidated by Russia.

1869: Jamaluddin Afghani exiled from Afghanistan. He proceeded to Egypt.

1871: Tunisia recognised suzerainty of Turkey through a Firman.

1876: Britain purchased shares of Khediv Ismail in the Suez canal and got involved in Egyptian affairs.

1878: Turkey handed over Cyprus to Britain.

1878: Adrianople fell to Russia.

1879: Jamaluddin Afghani exiled from Egypt.

1879: Treaty of Berlin. Turkey lost 4/5 th of its territory in Europe.

1881: France invaded Tunisia and the Bey acknowledged supremacy of France as a result of the treaty of Bardo.

1881: Muhammad Ahmad declared himself Mahdi in northern Sudan.

1882: Egypt came under British military occupation.

1883: Death of Amir Abdul Qadir in Damascus.

1885: Muhammad Ahmad declared free Government of Sudan under his rule.

1885: Death of Mahdi Sudani five months after the occupation of Khartum.

1890: End of Banbara State.

1895: Afghanistan got Wakhan corridor by an understanding with Russia and

British India making Afghan border touch China.

1895: Mirza Ghulam Ahmad of Qadian claimed prophethood.

1897: State of Bagirimi occupied by the French,

1899: Fall of Mahdi State occupied by the British and the Egyptians jointly.

ISLAMIC HISTORY (CHRONOLOGY) 20TH CENTURY (1900-1992) C.E.

1901: Ibn Saud (Abd al-Aziz) captures Riyad.

1901: French forces occupy Morocco.

1904: Morocco becomes a French protectorate under the Conference of Algeciras.

1904: The Presian constitution is promoted.

1905: The beginning of the Salafiyyah movement in Paris with it's main sphere of influence in Egypt.

1907: The beginning of the Young Turks movement in Turkey.

1912: The beginning of the Muhammadiyyah reform movement in Indonesia.

1914: Under Ottoman rule, secret Arab nationalist societies are formed.

1914: World War I.

1916: Arab revolt against Ottoman (Turkish) rule. Lawrence of Arabia leads attacks on the Hijaz Railway.

1918: Armistice signed with Ottomans on October 30.

1918: World War I ends on November 11.

1918: Syria and Damascus become a French protectorate.

1921: Abd Allah bin Husayn in made King of Transjordan. His father was the Sharif of Mecca.

1921: Faysal bin Husayn is made King of Iraq. His father was the Sharif of Mecca.

1921: Abd al-Karim leads a revolt against colonial rule in Moroccan Rif, and declares the "Republic of the Rif".

1922: Mustafa Kemal abolishes the Turkish Sultanate.

1924: The Turkish Caliphate is abolished.

1924: King Abd al-Aziz conquers Mecca and Medina, which leads to the unification of the Kingdoms of Najd and Hijaz.

1925: Reza Khan seizes the government in Persia and establishes the Pahlavi dynasty.

1926: Abd al-Aziz (Ibn Saud) assumes title of King of Najd and Hijaz.

1927: Death of Zaghlul, an Egyptian nationalist leader.

1928: Turkey is declared a secular state.

1928: Hasan al-Banna founds the Muslim Brotherhood.

1932: Iraq granted independence by League of Nations.

1934: War between King Abd al-Aziz and Imam Yahya of the Yemen.

1934: Peace treaty of Ta'if.

1934: Asir becomes part of Saudi Arabia.

1935: Iran becomes the official name of Persia.

1936: Increased Jewish immigration provokes widespread Arab-Jewish fighting in Palestine.

1939: World War II.

1941: British and Russian forces invade Iran and Reza Shah is forced to abdicate in favor of his son Mohammad Reza Shah in Iran.

1943: Beginning of Zionist terrorist campaign in Palestine.

1945: End of World War II.

1946: Jordan, Lebanon, and Syria are granted independence from Britain and France.

1947: Creation of Pakistan from Muslim Majority area in India.

1948: Creation of state of Israel. Arab armies suffer defeat in war with Israel.

1949: Hasan al-Banna, leader of the Muslim Brotherhood, is assassinated.

1951: Libya becomes independent.

1952: King Faruq of Egypt forced to abdicate.

1953: General Zahedi leads coup against Musaddeq, Shah returns to power.

1953: Death of King Abd al-Aziz (Ibn Saud) of Saudi Arabia.

1953: The foundation stone is laid to enlarge the Prophet's mosque in Medina.

1956: Morocco becomes independent.

1956: Tunisia becomes independent.

1957: The Bey of Tunisia is deposed, and Bourguiba becomes becomes president.

1957: Enlargement of the Haram in Mecca begins.

1962: Algeria becomes independent.

1962: Death of Zaydi Imam of Yemen (Ahmad). Crown Prince Bahr succeds him and takes the title Imam Mansur Bi-Llah Muhammad.

1965: Malcom X is assassinated.

1968: The enlargement of the Haram in Mecca is completed.

1969: King Idris of Libya is ousted by a coup led by Colonel Qadhdhafi.

1973: King Zahir Shah of Afghanistan is overthrown.

1975: Death of Elijah Mohammad, leader of Nation of Islam among African Americans in North America.

1975: Wallace Warith Deen Mohammad assumes leadership of Nation of Islam and shifts movement toward Islamic Orthodoxy renaming it American Muslim Mission.

1978: Imam Musa Sadr is apparently assassinated after he disappears on a trip to Libya. He was the religious leader of the Lebanese Twelve-Imam Shi'ites. He promoted the resurgence of Shi'ites in Lebanon and set the foundation of Amal.

1979: The Shah leaves Iran on January 15, thus bringing the Pahlavi dynasty to an end.

1979: On 1 Muharram AH 1400/21 November, the first day of the 15th Islamic century, fanatics led by students of the Theological University of Medina attempt to promote one of their group as Mahdi and thus fulfill a certain prophetic Hadith: "A man of the people of Medina will go forth, fleeing to Mecca, and certain of the people of Mecca will come to him and will lead him forth against his will and swear fealty to him between the rukn (Black Stone corner of the Kabah) and the Maqam Ibrahim." They hold the Haram of Mecca against the army for two weeks. Sixty-three of the 300 fanatics are captured alive, the mosque is recovered, and the conspirators are all put to death.

1980: Beginning of the Iran-Iraq war.

1989: Iran-Iraq comes to an end with much loss of life.

1990: Military annexation of Kuwait by Iraq, under Ba'athist leader Saddam Hussain, is reversed in 1991 by a coalition of United States-led forces.

Bibliography

Abdali, M.R. : *Scientific Thought in Islam,* Pious Publications, Hyderabad, 2001.

Adil, H. M. : *Letters of Hadrat Usman Ghani (R.A.A.),* Kitab Bhavan, New Delhi, 1992

Ahmad, Ilyas : *Sovereignty, Islamic and Modern,* Allies Book Corporation, Karachi, 1965.

Ali, Ameer : *Muhammadan Law,* Kitab Bhavan, New Delhi, 1986.

Ataur-Rahim : *Jesus a Prophet of Islam,* Idara Ishaat-e-Diniyat Pvt. Ltd, New Delhi, 1995.

Azam, Zaki : *The Ideas of Arab Nationalism,* Cornell University Press, New York,1956.

Beverly, Milton : *Islam and Politics in the Contemporary World,* Blackwell, New York, 1987.

Charles Howard : *The Constitutionalism,* Great Seal Books, New York, 1947.

Edwin, Elliot : *Worship in Islam,* University of Madras, Madras, 1925.

Fauzi M. : *The Islamic State : a Study in Traditional Politics,* Oxford, New York, 1967.

Glubb : *The Story of Arab Legion,* Feroz Pub., Lahore, 2000.

Herbert, Friedman : *The Amazing Universe,* National Geographic Society, Washington D.C., 1980.

Hussain, Ahanger : *Customary Succession among Muslims,* Uppal Publishibng House, New Delhi, 1997.

Hussain, M. : *Imam Abu Hanifah : Life and Work,* Kitab Bhavan, New Delhi, 2001.

Hussain, S. : *Human Rights in Islam,* Kitab Bhavan, New Delhi, 2001.

Ikbal Ali : *Islamic Sufism,* Idarah-I-Adbiyat-I-Delhi, Delhi, 1979.

Jafar, Sharif : *Islam in India,* Oxford, New Delhi, 1972.

James, Piscarton : *Islam in the World of National States,* Macmillan, New York, 1982.

John L. Esposite : *Islam in Transition,* Oxford, New York, 1969.

Kaur, R. : *Islamic Co-operation and Unity,* Deep & Deep Publications, New Delhi, 1993.

Mac, Closky : *Pacts for Peace,* New Century Pub., London, 1980.

Meer, Ali : *Observations on the Musulmauns of India,* Macmillan & Co., London, 1832.

Muhammad, Asad : *Islam at the Crossroads,* Kitab Bhavan, New Delhi, 2003.

Muslehuddin, M. : *Islam : its Political System,* Kitab Bhavan, New Delhi, 1999.

Palamer, E.H. : *The Quran,* Atlantic Publishers, New Delhi, 1996.

Robert, D. : *Exploring our Living Planet,* National Geographic Society, Washington, 1989.

Rodinson, Maxime : *Islam and Capitalism,* Penguin, London,1974.

Rosenthal, E.I.J. : *Islam in the Modern National State,* University Press, Cambridge,1965.

Schwartz, E. : *Science and Civilization in Islam,* Cambridge, London, 1966.

Setalvad : *War and Civil Liberties,* Feroz Pub., Lahore, 1992.

Siddiqi, M.Z. : *Hadith Literature,* Deepali Pub., Calcutta, 1961.

Sir, Thomas : *The Caliphate,* MacMillan, London, 1965.

Syed Husain : *Three Muslim Sages,* Cambridge, New York, 1959.

Syed, Amir Ali : *The Spirit of Islam,* Royal Pub.,Lahore, 1979.

Walker, Benjamin : *Foundation of Islam : the Making of World Faith,* Rupa & Co., New Delhi, 2001.

Watt, W.M. : *Islam and the Integration of Society,* Routledge, London, 1961.

Yezbeck Haddad : *Islamic Values in the United States,* Oxford, New York, 1999.

Zahid, Malik : *Subjects of Quran,* Kitab Bhavan, New Delhi, 1998.

Zaydan, Jurji : *Umayyads and Abbasides,* Luzac & Co., London,1907.

Index

□□□

Islam